RUSSELL HARLAN, ARTIST
© BY THE REVIEW AND HERALD

Uncle Arthur's
BIBLE BOOK

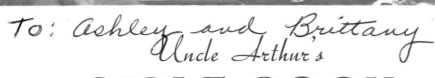

To: Ashley and Brittany

Uncle Arthur's
BIBLE BOOK

Seventy-one Choice Stories From the World's Best Book

An Introduction to Bible Reading for Boys and Girls

By ARTHUR S. MAXWELL

Author of *Uncle Arthur's Bedtime Stories, The Bible Story,*
Your Bible and You, Good News for You, etc.

REVIEW AND HERALD PUBLISHING ASSOCIATION
WASHINGTON, D.C.

FROM: Grandma Ida 1990

Artists participating in the illustration of this volume are Harry Anderson, Harry Baerg, Kreigh Collins, Corine B. Dillon, Frank Ford, Arlo Greer, Russell Harlan, William Heaslip, William Hutchinson, Manning de V. Lee, T. K. Martin, Lester Quade, Herbert Rudeen, and Jes Schlaikjer, N.A.

OFFSET IN U.S.A.

Russ Harlan

FOREWORD

In these days when the minds of so many children are being warped and bent toward evil by crime "comics" and horror TV programs, it is more urgent than ever that something be done to counteract this tragic trend. Somehow boys and girls must be helped to perceive the true values of life and develop a love for goodness, honesty, purity, and truth.

Uncle Arthur's Bible Book has been written for this purpose. It is designed to help children learn to love the Bible and to discover in it the source and wellspring of all that is noble and pure and good. It retells "the old, old story" in such a way that boys and girls will find delight in reading the Bible—so much so that they will put it above all other interests, even the most alluring TV program.

These stories appeared originally in the five-volume set of *The Children's Hour.* When that set was discontinued in 1964 the publishers decided to reissue them in a single volume. Now, revised and reillustrated, they even more effectively help to make the Bible a thing of beauty and wonder to the rising generation.

Uncle Arthur's Bible Book is not intended to deal with the whole Bible. Rather it is an introduction to *The Bible Story*—the author's ten-volume set which, with its more than 400 stories for children, covers the whole Bible from Genesis to Revelation.

When you have read all the stories in this volume, by all means proceed to *The Bible Story* and discover what a marvelous and fascinating volume the Bible really is.

May this new *Bible Book* lead many a boy and girl to love God's Word and find in it the way of salvation.

ARTHUR S. MAXWELL

What fun it is to blow on the dandelion seed balls and see the soft furry particles fly away into the air. This is how the wind scatters the seeds of trees and of plants everywhere.

CONTENTS

This treasure-trove of Bible stories adapts itself to the responsive heart, inquiring mind, and spirit of discovery that are the heritage of happy children of all ages in every land.

8

CONTENTS

The Moffatt excerpts in this book are from *The Bible: A New Translation* by James Moffatt. Copyright by James Moffatt 1954. Used by permission of Harper & Row, Publishers, Incorporated.

How Things Began

≈≈≈≈≈≈≈≈≈≈≈≈≈≈≈≈≈≈≈≈≈≈

DID you ever wonder how everything in the world began? Most boys and girls do at some time or other. A little girl I know has just started thinking along this line. Such questions she asks! How was this made? Who started that? Until at last I have to say, "Well, that's all for now, thank you!" Then she is quiet for a little while, storing up more questions for the next time she gets me alone.

One evening, as I was reading her a story, she stopped me in the middle and said, "How are books made?" So I left the story and began to explain that books are made of paper.

"Yes, but how is paper made?"

"Well," I began, thinking hard, "paper is made from wood, which is ground up into very small pieces, then boiled until it becomes a pulp. Then it is passed through great rollers which press it all out flat——"

"But how is wood made?" she interrupted.

So I stopped telling her about papermaking and started

11

How fortunate are the children of a family who have a grandfather with plenty of time to answer their questions and satisfy their curiosity about the things God has made.

to tell how wood and lumber come from trees in the forests.

"Lumbermen go into the woods," I said, "and with great saws and sharp axes cut down the trees. Then the trunks are hauled to sawmills and cut up into boards and——"

"But how are trees made?"

I could see we were heading into difficulties.

"Trees aren't made," I said. "They grow."

"I know," she said. "But what do they grow from?"

"A little seed in the ground."

"But where did the seed come from?"

"Another tree."

"But where did that tree come from?"

"A seed from another tree before it."

PAINTING BY RUSSELL HARLAN

HOW THINGS BEGAN

"Then," and here came the sixty-four-dollar question, "where did the first tree come from?"

"God made it," I said, and that settled that, for the time being.

Another evening when I was saying good night to her, she said, right out of the blue, "How is light made?"

"Light!" I said, stalling for time. "What light?"

"That light," she said, pointing to the electric light globe.

"Well," I said, "you just turn the switch and——"

"I know that," she said, "but what makes the light come into the globe?"

"Well—cr—um—electricity," I said. "An electric current runs along the wires that are hidden in the wall and heats a

very thin wire inside the globe. When that thin wire becomes white hot, which it does very, very quickly, well—er—it makes a light."

"I see," she said, thinking up more trouble for me. "But where does the electric current come from?"

"The power station," I said. "The big one, you know, that we saw once up by the dam."

"Why is it up by the dam?"

"Because the dam piles up the water behind it, the water is forced through pipes to drive big dynamos, and the dynamos make the electricity."

"What is a dynamo?"

"Now look here," I said, "it's about time for you to go to sleep."

"But, Daddy," she said, "just one more question."

"What is it?" I asked anxiously.

"Who made electricity first?"

"God did," I said with finality and kissed her good night.

But if I thought I had finished with her questions I was sadly mistaken. A few evenings later she started on another line. This time it was chickens. Her older brother had a number of them—too many of them, I always thought—in a wire pen opposite the back door. The chickens were always a source of interest to her, and she loved to feed them and listen to them peep. That is why I was met one evening with the following:

"Daddy, where do chickens come from?"

"From eggs," I said, thinking I had got out of this one easily.

14

"I know that," she said. "Some of our eggs hatched the other day."

"Well, then," I said, "what more do you want to know? Those eggs were laid by the hens."

"Of course, Daddy," she said. "But listen; those eggs were laid by hens, which were hatched out of eggs laid by other hens, which were hatched out of eggs——"

"That's enough," I said. "I understand perfectly. What you want to know is whether the egg came first or the chicken. Isn't that right?"

"That's right," she said.

"It was the chicken."

"Then how came the chicken?"

"God made it," I said, kissing her good night again.

But worse was to come. Thinking about how chickens began led her to question the origin of dogs. And this was but natural, for only a few weeks before, Sooty, the black cocker, had just presented her with triplets, two brown and one black.

"Daddy," she said the next evening, "let's talk about dogs tonight."

"All right," I said. "Anything to please you."

"I've been wondering," she said, "where dogs come from."

"Well," I said, "you know yourself that they come from puppies. Sooty has just had her puppies; but a year or so ago she was a puppy too."

"I know that," she said. "I remember when we bought her. But her mother was a puppy once, and her mother was a puppy once, and her mother——"

15

"Yes, darling," I said, wondering how far back she really intended to go. "Of course, that is how dogs have come for hundreds and thousands of years."

"I suppose so," she said. "But when you get far, far back, just as far as you can go," and she screwed her whole face into a puzzled frown, "do you get to a tiny puppy or a mamma dog?"

"A dog," I said. "I am confident of that. A dog."

"Then where did that dog come from?"

"God made it," I said. And, of course, there was nothing else to say. So I kissed her good night once more and begged her to start thinking up questions on some easier subject next time.

But she didn't. Instead, she got me panting over such questions as, How does the grass grow? and, What makes the sun shine? and, Why do we have daisies and daffodils in the garden? She asked so many questions that there isn't room here to tell you about them all. At last I thought it was about time I told her something she really ought to know about all these things; and this is what I'll tell you, too, in the next story.

As in every home the baby of this happy family was a source of joy to all the children.

The Book of Beginnings

IF YOU really want to get right back to the beginning of things; if you want to know, for instance, how light began, how trees began, how fishes began, how birds began, how animals began, there is just one place to go to find out. And that is to the very first chapter of the Bible. The first four words of it are among the most wonderful in this whole wonderful Book. Look at them: "In the beginning God."

How much these four words say! *In the beginning,* farther back than you or I can think, there was God. Before there was a man or a dog or a chicken, or any kind of animal or bird, there was God. Before there were any flowers, or trees, or mountains, or rivers, before there was anything at all on this old world, there was God. He did not begin. He always was, "from everlasting to everlasting."

And that is such a comforting thought. He was there when the world began. He will be there when it ends. And He is there all the time between. As the Bible says, He is "the same yesterday, and to day, and for ever." Forever and forever.

But look at that first verse of Genesis. It goes on to say, "In the beginning God created the heaven and the earth." In other words, everything we see in nature, whether in the sky or in the earth about us, came from Him. He created all. That is, He made it out of something that did not exist before.

How did God do it? That is something we shall never fully understand. In the Psalms we read: "By the word of the Lord were the heavens made; and all the host of them by the breath of His mouth." "For He spake, and it was done; He commanded, and it stood fast." Psalm 33:6, 9.

Evidently all God had to do to make things was to speak. He said what He wanted to happen and it happened.

If you say, "Well, I can't believe that," then all I can say is, this is one of the things we must believe or we have no starting point for anything. As one Bible writer says, "Through faith we understand that the worlds were framed by the word of God." And that is a good thing to say. In fact, it is the only thing one can say. "By faith I understand God did it this way." Or, "I can't explain just how God did it, but I believe He is wise enough and strong enough to do just what He says He has done."

And now let us see what things were like "in the beginning" of the history of this world. In the second verse of the first chapter of Genesis we read, "And the earth was without form, and void; and darkness was upon the face of the deep."

That sounds like a pretty gloomy picture. If you have ever

tried to look over a rough sea on a dark night, you will know what the world looked like "in the beginning." There was not a man to be seen anywhere, not a single boy or girl, not a dog or a chicken, not a tree or a flower—only water and darkness everywhere.

Then God said, "Let there be light: and there was light."

This was the beginning of light as far as this earth is concerned. What a wonderful moment it must have been when the light came on! Just as when we turn a switch today.

Then we are told, "God divided the light from the darkness. And God called the light Day, and the darkness He called Night. And the evening and the morning were the first day."

Here we learn of the beginning of night and day. That was the very first night and the very first day in the history of the world. Yet there was nobody alive anywhere. Nobody.

Light was all God made that first day, but, as the second day dawned, God spoke again. And God said, "Let there be a firmament . . . , and let it divide the waters from the waters. . . . And God called the firmament Heaven. And the evening and the morning were the second day."

If you think of the word "firmament" as meaning the atmosphere that surrounds the earth, you can better understand what God did on that second day. He made it possible for men and animals to live and breathe. That's why, after making light, He made the firmament, or atmosphere. He was getting ready to make the earth a place for living creatures.

Then came the third day. If you could have been there, say with an airplane, able to fly about quickly from place to

19

place, what activity you would have seen! For God said, "Let the waters under the heaven be gathered together unto one place, and let the dry land appear: and it was so. And God called the dry land Earth; and the gathering together of the waters called He Seas: and God saw that it was good."

What a sight it must have been—continents and islands rising up hither and yon out of the ocean depths! Great areas of land appearing where before there had been only water. And the light glistening and shimmering on myriads of streams rushing downhill to meet the waves that lapped the shore lines of these countries to be.

That third day! What a day it was! For scarcely had the land appeared above the sea than God spoke again. And He said, "Let the earth bring forth grass, the herb yielding seed, and the fruit tree yielding fruit after his kind, whose seed is in itself, upon the earth: and it was so."

Suddenly, as the voice of God echoed and re-echoed around the globe, an amazing thing happened. All the mountains and the hills, so brown and barren looking, suddenly turned to every glorious shade of green, from the yellow green of the grass to the deep green of the fir trees. Everywhere the

20

newborn land became one beautiful countryside, covered with lovely meadows and magnificent forests.

And it was not all green, for there were flowers, too, on trees and shrubs and plants, making wondrous patches of scarlet and gold, of blue and yellow, orange and violet. What a picture!

How the angels must have exclaimed at its loveliness! No wonder we read, "God saw that it was good." It *was* good. It was the best that God Himself could create.

And this was to be the home of man!

But not yet. God had something else in mind. Delightful as was the earth already, it was to be more radiant still. All this verdure—these trees and shrubs and bushes and grasses and flowers—needed sunshine to bring out its full perfection. So upon the fourth day God said: "Let there be lights in the firmament of the heaven to divide the day from the night. . . . And God made two great lights; the greater light to rule the day, and the lesser light to rule the night. . . . And God saw that it was good. And the evening and the morning were the fourth day."

That was the very first time that the sun had ever shone upon the earth. As its warm, brilliant rays flashed through the overcast upon all that God had made the day before, the scene must have sparkled and flamed like a fairyland. No wonder the Bible says that at that moment "the morning stars sang together, and all the sons of God shouted for joy." Job 38:7.

The Birds Start Singing

FOUR days had now passed, during which, out of a dark, ugly, shapeless mass, God had brought forth a world of plenty and beauty, fit for kings and queens to live in.

As yet, however, there was not a single creature anywhere. Not a man or an animal, not even a sparrow or a butterfly. Nor was there one single little trout in a river nor a sardine in the sea.

So on the morning of the fifth day God said: "Let the waters bring forth abundantly. . . . And God created great whales, and every living creature that moveth, which the waters brought forth abundantly, after their kind, and every winged fowl after his kind: and God saw that it was good."

What a day that must have been! The first fish swimming in the sea. Great whales moving majestically through the oceans like giant submarines. Schools of minnows dashing hither and yon like crowds of children fresh from school. Fish of every size and shape, of every kind and color. What joy God

22

must have had inventing them! But that wasn't all. Minutes later He sent the first birds flying through the air. Mighty eagles and tiny sparrows. Storks and cranes and robins. Bluebirds and blackbirds. Bright-red parrots and pale-yellow canaries. Singing birds and hummingbirds and maybe talking birds too. What a wonderful variety God thought out!

And—did you ever stop to think of it?—the first sound ever heard upon the earth, besides the noise of the wind and the waves, was the song of a bird. Perhaps it came from the first skylark to leap from the hand of God, or the first thrush or the first sweet nightingale. They were singing before a lion roared or a horse neighed or a dog barked or the voice of man was heard. For still there was no man anywhere. God was not ready for him yet.

So ended the fifth day, to the singing of birds, the spouting of whales, and the leaping of flying fish from the sea.

The next morning God said, "Let the earth bring forth the living creature after his kind, cattle, and creeping thing, and beast of the earth after his kind: and it was so. . . . And God saw that it was good."

If you could have been hiding somewhere in one of the

forests that morning, perhaps in a beautiful, sunlit glade, what marvelous things you would have seen! Up to that moment all the forests had been empty. There wasn't a footprint anywhere of any man or animal. You could have walked clear round the world and not found a single living creature except, of course, the birds in the air and the fish in the sea, created the day before.

Then, all of a sudden, you would have seen, perhaps, a majestic lion walking toward you, or a sleek tiger or an immense elephant. And you wouldn't have been frightened, for the animals were not ferocious then as they are now.

Turning round at a strange sound, you might have seen some sheep and goats or dogs and cats, frolicking about with all the happiness and energy of newly created beings. You would have petted them and fondled them and found them all as friendly as could be.

Now everywhere was life. Squirrels running up and down trees. Frogs hopping about in pools. Bears lolling in the sunshine. Horses capering about in sheer delight at being alive.

Again what marvelous variety! Giraffes with their great long necks. Zebras with their colored stripes. Leopards with their black spots. Hippopotamuses with their huge mouths.

24

Elephants with their funny trunks. Rabbits with their long ears.

"And God saw that it was good." It was good. Very good. A beautiful, parklike home, filled with wonderful, living creatures of every type and description, all dwelling together in peace and friendliness like one great happy family.

Yet there was something missing. Something of very great importance in the mind of God. Far more important indeed than anything He had created hitherto. It was man.

For God did not create the earth, with all its natural wonders, merely to be a place for birds and beasts and fishes to live in. He didn't intend it to be merely a zoo and an aquarium. He had made it to be a home for man. As we read in the book of Isaiah, "He formed it to be inhabited."

For man, then, were all these preparations made. For man all this creative energy was put forth. For man was the land raised out of the sea and clothed with trees and flowers; for man were the light and warmth of the sun caused to shine upon its surface. For man's delight were the birds created. For his pleasure and service were the animals formed. So much did God think of him and love him!

But as yet there was no man, and the sixth day was already drawing to a close.

STORY 4

The First Man

AT JUST what moment on the sixth day God made the first man, the Bible does not say. Perhaps it was late in the morning or early in the afternoon. Or it may have been just before sunset; who can tell? But sometime that day God crowned His work of creation by forming the most wonderful being that had come from His hand.

Everything was ready for him, the best that God could provide out of the infinite riches of His wisdom and love. Nothing was left undone to prepare the loveliest home anyone could ever hope to live in. And then God said, "Let us make man in our image, after our likeness."

What a wonderful thing for Him to say! He might have said, Let us make man like a lion, only bigger and stronger. Or He might have said, Let us make him like an eagle, only with wings ten times as large. Or He might have said, Let us make him a mixture of animal and bird and fish so that he can move anywhere he pleases and be at home on land or in the air or

27

Before God made man He had everything ready for his happiness. A beautiful garden was prepared for him to live in. Then with loving care He created him in His own image.

under the sea. He might have given man four legs and a horse's mane and a monkey's tail. He might. But He did nothing of the kind. He had something far greater and nobler in mind. For the pattern of this masterpiece of creation He looked upon Himself!

"So God created man in His own image, in the image of God created He him."

Notice that He didn't say this time, Let there be man, as He had said, "Let there be light," and "Let there be a firmament," and "Let the waters bring forth abundantly." This was different. This was the most important thing He had done up to now. Greater than making continents and oceans. More important than filling the earth with trees and flowers and animals and birds and fish. He was about to make someone like Himself.

So we read, "The Lord God *formed* man of the dust of the ground, and breathed into his nostrils the breath of life; and man became a living soul."

If only we could have been there to watch! If you and I could have seen the loving, tender care with which God took the dust in His hands and formed it—formed it with infinite skill—into a brain, a heart, a pair of lungs, and all the organs of a perfect body, connecting them by means of a nervous system and a glandular system, and binding them all together with muscles and flesh.

He made eyes, that man might see, and ears, that he might hear. He gave him a tongue, that he might taste, and a nose, that he might smell, and skin, that he might feel. And He arranged that the brain should not only take note of every impression on the eye, the ear, the nose, the tongue, the skin, but also record these impressions so that they might be remembered. He made memory possible.

Swiftly the task was completed. The beautiful figure, like an exquisite statue, lay upon the ground. God must have looked down upon it in great satisfaction. Then He drew near again and "breathed into his nostrils the breath of life."

How near He must have come! So close to his mouth that perhaps He kissed him! Who knows? But we do know that as the breath of God filled the man's lungs, he came to life and stood upon his feet. Tall, graceful, handsome, with flashing eye and kingly bearing, he must have been a glorious sight to behold. I can almost see the angels as they crowded close to get the first glimpse of this magnificent being, fresh from the hand of God. And I can imagine that they cried out in wonder: "Great and marvellous are Thy works, Lord God Almighty."

Long years afterward King David said, "I am fearfully and wonderfully made," and never was a truer word spoken. After studying the human body for thousands of years, doctors and surgeons and nerve specialists and bone specialists and gland specialists are still discovering new wonders in it that no one knew about before. Yes, when God made the body of the first man, it was indeed His masterpiece. He gave it His best. And that is why it seems to me such an insult to God

when some people say that He didn't make man at all; that man just "evolved" mysteriously from a speck of slime in the sea. That's just as though, after you had made a toy airplane of which you were very proud, the boy next door said, "Bah! You didn't make it; it just came together all by itself." You know how you would feel if anybody said that. And maybe God feels that way, too, when people say He didn't make man —when man was His greatest and best creative work.

But now let us look again at Adam, the first man. Already he is striding over the lovely earth, his keen eyes taking in all the beauty of land and sea and sky, his whole being athrill with the glory of being alive. Animals come to meet him, and birds sing the sweeter for his presence. The forests are alive with happy cries of welcome, as though all creation knew that God had said, This is your leader, your ruler, and he shall "have dominion over the fish of the sea, and over the fowl of the air, and over every living thing that moveth upon the earth."

A lion comes out from some bushes and walks beside him—two kings together! A zebra, a horse, a deer, a goat, and some sheep crowd him, while a little black dog sniffs at his heels. It is a grand procession through the woods, over the hills, down by the shore, and back again.

Adam feels hungry and wonders what to eat. He looks at the clusters of purple fruit on the vines, the big red berries on the bushes, the nuts hanging from the trees. He wonders whether he should pluck any, and God says to him—for God was not far away, I am sure of that—"Behold, I have given you every herb bearing seed, which is upon the face of all the

31

← PAINTING BY HARRY ANDERSON   © BY REVIEW AND HERALD

When God made Adam the ruler of all His created beings in the Garden of Eden, the animals lived in happy harmony and mingled together without fear of one another.

earth, and every tree, in the which is the fruit of a tree yielding seed; to you it shall be for meat."

So Adam eats his first meal. I wonder what he chose? Walnuts, perhaps, or almonds or pecans. Then some raspberries and gooseberries and, of course, some bananas and grapes. And what beautiful fruit it must have been, just created by the voice of God only three days before!

I can imagine the animals standing around as Adam ate all these lovely things. Then they ate, too, of the leaves and the grass, for God had said to them: "To every beast of the earth, and to every fowl of the air, and to every thing that creepeth upon the earth, wherein there is life, I have given every green herb for meat."

The wonderful thing about this is that during the very same week God had so constructed the grass, the plants, and the trees, that their green leaves would provide the animals with all that they would need to sustain life. How carefully did He plan every detail of this marvelous new world of His!

And His work was not finished yet. He had one more beautiful thing to do—the loveliest, kindest, sweetest act of all Creation week.

As Adam sat there in the forest glade, with the animals crowding around, looking at him with their big, friendly eyes and sniffing at him with their long, pointed noses, or their short, stubby noses, he noticed something about them he had not seen before. To each one God had given a mate. To the lion, a lioness. To the tiger, a tigress. And so on. But he was alone. There was no creature anywhere that looked like him.

32

THE FIRST MAN

Then he began to realize that though the animals might be his friends they could never be his close companions, thinking his thoughts, sharing his joys, talking over with him his hopes and plans.

Suddenly, as he thought of these things, he became very, very sleepy. Inasmuch as he had never slept before, he must have wondered what the sleepy feeling meant, and what was going to happen to him. Perhaps he tried to wake himself up and shake off the feeling of drowsiness. But if he did, it was no use. He became more and more sleepy, until at last, in a secluded part of the forest, under the shade of some big, beautiful tree, he lay down and went fast asleep.

"And the Lord God caused a deep sleep to fall upon Adam, and he slept."

No sooner was he asleep than God did a strange thing. With infinite skill He performed an operation on Adam, the first in human history. The Bible says, "He took one of his ribs, and closed up the flesh instead thereof; and the rib, which the Lord God had taken from man, made He a woman."

Perhaps you wonder why God did this; why He didn't choose some other way. If He could make light by saying, "Let there be light"; if He could make the trees by saying, "Let there be trees," why didn't He just say, "Let there be a woman"?

There must have been a very good reason, or God would not have worked the way He did. I think He did it this way that man might ever remember that his wife is truly part of

3

him and so treat her as he would himself.

And now let us watch God at work again. Of that rib it says (in the margin) that He "builded" a woman. Just as a little while before He had "formed man of the dust of the ground," fashioning the most wonderful creature He had ever made, so now all His infinite knowledge and wisdom were used in the creation of the one who was to become the mother of the whole human family. How perfectly He molded the features of her lovely face! How gracefully He arranged her long, flowing hair! With what loving thought He placed within her heart all the tenderness, all the gentleness, all the sweetness, and all the endless store of love He wanted every mother to have!

When Adam looked upon his beautiful companion Eve he said, "This is now bone of my bones, and flesh of my flesh: she shall be called Woman, because she was taken out of Man."

THE FIRST MAN

At last this fairest creature of Creation was completed. Then in all her perfect loveliness God "brought her unto the man."

Perhaps Adam was still asleep. I don't know. Perhaps he was dreaming—dreaming of the companion he hoped to find someday, somewhere in the woods or fields. Then perhaps God called to him, "Adam, wake up, wake up! See what I have made for you."

Then Adam awoke, rubbed his eyes, and looked. There before him was something more beautiful than any dream, a being so choice, so noble, so altogether lovely that his heart leaped within him. As he looked upon her lovely form and gazed into her bright, kindly, understanding eyes, he knew instantly that this was his mate. This was the companion he had been seeking.

"And Adam said, This is now bone of my bones, and flesh of my flesh: she shall be called Woman, because she was taken out of Man."

And now I see them—dear, beautiful creatures, walking arm in arm through the forests and fields, exploring all the wonders of creation. King and queen of the glorious new earth, they wander hither and yon, admiring the beauties of their lovely kingdom. They talk together of the marvels they have seen and the wonders of God's power. And they praise Him for all His goodness to them.

And I think, too, that I see God, silently watching them, smiling upon their perfect happiness.

STORY 5

Man's First Home

~~~~~~~~~~~~~~~~~~~~~~~~~~~~~~~~~~

T HE Lord God planted a garden eastward in Eden; and there He put the man whom He had formed."

Did you ever plant a garden? How exciting it is to sow the seeds, then watch the little plants grow, and finally gather the crops or pluck the flowers!

But when God planted a garden it was different. He didn't need to plant seeds. As the great Creator He could say, I want a cluster of giant redwoods here and a grove of silver birches there, and they appeared at His word. He called for a hill to be covered with pines and another with oaks, and it was so. He called for a valley to be carpeted with yellow buttercups, another with scarlet anemones, another with sweet-smelling hyacinths, while everywhere through the meadows He summoned the little white daisies. And it was so.

All the earth was beautiful then; there were no deserts or marshes or bare, rocky crags; everywhere was breathtaking loveliness. But there was one place more beautiful than all.

37

Before sin entered the world, all the earth was beautiful. No rocky crags or dismal marshes marred the scene. All was lovely in every direction Adam and Eve looked.

This was Eden, the garden that God planted, man's first home.

Notice that when God made the first man and the first woman He didn't build them a house; He planted a garden. He didn't give them a log cabin or an apartment with hot-and-cold water or a three-story stucco house or even a palace such as a king and queen might have expected; instead He gave them a home amid the trees and flowers. Its walls were pines and firs and oaks; its floors were bluebells, cowslips, and primroses. Its roof was the great dome of heaven, while for light the sun shone by day and the moon and the stars by night.

No shelter, of course, was needed in those days, for there was no rain. Instead "there went up a mist from the earth, and watered the whole face of the ground." Genesis 2:6.

This home had no bedroom, as we think of bedrooms, only cozy, moss-covered nooks anywhere one wished to rest. Its parlor was a hillside overlooking some delightful bay or a sandy, lakeside cove. Its music room was a low branch of a tree, where the songs of birds could be heard. Its pantry and kitchen were the vines, bushes, and fruit trees, ever loaded with good things to eat.

No home ever built by man has been like this garden planted by God, so beautiful, so peaceful, so happy, so altogether perfect.

Now, as Adam and Eve, hand in hand, hasten here and there to see everything they can of all that God has given them,

they come suddenly upon something so unusual that they stop to look at it in amazement. It is a tree the like of which they have not found anywhere else in the Garden. Tall, graceful, magnificent, it is covered with brilliant fruit. Not far away they see another wonderful tree also loaded with lovely fruit. Just as they are wondering what these two trees can be, God draws near and tells them that they are now in the very center of their garden home, that one of these trees is "the tree of life" and the other "the tree of the knowledge of good and evil."

"And the Lord God commanded the man, saying, Of every tree of the garden thou mayest freely eat: but of the tree of the knowledge of good and evil, thou shalt not eat of it: for in the day that thou eatest thereof thou shalt surely die."

No doubt they both wondered why God had put a tree in their garden of which they mustn't eat. And what did He mean by saying that if they should eat of it they would die? What did He mean by "dying"? What was "dying"?

Still wondering, they go on their way, looking for more of the treasures God had placed in the Garden for them.

It is still the sixth day of Creation week, though late in the afternoon. How much has happened upon this great, this wonderful day!

And now the sun, which has been high in the heavens, is moving toward the horizon. The heat of afternoon is giving place to the cool of evening, something that neither Adam nor

Eve has ever known before. Birds are twittering as they prepare to sleep, while new sounds come from the forest as the animals sense that night is near.

The happy pair, gazing westward, behold the blazing glory of the sunset. As the red orb plunges earthward, the sky is filled with wondrous colors and a new beauty glows upon every tree and flower.

Adam and Eve bow their heads in worship of their Maker while God looks down in delight at the completion of His work.

"And God saw every thing that He had made, and, behold, it was very good."

All had turned out well. All was the best that could be.

The earth with its rich stores of gold and silver and precious stones, its bright covering of grass and flowers and trees. The fish and birds and animals in all their marvelous variety. And now this man and this woman bowing in worship, recognizing their God.

Again the stars sang together and all the sons of God shouted for joy.

"And, behold, it was very good."

And the sixth day slowly faded into night.

The First Sabbath

I SUPPOSE you go to church every week. I hope so. It's a good thing for boys and girls to do. We all miss something when we don't worship God.

But when you go to church I wonder whether you ever ask yourself how "going to church" started, and who began the idea of keeping the Sabbath? You know, of course, that many people kept it last week and the week before that and the week before that and the week before that. You have a pretty good idea that some people at least kept it all last year and the year before that and the year before that. But how far back have people kept the Sabbath? A hundred years? Five hundred years? A thousand years?

Yes, and much longer than that. For almost six thousand years, without a break, the Sabbath has been kept by somebody or other on this old earth. Every week, without fail, some group of people has worshiped God on this day.

The fact is that it all began in that garden home which

God planted for Adam and Eve. Indeed, the very first Sabbath ever observed was kept by God Himself, together with these two wonderful creatures fresh from His creative hands. It was when the sun set on the sixth day of Creation week that the first Sabbath of all time began.

But how did the seventh day come to be a Sabbath, or rest day?

The Bible says that "on the seventh day God ended His work which He had made; and He rested on the seventh day from all His work which He had made. And God blessed the seventh day, and sanctified it: because that in it He had rested from all His work which God created and made."

I don't think this means that God rested because He was tired, for God does not get tired. Rather, He rested because He had finished His work of creation. Then, too, I think He rested because He wanted to set Adam and Eve an example that He wished them and their children to follow.

But God not only "rested" on this day. He "blessed" it and "sanctified" it.

To "sanctify" means to set apart as holy, and this is exactly what God did with the seventh day. He set it apart from the other days of the week as a holy day of rest and worship.

How did God "bless" the Sabbath day? Surely by putting a blessing into it which only those who keep it properly can find. And it is a fact, even after all these thousands of years, that anybody who keeps the Sabbath as a holy day does find a joy and peace that others know nothing about.

But we must get back to our story of Adam and Eve. On

42

God planned that the weekly Sabbath should be kept from eventide to eventide, and the going down of the sun on the sixth day of the week marked its beginning.

the afternoon of the sixth day they did not know anything about the Sabbath, for they had just been created. Therefore, as the sun set that evening, and the seventh day began, God must have told them of His plan. "This day, this seventh day," He may well have said to them, "we will spend together."

And that is exactly what they must have done, for at that time there was but the one man and the one woman in all the world, and God. It is therefore reasonable to suppose that since God did rest on that day, since He blessed and sanctified it, they must have shared it with Him.

I wonder what they did together? Perhaps they walked through the beautiful Garden while God explained to Adam and Eve all the marvels of creation. Perhaps He told them how trees draw their food from the soil, and how the sap rises through the trunk and so out into the branches, the twigs, and the leaves. Perhaps He told them how a beautiful white lily grows from a little brown bulb or how white milk comes from a red cow that eats green grass. Perhaps He showed them the secret of how birds fly or the marvel in a butterfly's wing.

No one knows, of course, what they discussed, but it must have been a wonderful experience to walk through creation with the Creator! What a marvelous Guide and Teacher He must have been! And as they talked together surely Adam and Eve must have been well-nigh overcome with wonder and praise, exclaiming again and again, from the depths of their hearts, "Great and marvellous are Thy works, Lord God Almighty!"

That first Sabbath was a day of rest and worship and communion with God, long to be remembered. And God

THE FIRST SABBATH

wants every Sabbath to be as nearly like it as possible, even today. We know this is so, because when He gave us the Ten Commandments He said, "Remember the sabbath day, to keep it holy. Six days shalt thou labour, and do all thy work: but the seventh day is the sabbath of the Lord thy God," and He added, "For in six days the Lord made heaven and earth, the sea, and all that in them is, and rested the seventh day: wherefore the Lord blessed the sabbath day, and hallowed it."

God will never forget that blessed day with Adam and Eve at the close of Creation week, and He wants everybody else to remember it too. So He told His people to keep every seventh day and to keep each one as nearly as possible as it was kept in Eden. Then, He said, a great blessing will be found in the Sabbath—the blessing that always comes from walking and talking with God, and worshiping Him as Creator of the heavens and the earth.

What One Sin Cost

HAVE you ever been on a picnic, perhaps in some beautiful park or down by the sea, with everybody having a wonderful time, then had it all spoiled because some of the boys or girls did something wrong? Perhaps they deliberately disobeyed the park rules or did something that the person in charge had said should not be done. If so, you know what happened. That one foolish act of disobedience ruined the picnic. It brought a cloud down on everything. Nothing was the same again. And on the way home the others said,

WHAT ONE SIN COST

"Oh, why did they have to do that! They wrecked the whole day for us, and we were so happy before!"

Well, if you ever had an experience like that, you will understand what happened to Adam and Eve in the Garden of Eden.

For some time after Creation life was one glorious picnic for them. They couldn't have wished for a lovelier place in which to live. Their work was easy and pleasant, for all that God asked of them when He placed them in their garden home was "to dress it and to keep it." There were no weeds or thorns or thistles to bother them. As for food there was abundance all about them. Had they been more careful they might have been living there yet.

But they made a mistake, a very big mistake, and it spoiled everything.

One day Eve went for a walk by herself to take another look at the two beautiful trees in the center of the Garden. They were so lovely, with all their bright-colored fruit, that she was fascinated by them. As she gazed with wondering eyes

upon "the tree of the knowledge of good and evil," she remembered, of course, that God had said that the fruit of this tree was not for them to eat. She could not understand why God had said this. It seemed strange to her that after He had given them so much He should hold back this one tree. But she had no thought of disobeying Him. She was sure God had some good reason for saying what He had about the tree, and would no doubt explain it all in good time.

Just as she was turning away, perhaps to look again at the beautiful "tree of life," she was startled to hear someone speaking to her.

Who could it be? The only voices she had heard up to then had been the voice of God and the voice of Adam. Now someone else was speaking. She looked about her and to her astonishment noticed that the voice was coming from a serpent. It was a very gracious and friendly voice, too, so much so that Eve's fears disappeared and she stood, listening. In a way it was nice to have someone else to talk to, even if it was only a serpent.

Who was this serpent? The Bible tells us that it was "the Devil, and Satan, which deceiveth the whole world." Revelation 12:9. He was leader of the rebel angels who were cast out of heaven, and he had come to this earth to take revenge on God by trying to spoil His plans for man's happiness.

But, of course, Eve did not know all this, or she wouldn't have listened to him. All she knew was that here was a most unusual animal talking to her in a pleasant, friendly voice. So she listened.

And the serpent said, "Yea, hath God said, Ye shall not eat of every tree of the garden?"

How strange! The serpent even knew just what she was thinking about!

She decided to reply to him.

"We may eat of the fruit of the trees of the garden," she said innocently; "but of the fruit of the tree which is in the midst of the garden, God hath said, Ye shall not eat of it, neither shall ye touch it, lest ye die."

In a confidential tone the serpent replied, "Ye shall not surely die."

This was stranger still, Eve must have thought. The creature was actually contradicting God! It didn't seem right. It didn't seem possible that anyone could ever do that! But—was God wrong? Could it be that He had not told the truth?

The first doubt entered Eve's mind.

Seeing he had made an impression, the serpent continued: "For God doth know that in the day ye eat thereof, then your eyes shall be opened, and ye shall be as gods, knowing good and evil."

This was a suggestion to Eve that God had been unfair to her and Adam; that He was holding something back that belonged to them. It was a sly hint that God was jealous of them and so would not give them their full rights.

It was a very mean thing the serpent did, when God had been so good. But the devil is always mean. And he is always

4

working against God. We need to beware of any suggestion that God is not fair. It comes from Satan.

The serpent also put the idea into Eve's mind that if she would take of this fruit her eyes would be opened and she would know both "good and evil." Up to that moment she did not know any evil. She must have asked herself, What does the serpent mean by "evil"? She became curious. She thought she would like to know what evil is like.

And that is always dangerous. It always leads to trouble and sorrow. If anyone ever suggests to you that you should try this or that wrong thing so that you may know "how it tastes" or "how it feels," turn your back on him and run away. It's the safest thing to do. You don't need to know evil. You are far better off without that knowledge. Remember, you don't have to put your hand in a bucket of tar to know it's black.

The serpent had done his deadly work. He had made Eve doubt God's word, and he had tempted her to taste the fruit of "the tree of the knowledge of good and evil."

Finally the temptation was more than she could stand. She reached out her hand, took of the fruit, and ate it. The taste was wonderful, so she gathered some more and took it to Adam, "and he did eat."

Perhaps he said to her, "But I thought we were not to eat this fruit." If so, she probably said, "Oh, it's quite all right. The serpent told me I wouldn't die and, you see, nothing has happened to me. God must have made a mistake."

But God had not made a mistake. He had purposely set aside one tree in the Garden in order to develop the characters of His newly made creatures. He did not want them to be just like clockwork figures, obeying Him merely because He said so. He wanted them to trust Him and serve Him because they chose to do so themselves. He wanted them to worship Him because they loved Him. The tree was only a test. If they truly loved Him they wouldn't touch it. Then they could live forever. If they doubted Him and couldn't be trusted to obey Him, then they would have to die and go back to the dust whence He had taken them.

No sooner had Adam and Eve eaten of the fruit than they were greatly worried about what they had done. It was the first time they had ever been worried about anything. Up to then they had not known a worry or a care. They began to

wonder what God would think of their disobedience. What would He say to them?

As the day dragged by they began to get frightened. All the happiness had gone out of life. Their lovely picnic was completely spoiled. They wanted to run away and hide themselves.

What a pity! But sin always works that way. It spoils everything it touches.

By and by Adam and Eve "heard the voice of the Lord God walking in the garden in the cool of the day." At other times they had been so pleased to hear that lovely voice, but now they ran away from it, "and Adam and his wife hid themselves from the presence of the Lord God amongst the trees of the garden."

As if they could hide from God! They couldn't do it then, and we cannot do it now.

"And the Lord God called unto Adam, and said unto him, Where art thou?"

What sorrow there was in His voice! It was as though He said, "Why don't you come to meet Me as you used to do? Why are you hiding from One who loves you so much?"

Then Adam, peering from behind a tree, said, "I heard Thy voice in the garden, and I was afraid."

Afraid! He had never been afraid before. He had never known what fear was. Now this grand, noble, beautiful creature was afraid. That is another thing sin does. It takes away all one's happy feelings and makes one want to run away and hide. It makes one hate to be in the presence of good people. It made Adam want to get away even from God, his Maker and his Friend.

Of course, all along God knew what had happened. God always does. So He said, "Hast thou eaten of the tree, whereof I commanded thee that thou shouldest not eat?"

Yes, Adam had, and so had Eve. They were both guilty of grave disobedience.

How sad it all was then!

God told them both what would have to happen because of their sin. They would have to leave their beautiful home. Instead of the pleasant time they had been having, they would have to work hard and long for their living. They would know pain and sorrow. They would learn the meaning of death. All nature, too, would suffer because of this evil thing they had done.

As they hung their heads in shame, and tears flowed down their cheeks, God spoke His final word. Looking at Adam in deepest pity, He said: "Because thou hast hearkened unto the voice of thy wife, and hast eaten of the tree, of which I commanded thee, saying, Thou shalt not eat of it: cursed is the ground for thy sake; in sorrow shalt thou eat of it all the days of thy life; thorns also and thistles shall it bring forth to thee; and thou shalt eat the herb of the field; in the sweat of thy face shalt thou eat bread, till thou return unto the ground;

for out of it wast thou taken: for dust thou art, and unto dust shalt thou return."

It was a hard sentence, but God wanted them and all their unborn children to know how terrible even the smallest sin appears in His sight. He knew how sin had already spoiled the harmony of heaven; now it was starting again on earth, spoiling this Paradise. Something had to be done.

So Adam and Eve left their beautiful garden home. With aching hearts they turned their backs on all that was so dear to them. Somehow I think I can see their friends, the animals, peering at them with wonder in their eyes, as though asking one another, What is the matter? Where are they going? And the birds hushed their singing as they listened in awe to the great, heartbroken sob of their lord and master as he and his lovely wife walked out into the night.

There was no way back. At least, so it must have seemed to them then. For, turning to take one last look at all that they had loved and lost, they saw a strange light over the way they had just come, "and a flaming sword which turned every way, to keep the way of the tree of life."

So great is the cost of just one sin! No wonder God wants us to be good and to love and obey Him with all our hearts.

The First Promise Ever Made

~~~~~~~~~~~~~~~~~~~~~~~~~~~~~~~~~~~~~

MANY times, I suppose, Adam and Eve must have talked over the good old days and the lovely Paradise home God gave them in the beginning. No doubt, too, they wondered if they would ever see it again.

Thinking of everything that had happened, going over all that had been said and done on that sad day when they made their terrible mistake, they tried to think whether God had given them any hope of returning to their home.

One thing that He had said stood out in their minds, something He had said to the serpent. Again and again they repeated it, wondering just what it might mean: "I will put enmity between thee and the woman, and between thy seed and her seed; it shall bruise thy head, and thou shalt bruise his heel."

What could this mean? they thought. Of course, it meant that Eve would have children, and she was glad of that. But how much more? "It shall bruise thy head." Surely that must

55

mean that one of her children would bruise, or crush, the serpent's head. And that must mean that someday the wicked serpent who had brought such sorrow and loss upon them would be destroyed. Then Eden might be restored to them!

How they loved this promise! It was the first promise ever made to man, and the first one mentioned in the Bible.

So Adam and Eve began looking forward to their first baby. Perhaps he would be the one to bruise the serpent's head! Perhaps they wouldn't have to wait so long to return to Eden after all!

When Cain was born they were very, very happy. Eve said: "I have gotten a man from the Lord." Some say that she said, "I have gotten a man, the Lord," believing that Cain would be the one who would crush the serpent and bring them back in joy and triumph to their beloved Eden.

But it was not to be Cain. He grew up to be a murderer and killed his own brother Abel.

And it was not to be their next boy, Seth, nor his son, nor his son after that. So the years went by, and no one came to restore them to their Paradise and the tree of life.

What, then, did God have in mind when He made that promise in the Garden? He was thinking of Jesus, of course, and all that He would do. For Jesus is the one who will finally destroy Satan and bring Adam and Eve and all who love God back to Eden again.

Of course, if God had said to Adam and Eve, "You will have to wait thousands and thousands of years before you see your first home again," they would have been very much dis-

57

Adam and Eve often talked about the promise God made to them just before they were driven out of the Garden of Eden. Eve clearly remembered how God cursed the serpent, and why.

couraged. So He told them just enough to let them know that all would be well at last. This cheered their poor, sad hearts, and led them to keep on hoping. And men have passed on the same blessed hope from one to another all down the years.

And this is how it came about that all the people who loved God began looking forward to the coming of Jesus. This is why Enoch, "the seventh from Adam," said, "Behold, the Lord cometh with ten thousands of His saints, to execute judgment upon all." Jude 14, 15.

Today we still hold the same hope. Boys and girls who love Jesus are everywhere looking eagerly for His return. They know that when He comes the first promise to Adam will be fulfilled and "that old serpent, the Devil," will be destroyed. Then, too, Eden—beautiful glorious Eden—will be restored.

STORY 9

The Man God Took

ADAM and Eve lived a long, long time. The Bible says that Adam was actually nine hundred and thirty years old when he died.

Nine hundred and thirty years! That's a long time.

If you say, "Oh, nobody could have lived that long," remember that Adam was created by God on that sixth great day of Creation week. Remember that he was the most perfectly formed man who ever lived. His heart, his lungs, his muscles, fresh from God's own hands, were good to last easily a thousand years. Indeed, they would have lasted forever had he been able to eat of the tree of life. Then, too, in those early days of the world, there were none of the diseases so common now, which carry so many people to an early grave.

I don't have any doubt that Adam lived nine hundred and thirty years, just as the Bible says. It may seem very old to us, but that's because we have become used to people dying much younger.

Now, if Adam lived to be more than nine hundred years old, he must have seen his sons' sons, and their sons, and their sons, for many generations. By the time he died he must have been a great-great-great-great-great-great-grandfather. I really don't know how many "greats" to put in. By that time, too, there must have been many thousands of people living on the earth, all related to him. What a crowd it must have been when they had a family get-together!

But not only Adam lived a long time. So did his children. One of his sons, Seth, lived to be nine hundred and twelve! And one of Seth's sons, Enos, nine hundred and five.

Then came Cainan, 910; Mahalaleel, 895; and Jared, 962. Enoch, 365, and Methuselah, the oldest man who ever lived, 969. After him came Lamech, 777, and Noah, 950.

You can read about these grand old men in the fifth chapter of the book of Genesis. And when you do, take a pencil and paper and draw lines to show how long each of them lived. Allow about half an inch to a hundred years. Work it out carefully and you will discover some very interesting facts.

First, you will notice that of these nine patriarchs that followed Adam, eight of them lived at the same time as he did. Only Noah never saw him.

Second, you will notice that two of them, Methuselah and Lamech, both of whom knew Adam personally, lived until just before the Flood. Noah was six hundred years old when the Flood came, and lived 350 years after it.

Third, you will notice that one line is much shorter than all the others. It is the line marking the life of Enoch. His

THE MAN GOD TOOK

father lived to be 962 years, and his son 969 years, but he only 365 years. Why was this? Did he become ill and die early?

No, he didn't die. That is the wonderful thing about Enoch. The Bible says, "God took him." This means that God took him away without his having to die. Why did God do that? There must have been a very good reason.

Now, God loved Adam very dearly, as we have seen, but God let him die, after he had lived for nearly a thousand years.

God loved Adam's son Seth, but He let him die, too, after he had lived just over nine hundred years. And so with all the others. God loved them, but He let them die. But Enoch lived so perfectly before God that He took him to heaven without seeing death.

Let us read exactly what the Bible says about it: "And Enoch lived sixty and five years, and begat Methuselah: and Enoch walked with God after he begat Methuselah three hundred years: . . . and Enoch walked with God: and he was not; for God took him."

There is the secret! He walked with God. That means he obeyed God's commandments and prayed every day for His guidance. That was what God wanted Adam to do in the beginning. There wasn't anything that God wouldn't have done for Adam had he faithfully walked with Him, instead of wandering away.

And God wanted Seth to walk with Him like that, and Enos and Cainan and all the rest, but none of them quite came up to His expectations.

THE MAN GOD TOOK

Only this man Enoch was different. He loved God with all his heart. His one purpose was to serve Him and to do His will. He thought of God in the morning, at noon, and at night. Always he was asking himself, Will God be pleased with this or that? His chief concern was to please not himself but God.

So God came very near to this man. Indeed, I can almost hear God saying, "This is a man after My own heart. This is what I hoped all men would be like. Dear Enoch! What a noble character!"

"And Enoch walked with God . . . three hundred years."

Three hundred years!

God didn't take him at once. He watched him, every day, every moment. And the more God saw of this man, the more God loved him.

Can we know what inspired Enoch to live such a life as this? Perhaps it was a talk he had one day with Adam—for Adam was still alive—of how God walked with him in the Garden of Eden before sin spoiled everything. Perhaps it was the thought of the great promise of deliverance of which he had heard so much. And yet it may have been something quite different.

The Bible says that Enoch walked with God "after he begat Methuselah." That is, after his little boy was born. It makes a lot of difference to some daddies when their boys are born, and perhaps it was as Enoch looked lovingly upon that little baby and thought of the wonderful power of God that had given him a child like himself that he gave his heart to God as never before and decided to love Him more than ever.

63

God came very near to Enoch. We can almost hear God saying, "This is a man after My own heart, a man perfect in character. This is what I hoped all men on earth would be."

Ever after that he "walked with God." And as he walked with Him he must have talked with Him many, many times. Then it was that God told him of His plans for the future, and how He would fulfill the promise He had made in the Garden.

It was after one of these talks that Enoch made that wonderful prophecy: "Behold, the Lord cometh with ten thousands of His saints." Jude 14. Although only "the seventh from Adam," as he was, the hope of the coming of Jesus was all aglow in his heart.

Then after he had lived three hundred years of such a life, "God took him." Where? The Bible does not say. It just says, "Enoch was translated that he should not see death; . . . for before his translation he had this testimony, that he pleased God." Hebrews 11:5. This is a beautiful thing to say about anybody. But this was written about three thousand years after "God took him." Just think! People still remembered that he "pleased God." Yes, and he was still alive then, still walking with God!

And Enoch will be there when Jesus comes in His glory. He will be there when Eden is restored.

STORY 10

The Old World Ends

≋≋≋≋≋≋≋≋≋≋≋≋≋≋≋≋≋

SAD to say, while some of Adam's children were good, like Enoch, some of them were bad, like Cain. All too soon many began to forget God. Then selfishness crept into their hearts. They became greedy and cruel. There was quarreling, fighting, and even killing.

How different from the peaceful days in Eden!

The old serpent, "which is the devil or Satan," who had deceived Adam and Eve in the Garden, rejoiced at the turn of events. He had come to this earth to take vengeance on God, and he was succeeding better than he had dared to hope. By filling men's minds with evil thoughts, he sought to complete the ruin of God's plans. Remembering what God had said to him in the Garden, about the Seed of the woman bruising his head, he set out to prevent the fulfillment of that prophecy.

So, led on by Satan and his evil angels, the children of Adam went from bad to worse.

No doubt Adam, out of his own bitter experience, did his

5

best to warn the wayward boys of the dreadful price of sin. Eve, with all her wonderful mother love, pleaded with the careless girls to turn back to God. For hundreds of years they sought to keep their children and their children's children in the good way "that leadeth unto life." But it was a hard struggle, for evil grew and spread. The wicked became bolder in their wickedness. They mocked at Adam's warnings and said that he was too old to understand young people. They complained at every restriction and murmured when anyone tried to make them keep good rules.

In the New Testament we are told that Jude, who was one of God's prophets, had a vision about Enoch, the man who walked with God away back there when Adam was growing old. Jude reports that Enoch protested about all the "ungodly deeds" of the people. He said they murmured, complained, and walked "after their own lusts" (verses 15, 16).

That was about nine hundred years after Creation. Five hundred years later things were much worse. By that time there was quarreling and fighting everywhere. Nobody's life was safe. The Bible says, "The earth was filled with violence."

THE OLD WORLD ENDS

What a pity! After all that God had planned for man's happiness! Once so peaceful and joyous, the beautiful earth was now a battlefield. Once so free from all sorrow and care, it was now filled with fears and tears.

How sorry God must have been! Remembering with what love and tenderness He made the first man and the first woman, we can understand how deeply pained He must have been.

The Bible says that "God saw that the wickedness of man was great in the earth, and that every imagination of the thoughts of his heart was only evil continually. And it repented the Lord that He had made man on the earth, and it grieved Him at His heart."

Conditions must have been terrible for God to say that!

Then with awful sadness He said to Himself, "I will destroy man whom I have created from the face of the earth; both man, and beast, and the creeping thing, and the fowls of the air; for it repenteth Me that I have made them."

Even so He decided to give the people yet one more chance to turn from their evil ways. "My spirit shall not always strive with man," He said: "yet his days shall be an hundred and twenty years."

He would wait just a hundred and twenty years, and see whether they would listen to His last call to repentance.

Looking for someone to give His message of warning, God found Noah, one of the ten grand old patriarchs of those ancient times, now nearly five hundred years old. He was one of the few good men still left on the earth. In the midst of the evil he had kept himself clean. The Bible says, "Noah was a just man and perfect in his generations, and Noah walked with God."

He must have been something like Enoch, for he, too, was walking with God. No doubt this is why God saved him and his family from the Flood.

"And God said unto Noah, The end of all flesh is come before Me; for the earth is filled with violence through them; and, behold, I will destroy them with the earth. Make thee an ark of gopher wood. . . . Behold, I, even I, do bring a flood of waters upon the earth, to destroy all flesh."

As Noah heard these words he must have wondered what God meant, and whether he had heard correctly. A flood of waters—what was that? And that ark of gopherwood he was to make—what a strange command! What would people think of him if he started to build a great big boat on dry land!

And the size of it! (For God was most careful to specify just what He wanted.) It was to be a huge vessel, big as a modern battleship. Yes, and in the same proportions used by the best ship designers today! It was to be about 600 feet long, 100 feet wide, and 60 feet in height.* That's a real ship, not a toy, as some people picture the ark. God designed it to sail the oceans and ride out the worst storms the world has ever seen.

Again Noah must have wondered. Whatever would the neighbors think when they saw him building a boat six hun-

---

* Assuming the cubit to be 24 inches long.

dred feet long! But, "Thus did Noah according to all that God commanded him, so did he." People do just that when they are walking with God.

So Noah started to work, building and preaching at the same time, with 120 years for his task.

What did the people do? Just as he expected: They laughed till their sides ached. "Look at old Noah!" they cried. "Whatever is he building? Is it a boat or a barn?"

But Noah replied, "God is about to send a flood of waters upon the earth because of your wickedness. Forsake your sins! Turn to God before it is too late!"

"A flood of waters!" they jeered. "Whoever heard of a flood of waters? The poor old man must be mad!"

But Noah went on building, and the great ship gradually took shape. The more the people mocked, the more earnestly he continued his work. Building and preaching. Building and preaching.

So the years, the last few years of that beautiful world, slipped away.

It is now the hundred and twentieth year, the last year of the old world. The great ship is completed, towering up sixty feet, twice as high as a three-story house! It looks gaunt and deserted, for only Noah is left with it, and his family. All his hired workmen have gone. They never had much interest in it anyway. They only worked for their pay and now, the job over, they have gone home. They never believed Noah's message, though they worked on his ark.

The great door stands open, inviting all who will to enter.

70

THE OLD WORLD ENDS

But nobody comes. To the few people who still bother to look, it seems as though Noah has wasted his time and money. Noah's folly, they call it. He has preached for 120 years that destruction is coming, and now nowhere is so peaceful as around this huge empty ark, where not even the sound of a hammer or a saw can be heard.

But look! Something is happening. Animals! What are they doing here? Look at them! Hundreds of them! Coming from all directions too. This is extraordinary. What can it mean?

As people come running to watch the strange sight, ani-

mals of every kind and description make their way to the ark, climb up the ramp that Noah has made for them, and in through the door. Lions, tigers, bears, giraffes, horses, zebras, elephants, donkeys, sheep, goats, and the rest. Two by two they go into the ark, each one with its mate, as though some unseen hand were guiding them.

And an unseen hand is guiding them—God's hand. For He has planned to save some of every kind of animal He created.

But the people looking on do not understand. It all seems strange to them, and funny. This ark isn't a boat after all, they say; just a new kind of zoo.

But when the last animal has passed through the door, Noah comes to the side of the ark and makes his final plea to the people to come in. "The Flood is coming. It is right upon you. Come into the ark! Come now, before it is forever too late!"

Again they mock him. "Go live with your animals!" they say. But repent of their evil deeds they will not.

So Noah leaves them. And the Bible says: "And Noah went in, and his sons, and his wife, and his sons' wives with him, into the ark, because of the waters of the flood. Of clean beasts, and of beasts that are not clean, and of fowls, and of every thing

72

that creepeth upon the earth, there went in two and two unto
Noah into the ark, the male and the female, as God had commanded Noah." "And the Lord shut him in."

As that great door mysteriously closed, there may have
been some looking on who wondered whether they had made
a mistake. Perhaps Noah was right. Perhaps they should have
gone in with him. But as nothing happened they soon stopped
worrying. There was no sign whatever of a flood such as Noah
had preached about. And there he was inside with all those animals!

The people became bolder in their ridicule, but after seven
days they changed their minds.

Great black clouds now cover the sky. Lightning flashes
and thunder roars. Drops of water begin to fall. It is raining
for the first time in the history of the world! Water from the
sky! This is what Noah said would happen. The old preacher
was right, after all.

It is a heavy downpour now, increasing every minute.
Water is pouring off the roofs of houses, rushing down the
roadways. Streams are filling up, overflowing their banks. Low-
lying land is becoming swampy. Pools and small lakes are
forming everywhere.

People are getting worried. Some look toward the ark

73

and wish they had gone inside before the door was shut. But it is too late.

Now there is water everywhere. Streets are flooded. It is coming into houses. People begin moving to higher ground.

But look! What is this? A wall of water is coming from the sea. A tidal wave! People run for their lives. They climb trees and hurry up hillsides. But the water chases them and there is no escape, for "the same day were all the fountains of the great deep broken up, and the windows of heaven were opened."

People climb up the ark and batter at the door. But there is no way to open it. They cry out that they are sorry for their sins, sorry that they laughed so at Noah and his preaching; but it is too late to be sorry.

How important it is to be sorry for our sins *in time!*

The water rises, rises, rises, until at last "all the high

hills" "and the mountains" are covered. "And all flesh died that moved upon the earth."

Even today the bones of animals that died in the Flood are found in some parts of the earth on the tops of the mountains where they had gone to escape the rising waters.

And so the old world, the beautiful world God created in the beginning, comes to its tragic end.

And all because of sin! All because people forgot their God! How much they lost by doing wrong!

Long years afterward, Jesus said, "For as in those days before the flood they were eating and drinking, marrying and giving in marriage, until the day when Noah entered the ark, and they did not know until the flood came and swept them all away, so will be the coming of the Son of man." Matthew 24:38, 39, R.S.V.

And He added—for you and for me: "Watch therefore: for ye know not what hour your Lord doth come."

The Rainbow of a New Beginning

~~~~~~

ONLY Noah and his family and the animals with him were saved from the Flood. Nobody else. In all the earth there was not a single animal or man left. Only in the ark, tossed on the wild waves of that storm-swept ocean, was there life.

How God must have watched over the ark through that whole terrible experience! How much it meant to Him! All His hopes and plans for the human race depended on the people within it. Only through them could His purpose be carried out.

"And God remembered Noah, and every living thing, and all the cattle that was with him in the ark: . . . and the rain from heaven was restrained. . . . And the ark rested . . . upon the mountains of Ararat."

But though the ark had touched ground again at last, there was no land to be seen—only water, water, everywhere. Noah felt sure that the water was going down, but there was no way to tell. He had to wait, trusting God to deliver him and his family in His own good time.

"And the waters decreased continually until the tenth month: in the tenth month, on the first day of the month, were the tops of the mountains seen."

What a shout must have gone up from them all at that moment! "Land! Land!" they must have cried.

Now it was that Noah "opened the window of the ark" and sent forth, first a raven, then a dove, "to see if the waters were abated from off the face of the ground."

But the dove returned. So Noah waited another week, then sent it out again. This time it came back with an olive leaf in its beak, which proved that the waters were going down and that some trees were still standing.

He waited yet another seven days, then sent out the dove again. This time it did not return.

THE RAINBOW OF A NEW BEGINNING

Feeling sure that there must now be much land exposed, "Noah removed the covering of the ark, and looked, and, behold, the face of the ground was dry."

At last the great door is opened. Eagerly all eight of them step into the open air again, while the animals, released from their pens, rush by to freedom.

What a sight meets their eyes! Around them lies the wreckage caused by the raging waters. Their beautiful world has gone! All is different. Great trees have been uprooted. Hills have been swept clean of soil and verdure. Mountains have become scarred and jagged. Fruitful plains have become deserts. Not a human dwelling can be seen anywhere. It is enough to break their hearts.

Suddenly, however, Noah looks upward. There in the sky, as though trying to encircle the ruined earth, is a great, glowing arch of many colors. Never have they seen anything so wonderful. With bated breath they stand looking at it, wondering what it may mean.

It is the first rainbow!

And God draws near and says: "I do set My bow in the cloud, and it shall be for a token of a covenant between Me and the earth."

So God has not forgotten them! This beautiful rainbow is only God's way of saying, "I will never forget you. I will never go back on My promises."

New hope fills their hearts. They know now that all will yet be well. And with the shining arch above them they go forth to a new beginning, to build a new world with God.

79

← PAINTING BY HARRY ANDERSON   © BY REVIEW AND HERALD

Suddenly there in the sky Noah and his family saw a great glowing arch of many colors, the world's first rainbow. It was God's promise there would not be another flood.

STORY 12

Starting Again

≈≈≈≈≈≈≈≈≈≈≈≈≈≈

MORNING dawned. Noah and his family had spent their first night on land after the long, weary months of confinement in the ark. How good it was to feel solid earth under their feet once more!

Yet it was not so solid as they had known it in the good old days before the Flood. Every now and then it was shaken by earthquakes as the land settled after the violent eruptions that had accompanied the Deluge, when "all the fountains of the great deep [were] broken up." Genesis 7:11. And as one quake followed another, Noah and his children must often have looked heavenward at the beautiful rainbow in the clouds, to remind themselves of God's promise to be with them and protect them "while the earth remains." Genesis 8:21, 22, R.S.V.

There was much to be done. Already the birds and animals had been released from the ark. One by one their cages and pens had been opened, and the happy exodus had begun.

What a sight it must have been! What a whirring of wings as great eagles, ospreys, and flamingos leaped into the air and flew out to freedom, with robins, sparrows, thrushes, and linnets singing and fluttering behind them! How the nightingales must have sung and the blackbirds squawked in that moment of glad liberation!

Lions and tigers, buffaloes and hippos, elephants and giraffes, dogs and cats, hurried through the great doorway, some leaping in their excitement, others lumbering heavily down the ramp, but all so glad to be out in the open again. And what a noise they all made, as elephants trumpeted, lions roared, horses neighed, and little dogs barked their loudest!

At first, no doubt, many of the animals stayed around, liking human companionship, and Noah may well have wondered what he was going to do with this huge menagerie. But one by one, and group by group, they began to move away, instinct telling them they could not continue to live on this mountaintop. So they wandered north and south and east and west, seeking food and shelter amid the wreckage of forest and field that the Flood had left.

How long Noah and his family stayed on Mount Ararat

6

no one knows. They may well have made the ark their home for some considerable time, using it as a store for the food and seed they had brought with them from their old home. No doubt they often discussed whether they should stay in the mountains or go down to the plains, where the land was easier to cultivate. Probably Shem, Ham, and Japheth made several explorations together, looking for a suitable location. At last some of them decided to go.

Packing their belongings on their backs, they started on their long, rough journey, leaving the ark behind them, perhaps to sink in the mud of some mountain lake or to be buried under the deep snow that in after years would fall upon it. Again and again they looked back at this mighty structure which had meant so much to them for so many years, until finally it faded from view, lost in the mist and the distance.

The downward trek was difficult, for there was no road, not even a pathway. The ground was dry, but everywhere there were evidences of the awful destruction wrought by the Flood. They clambered over jagged rocks, massive boulders, and fallen trees. They came across large bodies of water in the hollows of the hills and vast areas of swampy land.

There was a surprise at every turn, for this was not the world they knew. Everything was different. Everywhere there was some mark of the curse that sin had caused.

There wasn't a house anywhere, nor any signs of one. The beautiful homes of the people who had turned against God and refused to listen to the warning messages of His servants had vanished completely, smashed to pieces and swept

82

away by the towering tidal waves. If these pioneers from the ark wanted a home on the plains, or elsewhere, they would have to build one from the foundations up.

And they needed a home badly, for there was a baby coming. The Bible says that Arphaxad was born "two years after the flood." Genesis 11:10. He was Shem's little boy, and Noah's grandson, and I am sure Noah was very proud of him. He is the first baby mentioned in the Bible as being born in the new world.

Lots of babies were born after him, of course. Shem, Ham, and Japheth all had very large families. Pretty soon the first home they built wasn't large enough to hold them all, and they began to spread out. As the children grew up and got married, they, too, went off and started homes of their own. Thus, slowly at first, and then ever more rapidly, the earth began to be repopulated.

By the end of the first century after the Flood the three families had multiplied till there were many hundreds of people and lots and lots of children. By the end of the second century these hundreds had become thousands.

One of the big questions that all these people talked about was where to live. The housing problem was important then as now. Some said they should divide up and go out and explore the world, but most of them did not want to leave home. They might never meet again. They said it was better to stick together. No doubt, too, they didn't want to go too far from Father Noah, who, by the way, was still alive, and actually lived for 350 years after the Flood (Genesis 9:28).

Another matter they discussed was the beautiful world that Noah and his sons had known in days gone by, and how it was destroyed because of sin. Nobody doubted the Flood in those days. Noah remembered it all too well, and so did Shem, Ham, and Japheth and their wives. And they talked about it to their children, who told it to their children. If anybody questioned whether it was true, he could climb Mount Ararat and see the ark for himself.

Then one day someone asked, "How do we know there will not be another flood? How can we be sure that we won't be drowned, too, like our forefathers?"

Someone else said, "But there's the rainbow. When we see that, we are to remember God's promise that He will never again destroy the earth by a flood."

"But rainbows are flimsy things," said the other. "We can't trust our future and our children's future to rainbows. Better far to trust in bricks and mortar, and make ourselves secure."

"And they said one to another, Go to, let us make brick, and burn them throughly. And they had brick for stone, and slime had they for morter. And they said, Go to, let us build us a city and a tower, whose top may reach unto heaven; and let us make us a name, lest we be scattered abroad upon the face of the whole earth." Genesis 11:3, 4.

And this is exactly what they did. By putting forth enormous efforts they gathered together the material for the great undertaking. Everybody helped—men, women, children—

though I doubt that Father Noah approved the plan, for he knew the power of God and had seen the rainbow over the ark in the day of the great deliverance.

Slowly but surely, week by week, month by month, the massive building rose above the plain of Shinar. As it grew higher and higher, the eagerness of the people mounted. This was what they wanted. A big city where they could all live together, and an escape tower, higher than the clouds, up which they could climb to safety should another flood come upon them.

But they had reckoned without God; and that is always a bad thing to do.

The Bible says that "the Lord came down to see the city and the tower, which the children of men builded." Genesis 11:5.

They thought they were getting along nicely without God, and here was God right beside them, looking at them, all the time! And it is that way with us, too. God still sees everything we do.

How small and paltry that tower must have seemed to God—to Him who made the mountains, who raised up the Himalayas of India, the Alps of Switzerland, the Andes of South America, and the Rockies of North America! What a pitiful little pile of earth this Tower of Babel was, after all!

Yet it was dangerous, for it might, all too soon, become the center of an empire, the heart of a tyranny controlled by evil men, which might thwart God's gracious purpose for the world.

© BY RGH

Sad it was, too, that these people, who knew God's providences and promises so well, should by this building prove that in so short a time they had forgotten Him, and that they had ceased to trust Him, just as had their forefathers before them, whom He had been compelled to destroy.

Something had to be done about it, and God chose a most effective means to upset their program. He confused their tongues! He led various groups of people to talk in languages that others about them could not understand.

STARTING AGAIN

Thus it came about one day that an overseer on the tower called for more stone, and a man brought him mortar. And he was angry. Another called for mortar, and someone brought him stone. And *he* was angry. Another demanded a certain size of stone and was brought a different size. And he, too, was angry. Pretty soon everybody was angry, and all were shouting at one another and striking one another, until confusion reigned everywhere. After that it wasn't possible to get anything done any more, so the work stopped and the people went home. There the trouble continued until the whole community was in a terrible commotion.

Then somebody said, "I'm going to get out of here; I can't stand this bedlam any longer." So he went, taking his family with him, and perhaps a few others who could understand what he said. Somebody else did the same, and so on until all the people were scattered.

It was all very sad, for in the general mix-up many old friends were separated. Children who had played together for a long time went off in different directions. And at the moment of parting they couldn't even say good-by! They may have nodded and smiled and squeezed hands, but the one last word they wanted to say most sounded strange, ugly, and meaningless. Nor could they make a single plan to meet again.

So God's purpose was carried out. At the time it may have seemed a hard thing for Him to do, but it was all for the best. The people needed this lesson. And we would do well to remember that it never pays to forget God or disbelieve His promises.

Work on the Tower of Babel on the plain of Shinar ceased when God confused the language of the laborers so that no one understood the orders that the leaders shouted.

HARAN

MT ARARAT

NINEVEH

TOWER OF BABEL

UR OF THE CHALDEES

THE COUNTRY OF ABRAHAM
*When God called him out of Ur
to the land of Canaan*

SODOM

QUADE

STORY 13

The Man From Ur

PICTURE if you can what happened after work on the Tower of Babel ceased.

Fifty years, a hundred years, pass by. The massive building still stands on the plain of Shinar, gaunt and unfinished. Passers-by point to it in fear as something cursed of God. They remember that in some mysterious way the language of the builders was confused so that they fell out among themselves, then scattered over the earth, never fully to understand one another again.

Because of this scattering an age of exploration has begun. Little groups of people are wandering on and on, finding their way into various parts of Europe, into India, China, Siberia, and, perhaps, even across the Bering Strait into North America.

Villages, towns, cities, are springing up. Industries are beginning. Precious stones and metals buried by the Flood are being discovered here and there. Goldsmiths and silversmiths

89

Our artist has painted a scene here showing how beautiful Canaan may have looked when God called Abraham out of Ur of the Chaldees to travel to the lovely land.

are busy making beautiful ornaments, some of which can be seen today in museums. Boatbuilders are busy on the river Euphrates and the Persian Gulf. The first sailors are setting forth to explore the oceans and the lands beyond.

Unfortunately, with all this activity and growing prosperity the people are again turning away from God. Some have even started to make idols and worship them.

Noah is an old, old man, nearly nine hundred years of age. His words do not carry the weight they once did. He continues to tell his thrilling story about the wonderful world he knew before the Flood and about what happened to it because of the wickedness of the people, but already it has become to many nothing but a fairy tale.

Most, if not all, are seeking their own pleasure and profit, caring less and less for the things of God as they think more and more of themselves.

God, looking down upon the scene, is saddened again; for He sees that man has not yet learned his lesson, and is fast becoming as sinful as he was before the judgment of the Deluge fell upon him. Perhaps the thought came to God just then that it might have been better if Noah had perished with the rest, and so have saved all this trouble and sorrow.

But that was impossible, for had not God promised Adam in the Garden of Eden that one day He would restore everything that was lost on that day of the first sin? Had He not said that the seed of the woman would bruise the serpent's head? Therefore her seed must not perish till the victory should be won.

90

THE MAN FROM UR

When God makes a promise He never goes back on it. And when He sets Himself to carry out some purpose, nothing can stand in His way. That is why He watched over the ark with such infinite care as it was tossed to and fro on the mountainous waves of the Flood; He had no intention of giving Satan the satisfaction of seeing the last remnants of the race blotted out by the raging waters.

And that is why, three hundred and fifty years later, His all-seeing eye turned one day toward a certain riverside city known in those far-off days as Ur of the Chaldees.

In this city was a boy upon whom God had set His heart— a good lad and godly. Someone, perhaps his mother, had told him the marvelous story of Creation and of God's wonderful love for His earthly children, whom He placed in the beautiful Eden home in the long ago, and of all the joy and glory that was theirs as they walked and talked with God. He had heard, too, how after sin had spoiled everything God had come near in tender forgiveness to save His beloved creatures from the full consequences of their disobedience. And as the dear old story had been told and retold to him from his childhood up— possibly, too, by Noah himself, or by Shem, Ham, or Japheth— Abraham had given his heart to God and made the great decision to serve Him all his days.

It wasn't easy for Abraham to do right, for most of the people of his city had already turned to idolatry. Indeed, his own father, Terah, had fallen into this wicked way (Joshua

24:2). So Abraham had to take his stand for God by himself, right there in his own home.

But God was watching him, just as He watches every boy and girl today. And He was glad when Abraham chose to do right, no matter what the cost. And God said, "I will take that boy and use him in a wonderful way in carrying out My great purpose for the good of man, but first I must take him away from his evil surroundings."

So one day, when Abraham was grown to manhood, his heart still set on following the Lord, he heard a voice speaking to him, and he knew it was the voice of God.

Perhaps it was while he was at evening prayer, or at night while looking up at the stars, marveling at the mighty handiwork of God. Wherever it was, in the sacred stillness of that moment God said, "Get thee out of thy country, and from thy kindred, and from thy father's house, unto a land that I will shew thee: and I will make of thee a great nation, and I will bless thee, and make thy name great; and thou shalt be a blessing: and I will bless them that bless thee, and curse him that curseth thee: and in thee shall all families of the earth be blessed." Genesis 12: 1-3.

It was a great crisis in Abraham's life and in the history of the world. For a moment all the future hung upon his decision. Would he go or would he stay? He was comfortable at home. Life was easy. All his friends lived around him in the old familiar town. To leave all this was to court danger and maybe poverty and disaster. Certainly it would be a venture into the unknown, with no certainty as to the outcome.

92

One day, when Abraham was grown to manhood, his heart still set on following the Lord, he heard a voice speaking to him, which he knew was the voice of God. That was enough.

What did he do? According to the record he did not hesitate for a moment. He took God at His word and obeyed Him at once—and God loved Him for doing so.

"So Abram departed, as the Lord had spoken unto him." Verse 4.

The people of Ur must have wondered what was happening as they noticed all the bustle and commotion around Abraham's house, and more so when they saw the whole of Terah's property go up for sale—for father had decided to go along, too, despite his age and his difference in religious belief. No doubt old friends came and asked why everybody was leaving town; and when Abraham said it was because he had been called of God to go out into a new country, they couldn't understand him.

"Called of God?" they said. "To leave Ur? How could that be?" It didn't seem reasonable to them that anybody would be so foolish as to leave a thriving little city like Ur.

But Abraham understood. He knew what he was doing. God had spoken, and that was enough for him. Yet how little he knew of what was before him, or of all that God had in mind to accomplish through his life for the blessing of mankind!

When God said to him, "In thee shall all families of the earth be blessed," Abraham no doubt wondered how such a thing could be, for the only families he knew just then were those around home and possibly a few others in various parts of Mesopotamia. He must have asked himself how *he* could ever be a blessing to them.

But before the mind of God there spread the whole picture of history to be, with Abraham becoming the father of the faithful, the head of a great line of godly men through whom at last Jesus would come and fulfill the promise of redemption made to Adam in the Garden of Eden.

Still further ahead God saw the glorious day when men and women and children from every nation under heaven would share in the final victory of good over evil, and with the faithful of all ages enter that eternal wonderland where sin will be no more.

Thus it is always when God calls us to do something for Him. We may not understand at first just what He has in mind for us, but we may be sure that it is always something for our good, something far greater and more wonderful than anything we could ever plan for ourselves.

Knowing this, let us do as Abraham did—trust Him, obey Him, and follow where He leads.

Abraham's Altars

MAYBE you think it didn't mean very much to Abraham to leave his home and set out for the land of Canaan. At most, the distance wasn't much over six hundred miles, a good day's trip in a car. But Abraham didn't have a car. And he didn't have a truck. People who traveled in those days walked, or rode on horses or camels. And they couldn't move quickly, because their possessions consisted mostly not of furniture and other household goods but of sheep and cattle; and the pace had to be kept down to that of the youngest calf or lamb.

So when you think of Abraham leaving Ur of the Chaldees, don't think of him as packing his things into a big truck just outside his door, but think rather of a long caravan made up of flocks of sheep, herds of goats and cattle, each with one or two hired men to look after them, and dogs to keep the animals from straying.

96

ABRAHAM'S ALTARS

These servants also brought their wives and children along with them, the boys and girls walking beside their mothers, who perhaps had babies strapped to their backs. And, of course, the caravan couldn't move any faster than these boys and girls could walk.

Then came Abraham and his wife, Sarah, and old Father Terah, all riding on camels, and followed by more animals and servants.

Then there was Lot. He was Abraham's nephew, whose father had died recently. He wanted to go along too. But he also owned some cattle, with servants to mind them, so that made the caravan longer still.

How far they traveled each day we do not know. But it couldn't have been more than a few miles at the most, with all the stops to feed the animals and the children, and to look after their many needs.

At last, after many days, they came to a place called Haran, and decided to call a halt. Many things had to be done for all this company of people and animals. Then, too, old Father Terah wasn't well, and couldn't stand the traveling. So they camped at Haran, and stayed a long time; in fact, until Terah died.

While at Haran, the animals multiplied, and lots of baby camels were born, and calves and kids and lambs. The families of the servants increased also, as boys and girls came to town.

7

So by the time Abraham was ready to proceed on his journey, his moving problems had increased considerably.

In addition there were many other people who wanted to go along—men and women who had heard Abraham tell about the God of heaven whom he worshiped, and who wanted to worship Him too. For Abraham had been a missionary there in Haran, living a godly life among the people, upholding right standards, and telling them of God's power and love.

So at last, when the caravan was ready to move again, we read: "And Abram took Sarai his wife, and Lot his brother's son, and all their substance that they had gathered, and *the souls that they had gotten in Haran;* and they went forth to go into the land of Canaan; and into the land of Canaan they came." Genesis 12:5.

Who gave the word to start we are not told, but it was probably Abraham himself. He didn't say, of course, "All aboard for Canaan," but it meant the same thing. His word of command passed down the long line of waiting people and animals, and the servants sprang into action. And all because

one man had heard the voice of God and obeyed Him.

It would have been easier, and more comfortable perhaps, to have stayed in Haran, where everything had gone so well; but it would not have fulfilled God's purpose, so on they went, seeking "the land of promise."

The journey was slow—indeed, slower than ever, with so many more people and cattle and children, but it was full of interest. The scenery was new and beautiful. Here and there they came across small settlements of people, and discovered that most of them were fairly close relatives, descendants of pioneers who had moved away from Mesopotamia years before. They were children of Canaan, a son of Ham; hence, the name Canaan for the land we now call Palestine.

These people, like so many others, had turned away from the true God and had begun to worship idols. But this made no difference to Abraham, except to cause him to witness more faithfully and openly for the Lord he loved. He began to see a new reason why God had called him out of Ur of the Chaldees. He was to be God's missionary, God's champion, letting these

people know that there was still someone in the world standing for right and truth, and who worshiped the Creator of heaven and earth.

"And Abram passed through the land unto the place of Sichem, unto the plain of Moreh. And the Canaanite was then in the land. And the Lord appeared unto Abram, and said, Unto thy seed will I give this land: and there builded he an altar unto the Lord, who appeared unto him." Verses 6, 7.

How glad he must have been to hear the voice of God again! Sometimes, perhaps, he had wondered whether he was going the right way and doing what God really wanted him to do, but now new assurance came into his heart. God was pleased with him, and that was all he cared. Overjoyed, he built an altar, and he, his wife, and all his followers bowed in worship.

Those altars of Abraham! He built them wherever he camped. The very next verse says: "And he removed from thence unto a mountain on the east of Bethel, and pitched his tent, having Bethel on the west, and Hai on the east: and there he builded an altar unto the Lord, and called upon the name of the Lord." Verse 8.

As the smoke of the sacrifice rose high in the air, people came from far and near, wondering what was happening. Then as they saw Abraham on his knees before God, and perhaps heard the whole company singing the praises of God, their hearts were moved, and they recalled some of the wonderful things they had heard from their fathers about the great Creator. And some of them said, *"We* should be worshiping God

100

The first thing Abraham did wherever he pitched camp was to build an altar. Then he and his household would reverently worship God while the heathen looked on in wonder.

like this, too, instead of bowing down to idols of wood and stone."

As Abraham and his great caravan passed on, he left his altars behind, silent witnesses to his faith. And when strangers came upon them and asked, "What are these? Who built them, and why?" there was always somebody to say, "These are the altars of Abraham, servant of the most high God."

That was a very beautiful thing that Abraham did, and we would do well to follow his example. Not that we should build altars of brick or stone today, but that wherever we go, wherever we stay, we should leave behind us some evidence that we are children of God.

We should be just as faithful in witnessing for God among people who do not know Him, or who do not like Him, as was Abraham among the people of Canaan.

At school or at work we should so live as to leave an impression on the minds of others that we are loyal and true followers of Jesus.

When you have left school or moved to a different class, and teacher looks at the desk which once you occupied, he should be moved to say, "That was a fine Christian lad who sat there," or "What a pure, upright girl she was, so different from all the others!"

Thus, as we move from place to place through life, let us try to leave behind us, as Abraham did, a trail of beautiful monuments to the faith we hold and to the Lord whom we love and serve.

STORY 15

Lot's Mistake

≈≈≈≈≈≈≈≈≈≈≈≈≈≈≈≈≈≈≈≈

I F THERE were two pieces of candy on the table, a large piece and a small piece, and you were asked to take one of them, which would you choose, remembering that the piece you left would go to your brother?

Most boys and girls would say, "The big piece!" But it would be the wrong choice. Far better is it to be generous and take the smaller piece, leaving the bigger piece for somebody else, for in so doing you build something noble into your character which will bring rich returns in days to come. You may seem to lose, but instead you gain.

The truth of this has been known for a long, long time. The people who journeyed with Abraham understood it, for they saw it work out before their eyes.

As you remember, when Abraham left Ur of the Chaldees he brought with him his nephew, Lot, son of Abraham's brother Haran, who had died in Ur some time before the family moved out. Perhaps it was because Lot had no father

that he became so selfish; but whatever the cause, he certainly knew how to look after his own interests first.

However, it was not until after the great caravan had traveled all the way to Egypt and returned to Canaan that serious trouble broke out. We are told that then "there was a strife between the herdmen of Abram's cattle and the herdmen of Lot's cattle."

One reason for the strife was that there was not enough pasture to feed the cattle, and there were not enough wells at which to water them. The Bible says Abraham had become "very rich in cattle, in silver, and in gold. . . . And Lot also, which went with Abram, had flocks, and herds, and tents. And the land was not able to bear them, that they might dwell together: for their substance was great, so that they could not dwell together." Genesis 13:2-6.

It may well have been, however, that the trouble was due not only to the shortage of pasture and water but also to the fact that Lot and his servants had begun to think that Abraham was getting the lion's share of everything and that they were not being fairly treated. They had forgotten that they were all Abraham's guests.

As for Abraham, he was too noble to permit himself to be upset by anything so trivial. As soon as he heard about the trouble he sent for Lot and talked it all out with him. With princely graciousness he said to him:

"Let there be no strife, I pray thee, between me and thee, and between my herdmen and thy herdmen; for we be brethren. Is not the whole land before thee? separate thyself, I pray

105

The servants of Abraham and Lot quarreled over the division of the land, but Abraham was a man of peace, and he settled the trouble by allowing Lot to have the fertile valleys.

thee, from me: if thou wilt take the left hand, then I will go to the right; or if thou depart to the right hand, then I will go to the left." Verses 8, 9.

What a generous offer! And what an example to Lot—and to us!

That Lot did not deserve such kindness is clear from what he did next. Of course, he should have said, "My dear uncle, in view of all that you have done for me, let the choice be yours. You take what you will and I will be content with what is left."

Did he say that? Oh, no. Instead, "Lot lifted up his eyes, and beheld all the plain of Jordan, that it was well watered every where, . . . even as the garden of the Lord. . . . Then Lot chose him all the plain of Jordan; and Lot journeyed east: and they separated themselves the one from the other. Abram dwelled in the land of Canaan, and Lot dwelled in the cities of the plain, and pitched his tent toward Sodom." Verses 10-12.

That is where he made his big mistake. He thought he was choosing the best for himself, but instead it was the worst thing he ever did.

As he looked down from the mountainside upon the beautiful valley below, so green and lovely in the morning sunshine, with the Jordan River running through the middle of it, he said to himself, "What a place for cattle! How rich I shall become down there!"

Then, as he noticed the villages and towns scattered about the valley he thought how nice it would be to be a little closer to civilization instead of forever roaming around the hill country with Abraham. Then, too, there was Sodom, the big city toward the south, with its fine markets and popular places of amusement. What a good time he and his wife would enjoy!

So Lot made his choice. He chose the plain of Jordan, with its fine pasture land, its abundant water supply—and its cities. And he "pitched his tent toward Sodom."

He must have known that Sodom was a wicked city. Everybody was talking about it. But Lot thought it would be all right for *him* to go there. It might be dangerous for others, but he could take the risk. Anyway, he would like to see for himself just what was going on there.

But no child of God should take a risk like that. Any place with a reputation like Sodom's is a place that should be avoided like something filled with poison or disease.

Lot did not know, of course, that this city and all the "cities of the plain" that appeared so attractive to him were soon to be destroyed because of their great wickedness. Nor did he know that war was about to break out. Even as he chose the "best" land for himself, the rulers of four distant cities were already plotting an attack on his future home! Not long after Lot was nicely settled in Sodom, he found himself in the midst of a battlefield. The soldiers of Sodom were defeated and its citizens carried away captive, including Lot and his family.

"And they took all the goods of Sodom and Gomorrah, and all their victuals, and went their way. And they took Lot, Abram's brother's son, who dwelt in Sodom, and his goods, and departed." Genesis 14:11, 12.

How Lot must have wished he had never chosen to live there! How he must have longed for the safety of the mountains and the good time he had had with his dear old Uncle Abraham!

"And there came one that had escaped, and told Abram the Hebrew. . . . And when Abram heard that his brother was taken captive, he armed his trained servants, born in his own house, three hundred and eighteen, and pursued them unto Dan." Verses 13, 14.

That was wonderful of him, wasn't it? Lot, having chosen the best land for himself, had left him for good. Now Abraham went to his rescue.

The pursuit was successful. Not only were the enemy soldiers overtaken and defeated, but Abraham "brought back all the goods, and also brought again his brother Lot, and his goods, and the women also, and the people." Verse 16.

Did Lot learn his lesson? No. He went back to his home in Sodom and continued to live there as before, even though he now knew only too well that "the men of Sodom were wicked and sinners before the Lord exceedingly." Genesis 13:13.

Gradually conditions in Sodom became worse and worse. Lot should have left, and taken his children away from such evil surroundings, but he did not, and they learned many bad things from their companions.

At last so much evil was going on there that God decided the city must no longer be permitted to exist. Before destroying it, however, God told His servant Abraham what He was planning to do.

And for whom was Abraham's first care? His nephew, of course. What would become of Lot and his family?

Then Abraham said to God, "Wilt Thou also destroy the righteous with the wicked? Peradventure there be fifty righteous within the city: wilt Thou also destroy and not spare the place for the fifty righteous that are therein?" Genesis 18: 23, 24.

In response to Abraham's prayers God sent two angels to Sodom to rescue Lot and his family. On the very last night before destruction fell, the angels came to Lot's house and urged him to leave. With great earnestness they said:

"Hast thou here any besides? son in law, and thy sons, and thy daughters, and whatsoever thou hast in the city, bring them out of this place: for we will destroy this place, because the cry of them is waxen great before the face of the Lord; and the Lord hath sent us to destroy it.

"And Lot went out, and spake unto his sons in law, which married his daughters, and said, Up, get you out of this place; for the Lord will destroy this city. But he seemed as one that mocked unto his sons in law." Genesis 19:12-14.

They didn't believe him. The very idea that Sodom could be destroyed seemed ridiculous. There wasn't a sign of trouble anywhere. The streets, the markets, the houses, looked just the same as ever. It was absurd for anyone to talk about their destruction.

Lot himself began to doubt. On that very last morning, when the fires of heaven were about to descend upon the city and burn it up, he still wanted to stay there.

"And while he lingered, the men laid hold upon his hand, and upon the hand of his wife, and upon the hand of his two daughters; the Lord being merciful unto him: and they brought him forth, and set him without the city." Verse 16.

"Escape for thy life," they said; "look not behind thee, neither stay thou in all the plain; escape to the mountain, lest thou be consumed." Verse 17.

"Then the Lord rained upon Sodom and upon Gomorrah brimstone and fire from the Lord out of heaven; and He overthrew those cities, and all the plain, and all the inhabitants of the cities, and that which grew upon the ground." Verses 24, 25.

Everything was destroyed. The cities, the people, the trees, the pastures. Everything that had seemed so good to Lot.

LOT'S MISTAKE

Nothing was left save a great burned-over area, like Hiroshima, Japan, after the atomic bomb fell on it. Even today, thousands of years later, the whole district is a wilderness and the site of Sodom is covered by the Dead Sea.

So Lot, who had tried to grab the best, found himself at last with nothing—nothing save the clothes he had on. His home was gone; his barns and livestock; his cattle, his sheep, his goats, his camels—all burned beyond recognition. His wife, too, was dead, and all his children and grandchildren—all except the two daughters whom the angels had dragged out with him.

"And he dwelt in a cave, he and his two daughters." Verse 30.

It never pays to be selfish and choose the best for ourselves. And there is nothing more dangerous than to pitch one's tent toward Sodom.

Sarah's Big Surprise

~~~~~~~~~~~~~~~~~~~~~~~~~~~~~~~~~~~~~~~

MEANWHILE exciting events had been taking place in the household of Abraham, not the least of which was the arrival of a baby, a very important baby.

Abraham had been worried about this baby for a long time. In fact, from the moment that God had called him to leave Ur of the Chaldees.

At that time God had said to him, "I will make of thee a great nation, and I will bless thee, and make thy name great." Genesis 12:2. After that he naturally expected that pretty soon he would have a baby boy of his own—to make a start, at least, on the "great nation" God had promised. But no little boy turned up.

Months and years went by, and still Abraham had no son. Again and again he must have wondered how God's promise would ever be fulfilled, but he trusted that in some way it would come to pass.

After the trouble with Lot over the land, and Lot's choice

112

of the best, God spoke to Abraham again and said: "Lift up now thine eyes, and look from the place where thou art northward, and southward, and eastward, and westward: for all the land which thou seest, to thee will I give it, and to thy seed for ever. And I will make thy seed as the dust of the earth: so that if a man can number the dust of the earth, then shall thy seed also be numbered." Genesis 13:14-16.

Like the dust of the earth—so should his children be; still he had no child. What did God mean?

Many times he and his wife, Sarah, must have talked it all over together, but they couldn't make it out. How could God keep on promising them lots of children and yet not give them one single baby?

Besides, they were both getting on in years, and it isn't usual for elderly people to have children.

One night when Abraham was feeling quite discouraged about it he had another vision from God, and heard that same wonderful voice he had heard so many times before.

"Fear not, Abram," said God: "I am thy shield, and thy exceeding great reward."

It was a beautiful promise, but Abraham wanted something more definite just then. So he said, "Lord God, what wilt Thou give me, seeing I go childless, and the steward of my house is this Eliezer of Damascus? . . . Behold, to me Thou hast given no seed: and, lo, one born in mine house is mine heir." Genesis 15:2, 3.

8

Already Abraham had been working out in his mind just how he would dispose of all his property. Having no son of his own, he supposed all would go to his chief steward. But God had no such purpose in mind.

"This shall not be thine heir," He said.

Then God took him outside the tent and said, "Look now toward heaven, and tell the stars, if thou be able to number them: and He said unto him, So shall thy seed be." Verses 4, 5.

First like the dust, now like the stars. And still no baby boy. It was hard to understand. But Abraham "believed in the Lord; and He counted it to him for righteousness." Verse 6.

Still more years went by. Abraham was now ninety-nine years of age. Nearly a hundred, and still no son. Surely it was hopeless now. Surely God must have meant something quite different. Perhaps Abraham had been mistaken. Perhaps it wasn't God who had spoken to him after all!

How often he must have been tempted to doubt! Yet he held on in faith, trusting, hoping, believing.

Now God spoke to him once more, saying, "A father of many nations have I made thee. And I will make thee exceeding fruitful." Genesis 17:5, 6.

Then He mentioned Sarah, poor old wrinkled Sarah, now over ninety.

114

SARAH'S BIG SURPRISE

"I will bless her," said God, "and give thee a son also of her: yea, I will bless her, and she shall be a mother of nations; kings of people shall be of her."

This astonishing announcement was too much for Abraham. His faith had held out till now, but, surely the Lord didn't expect him to believe this.

"Then Abraham fell upon his face, and laughed, and said in his heart, Shall a child be born unto him that is an hundred years old? and shall Sarah, that is ninety years old, bear?" Verse 17.

Yes, he laughed. And when Sarah heard about it, she laughed too (Genesis 18:12).

And I dare say that God smiled also, saying to Himself, "Just wait and see! What a surprise you are both going to have soon!"

And the surprise came, all right; just when least expected, and when it seemed altogether impossible.

"And the Lord visited Sarah as He had said," and she "bare Abraham a son in his old age, at the set time of which God had spoken to him." Genesis 21:1, 2.

Thus was Isaac born, the son of promise—indeed, of many promises—and great was the rejoicing in the camp of Abraham. We can hardly imagine how happy those two dear old people must have been after waiting so long. No wonder we read that "Abraham made a great feast the same day that Isaac was weaned." Verse 8. He had something to celebrate in a big way.

And I like to think that in the midst of the feasting and the rejoicing, when all the people from far and near were crowding around to offer their congratulations, Abraham lifted up his heart to God and said, "Thank You, dear God; thank You for my baby son."

And Sarah? I can hear her saying, as she held her baby tight in her arms, "You were right, dear Lord, You were right after all; there is nothing too hard for You."

116

STORY 17

Tried and Tested

~~~~~~

I DOUBT whether any boy who ever lived was loved as much as Isaac. That his parents loved him most dearly goes without saying, for he had come to them in such a wonderful way and after so long a time of waiting; but God loved him most of all.

For God had thought about him a long time too. To Him Isaac was a most important link in the chain of salvation. All the future descendants of Abraham, including Jesus, were to come through him. How precious, then, was this child in the sight of God!

Then God did a strange thing. He asked Abraham to kill the boy!

Just as Isaac was growing up into sturdy young manhood, the joy of his parents' hearts, and the pride of the whole camp, God said to Abraham—and it was the same voice that had spoken to him first in Ur of the Chaldees, so that there could be no mistaking it—"Take now thy son, thine only son Isaac, whom thou lovest, and get thee into the land of Moriah; and offer him there for a burnt offering upon one of the mountains which I will tell thee of." Genesis 22:2.

Surely no greater test of faith ever came to any man. Poor Abraham! After waiting for years and years for this boy; after showing him off to all his friends and servants as the miracle child of promise, destined to become his heir; after loving him with all the intense devotion that an old man has for his only son, he was now asked to lay him on an altar and kill him!

It was enough to make most men rebel against God and turn from Him forever. But not so Abraham. Although he could not understand the command, he made up his mind that it must be right, and he decided to obey it.

When he was first called to leave his home country, the record says, "So Abram departed." Genesis 12:4. Now in this new crisis in his life the Bible says that he "rose up early in the morning, and saddled his ass, and took two of his young men with him, and Isaac his son, and clave the wood for the burnt offering, and rose up, and went unto the place of which God had told him." Genesis 22:3.

All day long they traveled, and all the next day. Just the two of them together, with the two servants following behind.

It was a sad journey for Abraham. His heart must have become heavier and heavier every step he took, and I dare say he could hardly look at Isaac without wanting to cry.

What did they talk about? No one will ever know; but we can be sure that when they did speak to each other, it was with great tenderness: Isaac out of loving regard for his aged father,

and Abraham because of what God expected him to do on the morrow.

"Then on the third day Abraham lifted up his eyes, and saw the place afar off. And Abraham said unto his young men, Abide ye here with the ass; and I and the lad will go yonder and worship, and come again to you." Verses 4, 5.

"And come again to you." What hope was in these words! Yet how could it be? If he obeyed God and killed his son, how could both of them ever "come again"? Unless—could it be?—unless God planned to work a new and still greater miracle for him. It had never been done before, but, yes, God could do it! Had He not said that nothing was too hard for Him? Perhaps, then, it might even be that He would raise Isaac from the dead.

So we read in the book of Hebrews: "By faith Abraham, when he was tried, offered up Isaac; and he that had received the promises offered up his only begotten son, of whom it was said, That in Isaac shall thy seed be called: accounting that God was able to raise him up, even from the dead." Chapter 11:17-19.

On the way up the mountainside Isaac began to wonder just what his father had in mind. Till now he had felt very proud and happy at being alone with him on this long journey to build a new altar to God; but now, as he looked over the equipment, he noticed something missing. There was no animal for the sacrifice. They had traveled all this long way in vain. The most important item had been forgotten!

"My father . . ." he said. "Behold the fire and the wood: but where is the lamb for a burnt offering?" Genesis 22:7.

HERBERT
RUDEEN

TRIED AND TESTED

So the moment Abraham had dreaded most had come! Isaac must be told the awful truth—but not yet. Not till the last moment. So Abraham replied—and we can almost hear the tremor in his voice—"My son, God will provide Himself a lamb for a burnt offering." Verse 8.

In saying this he said much more than he realized. His words were prophetic. For, long years in the future, God would do this very thing, not only for Abraham, but for everybody. He would "provide a Lamb" to die on Calvary—Jesus, "the Lamb of God, which taketh away the sin of the world."

On they went together, with slow and weary steps, until at last they came to "the place which God had told him of; and Abraham built an altar there, and laid the wood in order." Verse 9.

Never had it taken him so long to lay the wood in order on an altar, for he kept wondering and wondering whether God would do something to make the next step unnecessary. But nothing happened; and at last, turning to Isaac, he explained, as best he could, what God wanted him to do.

And here the beauty of Isaac's character is seen. He was young, strong, and vigorous. He could have resisted. He could have overpowered his old father and run for his life. But he didn't. When he understood that it was God's will that he should die, he yielded himself willingly, and Abraham "bound Isaac his son, and laid him on the altar upon the wood."

If ever heaven and earth were close together, it was at that moment. There was Abraham, standing by the altar, with tears running down his cheeks as he took one last look at the

121

← PAINTING BY HARRY ANDERSON   © BY REVIEW AND HERALD

After three days' journey Abraham reached Mount Moriah, built an altar, and arranged the wood for the fire. He then prepared his son Isaac for the sacrifice as God instructed.

son he loved so dearly; and there was God right beside him, watching with infinite eagerness, wondering whether His faithful servant could make so great a sacrifice without a question, without a word of complaint.

Would Abraham stand this awful test? Would he go through to the bitter end rather than disobey God?

"And Abraham stretched forth his hand, and took the knife to slay his son."

Isaac closed his eyes, awaiting the fatal cut. The knife flashed in the morning sunlight. But it never touched him. Suddenly the silence of that mountaintop was broken by the sound of a voice, loud, urgent, commanding, as though God Himself were anxious now.

"Abraham, Abraham. . . . Lay not thine hand upon the lad, neither do thou any thing unto him."

The voice came just in time. Another moment and all would have been over. Now the knife that might have killed the lad, cut his bonds and set him free.

How the two of them, father and son, must have embraced each other in speechless joy at this amazing deliverance! And how God must have smiled upon them both for their love and devotion to Him!

Said the voice again, "Now I know that thou fearest God, seeing thou hast not withheld thy son, thine only son from Me."

Then it was that Abraham saw a ram "caught in a thicket." Probably it had been there all the time, but both of them had been too concerned to notice it. "And Abraham went and took the ram, and offered him up for a burnt offering in the stead of his son."

Then the voice came again, for God was still close by, happy in the knowledge that here was a man who loved Him with all his heart, who was willing to give up his dearest treasure at His command.

And the voice said: "By Myself have I sworn, saith the Lord, for because thou hast done this thing, and hast not withheld thy son, thine only son: that in blessing I will bless thee, and in multiplying I will multiply thy seed as the stars of the heaven, and as the sand which is upon the sea shore; and thy seed shall possess the gate of his enemies; and in thy seed shall all the nations of the earth be blessed; because thou hast obeyed My voice." Verses 16-18.

Wonderful promise of blessing! The whole treasury of heaven suddenly opened for this loyal and faithful servant! Everything God owns was made his forever.

And such is the blessing God offers to all who love Him as did Abraham, who are willing to lay their best and choicest things upon the altar of sacrifice for Him and His service.

Are you willing, dear boy or girl, to lay yourself upon that altar? Will you say to God—

> "Take my life and let it be
> Consecrated, Lord, to Thee"?

If so, then the voice of God will speak from heaven to you, saying, "John, John," "Mary, Mary," "in blessing I will bless thee, . . . because thou hast obeyed My voice." And all your life to come will be radiant with the presence of the Lord.

One Kind Deed

~~~~~~~~~~~~~~~~~~~~~~~~~

WHEN Sarah died at the good old age of one hundred and twenty-seven, Isaac felt very sad and lonely. As an only son, his mother had meant much to him. And not being married yet, he felt the loss more keenly still.

The question of Isaac's marriage was often discussed in the camp. As he was the only heir to his father's great possessions, it was a very important matter. Whom would he marry? Whom *could* he marry? Not one of the servants, for that would not have been thought fitting in those days. Not a daughter of one of the heathen families around, for the girl might lead him away from God.

Abraham was especially worried about it, for he was old now, and he knew that he had not many years to live. And here was Isaac, his heir, the one and only hope for the fulfillment of God's promises, without a wife. It was serious.

So Abraham called his most trusted servant and asked him

125

God honored Abraham's faith by restoring to him his son Isaac from the altar of sacrifice. They lovingly embraced each other in gratitude to God for His wonderful goodness.

to go back to the home of Nahor, Abraham's brother, to see
whether one of his daughters would make a good wife for Isaac.

Of course, if Isaac had lived today he would have gone
himself and looked them all over personally; but in Abraham's
time that would not have been proper. That is why the servant
was sent first to "spy out the land" as it were, and see whether
any suitable girl could be found. Isaac trusted his father so
much that he was quite willing for it to be done this way.

Just before the servant left on his long journey, Abraham
gave him much good advice as to the kind of girl he should look
for and the kind he was *not* to bring back. No doubt Isaac also
added a word or two of his own.

Taking ten camels with him, the servant prepared quite

126

a caravan. He wanted to make a good impression on the young lady and her parents.

Many times on his journey he asked himself how he would go about finding the right young lady when he got there. It was no small task he had taken on—finding a wife for somebody else, and that somebody his master's son and heir. Suppose he should bring back the wrong girl!

At last he came to the city of Nahor, named after Abraham's brother, who was probably the chief man in it. Making his way to the well outside the city gate, he arrived there in the early evening and made his camels kneel down ready to be watered. Then he stood back and waited, for it had occurred to him that at this time of day the maidens of the city would probably come to get water at the well for their homes and their animals, and this would give him a wonderful chance to see them.

But he was still worried about how to choose the right one. How could he tell? He might pick a pretty one, and yet she could be mean and selfish in her heart. He might pick one that looked well dressed and attractive, only to discover later that she was worldly and untrue to God.

Dear, dear, what to do?

Some girls were coming toward the well now, their water pitchers on their shoulders. Which was the one for Isaac?

He decided to ask God to help him make the right choice.

"And he said, O Lord God of my master Abraham, I pray Thee, send me good speed this day, and shew kindness unto my master Abraham." Genesis 24:12.

Then he suggested a simple test:

"Behold, I stand here by the well of water; and the daughters of the men of the city come out to draw water: and let it come to pass, that the damsel to whom I shall say, Let down thy pitcher, I pray thee, that I may drink; and she shall say, Drink, and I will give thy camels drink also: let the same be she that Thou hast appointed for Thy servant Isaac." Verses 13, 14.

This test, you notice, was based, not on the prettiness of the girl's face, but on the kindliness of her heart; not on her fine clothes or her make-up, but on her thoughtfulness for others.

Carefully he watched the group of girls, wondering

128

whether any one of them would do this thing he had mentioned. Some were plain and some were good looking. Some were cheerful and others glum and sulky. Some noticed the stranger with the camels and smiled at him; others turned their backs and ignored him.

Then one of them, sweeter than all the rest, went to the well and filled her pitcher with water. Feeling impressed to speak to her, Abraham's servant said, "Let me, I pray thee, drink a little water of thy pitcher."

And she said, "Drink, my lord."

Then she took the pitcher from her shoulder and gave him a drink.

The servant was greatly pleased, and still more so when she said, "I will draw water for thy camels also, until they have done drinking.

"And she hasted, and emptied her pitcher into the trough, and ran again unto the well to draw water, and drew for all his camels." Verses 19, 20.

How much water those ten camels drank, I don't know, but I am sure that it must have meant a lot of work for that girl to draw it out of the well and carry it over to the trough. But she did it, and did it happily and graciously, while the servant looked on with increasing admiration, feeling more and more sure that this was the girl he had come to find.

Then what a surprise was hers! For now the servant, opening one of his bags, took out some beautiful gold ornaments and gave them to her. I can almost hear her crying out in surprise, "For me? I didn't expect any reward for doing a little kindness, sir, but, oh, they are pretty!"

Then the servant asked who she was and where she lived. She said her name was Rebekah, a granddaughter of Nahor.

So she belonged to the very family he had come to seek! How wonderful! Everything was turning out well after all.

Rebekah then invited him to come to her home to meet her people. With her generous disposition she said, smiling, "We have both straw and provender enough, and room to lodge in."

The servant accepted the invitation, and she ran to tell the folks about the nice old man who had given her such lovely presents just for watering his camels. Greatly interested, her brother Laban went down to the well to see who had been so kind to his sister. When he learned that the stranger was Abraham's servant, there was great excitement, for visitors

130

to Mesopotamia from so far away were rare in those days.

"Come in, thou blessed of the Lord," he cried. "Wherefore standest thou without? for I have prepared the house, and room for the camels."

Once indoors, the servant came right to the point, telling why he had come and how Abraham had sent him to find a wife for Isaac. Then he told of his prayer; how he had asked God to help him, and how Rebekah had done just the right thing at the right time.

As Rebekah listened, a blush came to her cheeks, and her heart pounded. This was too wonderful! First the gold ornaments, and now this! To be the wife of the only son of Abraham—the great Abraham of whose riches and goodness she had heard from her childhood! It was too good to be true!

When the servant had finished his story, Rebekah's father and brother said, "The thing proceedeth from the Lord. . . . Behold, Rebekah is before thee, take her, and go, and let her be thy master's son's wife, as the Lord hath spoken."

Then they turned to Rebekah to find out what she would say. "Wilt thou go with this man?" they asked. And she said, "I will go."

And she went, the very next day, still wondering how such great good fortune could have come to her so suddenly.

And did you ever stop to think how much depended on

that one kindly deed she did for a stranger? And of what might have happened if she had been cross and mean that evening? Destiny hung upon that moment—all the future, for herself, her children, and her children's children; and her part in God's plan of salvation.

How did it all come out?

Most happily. As Isaac—poor, lonely Isaac—"went out to meditate in the field at the eventide: . . . he lifted up his eyes, and saw, and, behold, the camels were coming." Verse 63.

How he had waited for those camels!

Had the old servant been successful? What sort of girl had he brought back with him?

And Rebekah, riding on one of those camels, was a little anxious, too, wondering what sort of man she was going to marry. And she "lifted up her eyes" and took a good look at Isaac. Evidently both were well satisfied with each other, for the Bible says that "Isaac brought her into his mother Sarah's tent, and took Rebekah, and she became his wife; and he loved her: and Isaac was comforted after his mother's death." Verse 67.

STORY 19

Trouble at the Wells

~~~~~~

D ID you ever start playing on a football field or a base-
ball diamond or a tennis court, and have another
group of boys or girls come up to you and say, "This
is our place; we were here before you were; now get out quick"?

Or maybe you were out on a picnic once and found just
the loveliest spot to have your lunch, only to have another
party come along and claim the spot for themselves.

It isn't nice to have such a thing happen; and it is very
hard on the temper. But what should one do? Fight it out—or
smile sweetly, say you're sorry, and let the other folks take
over?

Some will say, Stand up for your rights! Fight it out! But
what then? Whoever may win, everybody is sure to be upset.
The fun is spoiled and you have made enemies. On the other
hand, if you are nice about it and talk in a kind, generous way,
the other folks may go somewhere else, or they may suggest
all taking turns. Then you will have made new friends.

133

Something like this happened back in Isaac's day. Only the trouble then was not over places to play in but over wells to drink from. In those days when there were no waterworks and no water pipes laid to people's houses, nothing was more valuable and important than a well. People who did not live near a stream had to dig a well; and the more land and cattle they owned, the more wells they had to dig.

Wells were so precious that when a man had gone to the work of digging one, he usually marked it in some way and set someone to guard it. Even then there was trouble, and battles were often fought for the possession of a well.

If an enemy wanted to do a man harm he filled up his wells when he wasn't looking!

Thus it happened to Isaac. On his travels he came to a place called Gerar, where he found that the Philistines had filled up the wells which his father Abraham had dug. So "Isaac digged again the wells of water, . . . and he called their names after the names by which his father had called them." Genesis 26:18.

No sooner had he done so, however, than the herdsmen of Gerar came along and said, "The water is ours!" and started a fight. But Isaac thought that a well, however precious, wasn't worth fighting about, so he ordered his men to go somewhere else and dig another.

But again, hardly had his men found water than along

© BY R&H

came some other people and claimed it, saying, "It's ours."

No doubt Isaac and his men could easily have driven them off, but as a servant of God, Isaac felt he couldn't do that. Always he had to remember that he, like his father, was a witness for the true God, and that God had sent him to win others to Him, not fight them.

So once again Isaac gave the word that the well was to be left to those who claimed it. "And he removed from thence, and digged another well; and for that they strove not." Verse 22.

So he won, after all, and he left behind friends instead of enemies.

Best of all, "the Lord appeared unto him the same night, and said, I am the God of Abraham thy father: fear not, for I am with thee, and will bless thee, and multiply thy seed for My servant Abraham's sake." Verse 24.

It was just as though God had said, "I know what you have been through with those selfish people; I know how unfair they have been to you; but I am glad you acted as you did. I love you for it. You are just like Abraham your father."

Certainly God was pleased with Isaac over those wells. And He is pleased with us also when we are kind and gracious and unselfish when others are mean and rude to us.

This, too, is what Jesus meant when He said: "Love your enemies, bless them that curse you, do good to them that hate you, and pray for them which despitefully use you, and persecute you; that ye may be the children of your Father which is in heaven." Matthew 5:44, 45.

The Boy Who Didn't Care

~~~~~~~~~~~~~~~~~~~~~~~~~~~

ISAAC had two sons, Esau and Jacob. They were twins, but Esau was born a few minutes before Jacob. Because of this, the "birthright" belonged to Esau. That is, according to the custom of those days, he became heir to the major part of his father's property, and was recognized as the future head of the family. Second sons and third sons—and daughters—just didn't count.

Such a plan doesn't seem very fair to us nowadays, for we are used to seeing all children share equally after a father's death; yet even today, in some countries the same practice is followed as in Abraham's time, and a father's title and estate go to his eldest son.

To be an eldest son in those days was a very great honor; and especially so in this case, for Isaac's heir would inherit not only most of his father's worldly possessions but also all the blessings promised by God to Abraham.

But all this meant nothing to Esau. He wasn't interested.

136

He didn't care. He loved to hunt and to have a good time out in the fields and woods with his bow and arrows. Indeed, he was away so much that he knew little of what was going on at home. It meant far more to him to be known as the best shot in the country and the most cunning hunter than to be the first-born son of Isaac.

Jacob was different. He didn't like hunting. He preferred to stay around home. He enjoyed talking to his mother, Rebekah, who once told him about what happened at his birth—how the Lord had said, "The elder shall serve the younger." Genesis 25:23. Jacob thought about that a lot, and wondered how it would come to pass. From that moment he had his eye on the birthright.

Gradually the twins drew farther and farther apart. It was sad, for surely twins were meant to love each other in a special way all through life. How much better it would have been if both of them had played and worked together! If Jacob had taken his bow and arrow and gone to the woods sometimes, and

137

if Esau had not stayed away from home and family worship so much, what a different story the Bible might have had to tell about them!

One day Esau came in from the fields feeling very hungry. He was a fine, well-built young fellow, healthy as the hills where he loved to roam, but this day he was exhausted. There was nothing he wanted so much in all the world as a good meal.

As he reached home he found Jacob cooking lentils in some form or other. It must have been an unusually good mixture, for the smell of it made Esau ravenous.

"Feed me, I pray thee," he said to his brother, "for I am faint."

But Jacob was in a mean frame of mind. He saw a chance to get something from Esau that he had wanted for a long time. So he refused to give him food unless Esau promised to trade with him.

"Trade what?" I can hear Esau saying.

"How about selling me the birthright for a nice, big bowl of lentils?" said Jacob.

Now the birthright, according to ancient Hebrew law, was the right of inheritance of his father's wealth by the oldest son of the family. In the case of Esau this would have been considerable, for his father, Isaac, was a rich man.

THE BOY WHO DIDN'T CARE

Without a thought of the seriousness of his bargain, Esau cried, "It's a deal!"

To make quite sure of the advantage he had gained, and that Esau would not go back on it, Jacob said, "Swear to me this day; and he sware unto him: and he sold his birthright unto Jacob. Then Jacob gave Esau bread and pottage of lentiles; and he did eat and drink, and rose up, and went his way: thus Esau despised his birthright." Verses 33, 34.

Afterward, of course, when Esau realized how much he had given away for one dish of lentils, he was very sick about it. He had treated the birthright as of no special importance. All the riches of Abraham and Isaac, all the blessings promised by God, all the honor of being the heir through whom the family name should be carried on—and through whom Jesus, the Messiah, at last should come—he had valued at the price of a "morsel of meat." He had made light of spiritual things. And now "he found no place of repentance, though he sought it carefully with tears." Hebrews 12:17.

Today we, too, should be careful not to despise our birthright. For we are "sons of God" and "heirs of the kingdom." As the apostle Paul says, we are "heirs of God, and joint-heirs with Christ." Romans 8:17. All the richest treasures of heaven have been promised to us if we will remain faithful to God and obey His word.

This means far too much to us, here and hereafter, for us to treat it lightly. Let us see to it that we do not exchange our birthright blessings for some passing worldly pleasure. Heaven is too rich a prize to sell for a mess of pottage.

139

The High Cost of Cheating

HAVE you ever wondered why some boys and girls cheat at school or in games? It is because they think they are smart and that by breaking some rule that others are too honest to break, they will get ahead and gain some advantage for themselves.

But cheating never pays. Sometimes, of course, someone seems to win by being mean, but he really loses. He makes himself cheap. He spoils his good name.

There is a high price to pay for cheating, and if you doubt it, then read the story of how Jacob cheated his brother Esau, and what it cost him.

It happened when Isaac had grown old and blind. Feeling that he had not long to live, Isaac decided that he would give his eldest son Esau his parting blessing as though the birthright still belonged to him.

So he sent for Esau, whom he loved dearly, and told him what he had in mind. Before giving him the blessing, however,

he asked Esau to take his bow and arrows, go hunting, and prepare a savory dish for him as he had done so often in days
gone by.

"Bring it to me, that I may eat," said Isaac; "that my soul
may bless thee before I die." Genesis 27:4.

Glad to be able to do something to make his old father
happy, Esau set out to hunt. Little did he know what would
happen while he was away.

Unfortunately, his mother had overheard what Isaac had
said to Esau about the "blessing," and she guessed the rest;
and she made up her mind that Jacob, who had always been her
favorite, should have it as well as the birthright.

So she told Jacob what she had overheard, and suggested
how he might deceive his old father and cheat his brother out
of the blessing.

The plan was this: Jacob was to dress up in some of Esau's
clothes, while his mother cooked a savory dish made from a
couple of young goats taken from the flock. Because Esau was a
"hairy man" and Jacob was smooth-skinned, the skins of the
goats were to be laid on his hands and neck where Isaac was
most likely to touch him.

When the dressing up was completed, Jacob carried the
savory dish to his father. So scared was he that I wonder he
didn't spill the food all over the floor. He was afraid that his
father would discover the deception and curse him instead of
blessing him; and he was frightened, too, lest Esau should come
back in the middle of it all and give him the punishment he
deserved.

THE HIGH COST OF CHEATING

But Isaac was completely taken in. At first he was a little suspicious, for he didn't expect the food to be brought to him so soon. And he couldn't understand why this person who had brought the meal should talk like Jacob, yet feel like Esau.

"The voice is Jacob's voice," he said, "but the hands are the hands of Esau. . . . And he said, Art thou my very son Esau? And he said, I am." Verses 22-24.

That is the worst of deceit. It leads from one falsehood to another. Now Jacob was guilty of an outright lie, told to his poor, blind father. He could hardly have done anything worse than that.

Isaac, never thinking that one of his sons would lie to him, gave Jacob the blessing he had planned for Esau. No doubt he had been thinking for days and weeks of just what he would say and of all the good things he would promise to his eldest son, so dear to his heart. Now he said it all to the wrong boy!

The blessing received, Jacob hurried out, tore off Esau's clothes, and tried to look as innocent as he could. But if he thought his brother wouldn't find out, he was greatly mistaken.

Hardly had Jacob left the room than Esau returned.

That was a sad, sad moment.

"And it came to pass, as soon as Isaac had made an end of blessing Jacob, and Jacob was yet scarce gone out from the presence of Isaac his father, that Esau his brother came in from his hunting." Verse 30.

Not dreaming that anything had gone wrong, he went on making the savory meal, then happily carried it to his father.

"Let my father arise," he said, with tender devotion, "and

143

With his mother's help Jacob put hairy skins over his arms and neck to deceive his blind father Isaac, so that he might receive the blessing intended for his older brother, Esau.

eat of his son's venison, that thy soul may bless me." Verse 31.

Then the blow fell.

"Who art thou?" demanded his father in a loud voice, angry that anyone should play with him like this.

Esau stood still, astonished. What could be the matter? Did not his father recognize him?

"I am thy son, thy firstborn Esau."

"Who?" cried Isaac, now trembling all over. "Who? where is he that hath taken venison, and brought it me, and I have eaten of all before thou camest, and have blessed him?" Verse 33.

Esau was heartbroken. His last labor of love for his father had been spoiled. The food he had so carefully prepared with his own hands was not wanted. And now the blessing he had been promised had been given to someone else. It was too much. He broke down and wept, crying out in his sorrow, "Bless me, even me also, O my father!"

No more pitiful words were ever spoken. But what could Isaac do? He had given the blessing to Jacob, and, according to the custom of those days, he could not take it back.

144

THE HIGH COST OF CHEATING

He gave Esau another blessing, truly, but it wasn't just the same, and Esau knew it.

"And Esau hated Jacob because of the blessing wherewith his father blessed him: and Esau said in his heart, The days of mourning for my father are at hand; then will I slay my brother Jacob." Verse 41.

He not only said it "in his heart." He told his friends, and someone passed it on to Rebekah, and she told Jacob.

From the moment of the deception Jacob had been afraid that this might happen; now he became more frightened than ever, and decided that his only safety lay in flight.

Rebekah suggested that he flee to her brother's home in Haran, and this he agreed to do.

"Tarry with him a few days," she said, "until thy brother's fury turn away; . . . and he forget that which thou hast done to him: then I will send, and fetch thee from thence: why should I be deprived also of you both in one day?" Verses 44, 45.

Little did she know of the future, or of the high cost of cheating.

By that one miserable deed she lost both of her sons "in one day"—and broke her own heart. For Esau hated her, and Jacob she never saw again.

She expected him back in "a few days," but he never came while she was alive.

As for Jacob, he lost his home and his mother. For years he suffered great loneliness and disappointment, and ever regretted the injustice he had done.

No, it doesn't pay to cheat.

10

STORY 22

The Ladder Up to Heaven

≈≈≈≈≈≈≈≈≈≈≈≈≈≈≈

IT DOESN'T seem possible that God could ever have forgiven Jacob for that mean trick he played on his brother
and on his old father Isaac. It was enough, one would think,
to have made God want to finish with him there and then
forever.

But that is the wonderful thing about God. He never
"finishes" with anybody who has done wrong as long as there is
any hope that he will say he is sorry and promise to live better.
He forgives the worst sinners and lets them try again.

To all who have done wrong He says, "Come now, and let
us reason together . . . : though your sins be as scarlet, they
shall be as white as snow; though they be red like crimson, they
shall be as wool." Isaiah 1:18.

"Who is a God like unto Thee," said Micah, "that par-
doneth iniquity, and passeth by the transgression of the remnant of His heritage? He retaineth not His anger for ever, because He delighteth in mercy." Micah 7:18.

THE LADDER UP TO HEAVEN

Jacob needed mercy all right. Plenty of it. He knew what a mistake he had made and what it had cost him. How little he had gained! How much he had lost! Though heir to all the riches of Abraham and Isaac, here he was penniless, fleeing for his life.

No doubt Jacob thought of his happy childhood home in which God was reverently worshiped each day, and of how he was loved by all his father's servants.

At last, weary to death and homesick, he flung himself upon the ground, hoping that sleep would cause him to forget his fears and sorrows. No comforts for him now, only the hard ground to lie on, as "he took of the stones of that place, and put them for his pillows, and lay down in that place to sleep." Genesis 28:11.

Never did he feel so low, so wretched, so far from God; yet never was God so near.

As he slept he dreamed, "and behold a ladder set up on the earth, and the top of it reached to heaven: and behold the angels of God ascending and descending on it.

"And, behold, the Lord stood above it, and said, I am the Lord God of Abraham thy father, and the God of Isaac: the land whereon thou liest, to thee will I give it, and to thy seed; and thy seed shall be as the dust of the earth, and thou shalt spread abroad to the west, and to the east, and to the north, and to the south: and in thee and in thy seed shall all the families of the earth be blessed. And, behold, I am with thee, and will keep thee in all places whither thou goest, and will bring thee again into this land; for I will not leave thee, until I have done that which I have spoken to thee of.

"And Jacob awakened out of his sleep, and he said, Surely the Lord is in this place; and I knew it not." Verses 12-16.

Yes, indeed, the Lord was there. Despite all his mistakes and failures and downright wickedness, the Lord had spoken to him. He knew he didn't deserve it. He had been too mean and unkind, and yet here was God renewing to him—him, of all people—the great promises He had made long ago to faithful Abraham. How kind was God! How tender and forgiving!

Overcome by this revelation of God's goodness and mercy, he exclaimed, "This is none other but the house of God, and this is the gate of heaven." Verse 17. It must have seemed so indeed, with that wonderful shining ladder stretching far up into the midnight sky, and the glory of the Lord above it, and His voice speaking such kind and tender words.

Deeply moved by what he had seen and heard, Jacob made up his mind to live a better life from this night on. So he made God a promise, saying, "If God will be with me, and will keep me in this way that I go, and will give me bread to eat, and raiment to put on, so that I come again to my father's house in peace; then shall the Lord be my God: . . . and of all that Thou shalt give me I will surely give the tenth unto Thee." Verses 20-22.

It was the prayer of a worried, hungry, homesick man taking his first faltering step toward heaven, but God was glad for it and accepted it. So, too, He rejoices when anyone today

148

In his dream, with only a stone of the field for his pillow, Jacob saw a wonderful ladder that reached from earth to heaven, with the angels of God ascending and descending on it.

comes back to Him, no matter in what feeble words he tells Him he is sorry for his sins.

Yes! That ladder up to heaven, with the angels ascending and descending upon it, was God's way of telling us all that the worst of sinners may return to Him; that for all who do wrong there is a ladder leading from just where they are right up to the throne of glory.

Is that ladder still there? It is. You may see it in your dreams tonight. And you may climb it when you will. For that ladder is none other than Jesus, who once said to Nathanael, "Hereafter ye shall see heaven open, and the angels of God ascending and descending upon the Son of man." John 1:51.

Yes, Jesus is the ladder up to heaven. He is "the way, the truth, and the life: no man cometh unto the Father" but by Him. John 14:6. "Neither is there salvation in any other: for there is none other name under heaven given among men, whereby we must be saved." Acts 4 :12.

When we know we have done wrong, and feel just as low as did Jacob as he lay on that pile of stones, we may think again of that beautiful Ladder and see it going straight up from our tear-stained pillow into heaven. And above it we can see God, waiting to forgive, waiting to say, "Behold, I am with thee, and will keep thee . . . ; for I will not leave thee."

Have you done something wrong today? Have you been cross, unkind, ugly, deceitful? Are you sorry? Do you want to be good? The Ladder is beside you. Use it. Climb back to God through Jesus. He is waiting for you now.

A Tale of Twelve Brothers

SWIFTLY the years rolled by. Away in Haran, Jacob worked hard and long for his Uncle Laban. Again and again he learned what it meant to be tricked as he had tricked others. Ten times Laban cheated him over his wages.

Twenty years later, when Jacob returned to Canaan, he was a wiser and a better man.

On the way he heard that Esau was coming to meet him with four hundred men. His old fear of his brother returned, but this time he looked to God for help, and spent a whole night in prayer. That was the night God changed his name from Jacob to Israel.

When Esau arrived, there was no argument and no fighting. Instead, like a real twin brother, "Esau ran to meet him, and embraced him, and fell on his neck, and kissed him: and they wept." Genesis 33:4.

After that Jacob settled in Canaan with his large family. And it *was* a large family, even for those days. He brought eleven sons with him from Haran, the oldest being Reuben and the youngest Joseph. After he reached Canaan, another little boy, Benjamin, turned up, making twelve in all.

As was the custom then, the boys helped with the farm chores, spending much of their time minding the flocks of sheep and the herds of goats and cattle belonging to their father.

Somehow Joseph did not quite fit in with his older brothers. They looked on him as the "little brother" and a bit of a nuisance. They were afraid that he might carry stories about them to their father. And they were jealous of him because Jacob favored him a lot, seeing he was "the son of his old age."

One day Jacob had a beautiful coat made for Joseph, but it only caused more trouble. The older brothers envied him,

153

When Jacob made Joseph a beautiful coat of many colors as a sign of his affection, it excited the envy of all Joseph's brothers and they began to plot how they might kill him.

and no doubt remarked that father had never given any of *them* a coat like that. They were suspicious, too, that this might mean that Jacob was going to give the birthright to Joseph.

The situation became worse when Joseph told his brothers about a dream he had had. He said that they were all binding sheaves of corn in a field when suddenly all their sheaves bowed down to his sheaf. Naturally they didn't like that.

Then he told them how he had dreamed that the sun, moon, and eleven stars bowed down to him; and they liked that still less.

The fact was, of course, that God had given Joseph these dreams to let him know what was going to happen in later years, and to give him courage for the trials that would come to him.

But his older brothers did not know about that, and so angry did they become with Joseph that they went so far as to talk about killing him, even though he was only seventeen.

One day, as his older brothers saw him coming across the fields toward them, "they said one to another, Behold, this

154

dreamer cometh. Come now therefore, and let us slay him, and cast him into some pit, and we will say, Some evil beast hath devoured him: and we shall see what will become of his dreams." Genesis 37:19, 20.

Just then Reuben, who had been absent for a while, came on the scene.

He disliked Joseph almost as much as the rest, but he wasn't willing to go so far as to kill him. Then, too, as the eldest son, he knew his father would hold him responsible for the boy's safety.

"Let us not kill him," he said to the others. "Shed no blood, but cast him into this pit"—his purpose being to take Joseph out of the pit later and send him back to his father.

The others agreed, and all waited for Joseph to come.

Meanwhile Joseph, who had walked a long, long way—almost fifty miles—looking for his brothers, was feeling very happy that at last he had found them. At the joy of seeing them again he almost forgot how tired and hungry he was. Imagine, then, his disappointment when he saw the ugly looks on their faces. This was not the welcome he had expected. Then, to his horror, some of them seized him, tore off his beautiful new coat, then carried him to a deep pit and threw him in.

A TALE OF TWELVE BROTHERS

In vain he cried to them to have mercy on him, but they wouldn't listen, and soon he found himself left alone at the bottom of the pit, hungry, cold, and heartbroken. He called and called, but no one came. For all he knew, he was to be left there to die of thirst and starvation.

Meanwhile Reuben had gone back to his work, and the others, left to themselves, started to talk about what to do with Joseph. They were in a fix. Having agreed not to kill the boy, they couldn't leave him in the pit to die; but if they let him go, he would surely run home and tell his father how cruel they had all been to him.

Just then they saw a caravan approaching, and discovered it was a company of Ishmaelites from Gilead "with their camels bearing spicery and balm and myrrh, going to carry it down to Egypt."

At this, one of the brothers, Judah, had a bright idea. "Come," he said, "let us sell him to the Ishmaelites."

The very thing!

The rest agreed at once, for not only would this get them out of a very difficult situation, but they would actually make some money as well.

So the caravan was stopped, and the bargaining began. Finally Joseph was lifted out of the pit and, despite his tears and pleadings, was sold to the Ishmaelites for twenty pieces of silver.

Thus within an hour or two of his arrival at his brothers' camp, poor Joseph, pride and joy of his father's heart, found himself a slave in a caravan bound for Egypt.

157

Joseph had never been far away from home, but now he was sold by his cruel brothers as a slave to rough strangers, who took him many days' journey from his home to Egypt.

Hardly had the caravan disappeared in the gathering dusk than Reuben returned. Making his way to the pit to release Joseph, he was shocked to find the boy was no longer there.

"And he returned unto his brethren, and said, The child is not; and I, whither shall I go?" Verse 30.

He couldn't bear the thought of facing his father without Joseph. And what would the old man say when he learned what had happened to the boy? If Jacob discovered that his beloved Joseph had been sold as a slave, he might disinherit all of them in his fury.

So, as often happens when people do wrong, they had to lie about it.

Which brother first suggested the false story we are not told, but between them they arranged to give their father the idea that Joseph had been killed by some wild animal while searching for his brothers. To make the plan quite foolproof, so they thought, they took Joseph's new coat, dipped it in the blood of an animal, and carried it to Jacob.

"This have we found," they said: "know now whether it be thy son's coat or no." Verse 32.

Jacob knew it, of course. No one but Joseph had had a coat like that.

"It is my son's coat," he said with a sob; "an evil beast hath devoured him; Joseph is without doubt rent in pieces." Verse 33.

So Jacob, who had deceived his father, was now deceived by his own sons.

"And Jacob . . . mourned for his son many days. And all his sons [imagine it!] and all his daughters rose up to comfort him; but he refused to be comforted; and he said, For I will go down into the grave unto my son mourning. Thus his father wept for him." Verses 34, 35.

But, unknown to his father, Joseph was not dead. Instead, sad, weary, and homesick, he was on his way to Egypt.

Trudging along the dusty trail with the Ishmaelite caravan, he wondered why all this evil had come to him; why his brothers had been so cruel to him; why they had sent him away from his father whom he loved so much. But in God's providence it was the best thing that ever happened to him. Though he did not realize it, though everything before him looked black and miserable, he was on his way to a great future, which otherwise he would never have known.

To all of us, boys and girls, there come sad times like this, when the way seems dark and hopeless. But if we trust in God all will be well. He will not forget us. And in His own good time He will bring us out of the night into a bright new day.

159

From Prison to Palace

A RRIVING in Egypt, Joseph found himself in a new world. Never had he seen so many people, nor such fine buildings. It was all so different from anything he had known in the land of Canaan, where he had been brought up. He looked around with great interest at all the new sights and sounds, wondering just what would happen to him in this strange, exciting country.

He had not long to wait. The Ishmaelites with whom he had traveled were eager to get rid of him at a profit, and they sold him to Potiphar, captain of the guard and an officer in Pharaoh's court.

That's how it was in those days. Boys and girls were bought and sold just like cows and sheep.

Poor Joseph! Now he was a servant in an Egyptian home, at the beck and call of a stranger. It was hard, but he made up his mind to make the best of it. Whatever he was asked to do, he did well and faithfully.

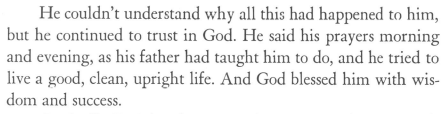

He couldn't understand why all this had happened to him, but he continued to trust in God. He said his prayers morning and evening, as his father had taught him to do, and he tried to live a good, clean, upright life. And God blessed him with wisdom and success.

Gradually Potiphar began to place more and more confidence in him. As the Bible says, "His master saw that the Lord was with him, and that the Lord made all that he did to prosper in his hand."

One day, to his great joy, Joseph was made overseer. Now he had servants under him, and was in charge of the whole household. And the wonderful thing was that from the time that Joseph took over this position, "the Lord blessed the Egyptian's house for Joseph's sake; and the blessing of the Lord was upon all that he had in the house, and in the field.

"And he [Potiphar] left all that he had in Joseph's hand; and he knew not ought he had, save the bread which he did eat." Genesis 39:5, 6.

Then, just as everything was going so well, trouble came again. Potiphar's wife accused him, falsely, of doing something

11

wrong. Her story was untrue, and most unfair, but Potiphar, in a fit of anger, commanded that Joseph be thrown into prison.

It was enough to break Joseph's heart. He knew he was innocent. He had taken a firm stand for right. "How . . . can I do this great wickedness, and sin against God?" he had said. And now he was in prison, chained in a dungeon like a common criminal!

Still he was faithful to God, and God did not forget him. "The Lord was with Joseph, and shewed him mercy, and gave him favour in the sight of the keeper of the prison." Verse 21.

There must have been something very fine about Joseph, for he made the same good impression on everyone he met or worked with.

Soon he found himself placed in charge of the other prisoners, and "the keeper of the prison looked not to any thing that was under his hand; because the Lord was with him, and that which he did, the Lord made it to prosper." Verse 23.

Those were hard years for Joseph, confined in that prison,

but they were all part of his training for the great responsibility that God was about to lay upon him.

While in prison Joseph helped the other prisoners in every way he could. He even gained quite a reputation as an interpreter of their dreams; and this fact finally got to the ears of Pharaoh himself, who also had dreams which he wanted someone to interpret for him.

One day, to Joseph's amazement, he was ordered to appear in court.

"Then Pharaoh sent and called Joseph, and they brought him hastily out of the dungeon: and he shaved himself, and changed his raiment, and came in unto Pharaoh." Genesis 41:14.

How excited Joseph must have been! All the way from the prison to the palace he must have asked himself, "Why has he called for me? What wrong have I done now?"

Then the great door opened and Joseph was led into the gorgeous throne room. Pharaoh was seated upon his golden throne with officials and servants all about him. It was a marvelous sight to Joseph after all the years he had spent in the drab and dreary prison. Then Pharaoh beckoned to him, and he knew that all was well.

"I have dreamed a dream," said Pharaoh, "and there is none that can interpret it: and I have heard say of thee, that thou canst understand a dream to interpret it." Verse 15.

Then Joseph answered Pharaoh very humbly. "It is not

in me, God shall give Pharaoh an answer of peace." Verse 16.

Then Pharaoh told him about two dreams he had had. One was about seven lean cows that ate up seven fat cows; and another about seven withered ears of corn that ate up seven good ears.

Joseph understood at once, and in a few words he told Pharaoh just what the dreams meant. Both dreams, he said, had the same meaning and were sent by God to warn Pharaoh of the coming of a great famine. There would be seven years of plenty, with wonderful harvests and lots of grain and other food-stuffs; but afterward there would be seven years of the worst famine Egypt had ever seen.

"Now therefore," said Joseph, "let Pharaoh look out a man discreet and wise, and set him over the land of Egypt. . . . And let him appoint officers over the land. . . . And let them gather all the food of those good years that come, and lay up

164

corn under the hand of Pharaoh, and let them keep food in the cities. And that food shall be for store to the land against the seven years of famine." Verses 33-36.

Pharaoh was greatly impressed, not only by the interpretation of his dream but by this sound advice from the fine young man before him. Turning to his counselors, he said, "Can we find such a one as this is, a man in whom the Spirit of God is?" Verse 38.

So Joseph was chosen to be food controller and director of famine relief, and Pharaoh made him ruler over all the land of Egypt. "Only in the throne," he said, "will I be greater than thou."

"And Pharaoh took off his ring from his hand, and put it upon Joseph's hand, and arrayed him in vestures of fine linen, and put a gold chain about his neck; and he made him to ride in the second chariot which he had; and they cried before him, Bow the knee." Verses 42, 43.

If only his brothers could have seen him now! Having sold him as a slave, they pictured him working at menial tasks in some rich Egyptian's home; and here he was riding through Egypt's cities in the royal chariot, with everybody bowing before him!

Thus does God work for those who love and trust Him, defeating the plans of their enemies and making everything come out right in the end.

Sometime you may find yourself in a pit or dungeon, but never fear. Be faithful, be true, for beyond is the palace and the throne. And God is leading you there.

Greatness in Victory

~~~~~~

EGYPT now enjoyed seven wonderful years of prosperity. Never had it known such harvests. "The earth brought forth by handfuls."

Joseph, faithful as ever, and keen to do his job well, drove from place to place in his chariot, arranging for the collection and storage of the grain. He built huge storehouses in various parts of the country and filled them to the bursting point. At first he began to count the bushels taken in, but gave up. There was too much to count.

"And Joseph gathered corn as the sand of the sea, very much, until he left numbering; for it was without number." Genesis 41:49.

Then, as suddenly as they had come, the good years ended, and the seven years of famine began. Crops dried up and harvests failed. Soon there was no food for man or beast. Then the word, "Corn in Egypt," was carried from country to country, and thousands began moving toward Joseph's granaries.

166

GREATNESS IN VICTORY

But Joseph held on to his vast stores of grain as long as he could, for he knew they must last for many years. He held them, indeed, until the Egyptians complained to Pharaoh and cried to him for bread. But all Pharaoh said was, "Go unto Joseph."

At last conditions became so bad that Joseph decided to open his storehouses and sell the corn to the hungry people. How glad they were then that he had been so wise and careful! Otherwise all might have starved to death.

Away up in Canaan, Jacob was beginning to get worried over the famine. In all his long life he had never seen anything like this. There was no grass for his cattle and no grain to make bread for his large family and household. His harvest had failed, and his supplies of food were getting dangerously low.

So Jacob called his sons together and said to them, "Behold, I have heard that there is corn in Egypt: get you down thither, and buy for us from thence; that we may live, and not die." Genesis 42:2.

So ten of his sons set out for Egypt, leaving only Benjamin behind with his father.

They followed the same trail that Joseph had traveled twenty years before, when they sold him as a slave to the Ishmaelites. Many times they thought about the wrong they had done to him then, and they wondered whether they might meet him in Egypt, if indeed he were still alive. But one thing they did not expect—and that was to find him the chief man in Egypt next to Pharaoh.

On arriving in Egypt, they inquired where they had to go to buy grain, and were told they must first obtain permission from the governor. So they went to see him and bowed low before him, never supposing for a moment that this fine big man, dressed in the splendid robes of the Egyptian court and speaking the Egyptian language, was their own brother whom they had sold into slavery.

But Joseph recognized them. And he was glad to see them; but before letting them know who he was, he decided to test them. So he put on a harsh voice and accused them of being spies. They were badly frightened, and said humbly that they were merely sons of an old man in the land of Canaan, and all they wanted was food. But Joseph kept on saying, "Ye are spies!"

At last he put them in prison for three days, perhaps to give himself time to think what to do next. What he wanted most was to see his younger brother again, his own dear Benjamin; but how could this be brought about?

Finally he thought of a plan, and sent for his brothers. Then he suggested that one of them should remain in prison while the rest took what corn they needed, returned home, and

came again with Benjamin. They agreed, and Simeon was chosen to be the hostage.

Then a strange thing happened. Suddenly it came over the brothers that all this trouble had come to them because of the way they had treated Joseph long ago, and they began to say one to another, in Joseph's presence, "We are verily guilty concerning our brother, in that we saw the anguish of his soul, when he besought us, and we would not hear; therefore is this distress come upon us. And Reuben answered them, saying, Spake I not unto you, saying, Do not sin against the child; and ye would not hear?" Verses 21, 22.

Of course they didn't know that Joseph understood every word they said; but he did, "and he turned himself about from them, and wept." Not till now did he know they were sorry for what they had done to him, and his tender heart overflowed at the thought.

Later, on their way home, they found all the money they had paid for the corn inside their sacks. This made them more afraid, for they did not know that Joseph, out of his love for them, had himself ordered this to be done.

169

When they arrived home, they told Jacob everything that had happened, and how the governor of Egypt had said that they could have no more corn unless they took their youngest brother back with them.

"Benjamin!" cried Jacob. "Never!" "Joseph is not, and Simeon is not, and ye will take Benjamin away: all these things are against me." Verse 36.

But there was no other course to follow. When the food they had brought from Egypt was eaten, they had to go to buy more, or die of starvation. And so, with Jacob's reluctant consent, they set out again, taking double the money with them—besides a gift for the governor—and Benjamin.

Joseph was expecting them. He knew they would have to return for more food, and when word reached him that they were in the city, he decided to give them the surprise of their lives. He sent them an invitation to dinner!

They couldn't believe their ears. Dine with the governor! It was too great an honor for them. They had never dreamed of any such thing. But it was true, and they had to go.

When they appeared before Joseph, he began to talk with them about their father. But when Joseph caught sight of Benjamin he was so overcome that he hurried out of the room and burst into tears. How he longed to throw his arms around his youngest brother! But he must not do it yet.

Presently Joseph returned to the dining hall, seemingly quite calm, and ordered the meal to be served. He sat at one table with his Egyptian officers, while his brothers, being Hebrews, sat at another table, looking in amazement at this magnificent meal that had been prepared for them. The Bible says they "marvelled one at another," and the more so when they saw how, by the governor's order, Benjamin's plate was heaped with five times as much food as anyone else's.

Yet still they did not guess who the governor was.

So Joseph played one more trick on them. He gave orders that when their sacks were filled with grain, his own silver cup was to be placed in Benjamin's sack.

Presently the brothers set off for home, very proud of themselves at having been invited to dinner with the governor of Egypt and very happy that everything had turned out so well after all. But soon they heard the sound of galloping horses, and, looking round, were horrified to find that it was the governor's steward, with a bodyguard, come to arrest them!

Roughly he accused them of stealing the governor's silver cup, which he greatly prized.

Of course they denied doing any such thing, and their blank looks were enough to convince anybody that they were

innocent. But the steward demanded that all the sacks be examined, and, of course, the cup was found in Benjamin's sack.

It was a sad journey back to the city! All the joy and pride of the morning were gone, and life didn't seem worth living.

Back at the governor's palace, they once more fell on their faces before Joseph, pleading their innocence. This was more than Joseph could stand. Suddenly he raised his voice in command, saying, "Cause every man to go out from me! And there stood no man with him, while Joseph made himself known unto his brethren." Genesis 45:1.

What a meeting was that!

"And he wept aloud: and the Egyptians and the house of Pharaoh heard."

At first the brothers wondered what all this might mean. Then as Joseph was able to control himself, he said, "I am Joseph; doth my father yet live?"

Then they were really afraid. Joseph! Could this be Joseph? If it were, what would he do to them in revenge for all they had made him suffer?

GREATNESS IN VICTORY

But there was no revenge in Joseph's heart. Only love. He had forgiven them long ago; all he wanted was to be friends.

In their fear they had moved away from him, but he said, so gently, "Come near to me, I pray you. And they came near. And he said, I am Joseph your brother, whom ye sold into Egypt. Now therefore be not grieved, nor angry with yourselves, that ye sold me hither: for God did send me before you to preserve life. For these two years hath the famine been in the land: and yet there are five years, in which there shall neither be earing nor harvest. And God sent me before you to preserve you a posterity in the earth, and to save your lives by a great deliverance. So now it was not you that sent me hither, but God." Verses 4-8.

How beautifully did he try to take all the worry out of their hearts! They weren't to blame; it was in God's plan.

Only a truly greathearted man could speak like that!

Then he told them of his plan to bring the whole family into the land of Goshen, close by him, where he could help them and feed them through all the years of famine.

"There will I nourish thee," he said; ". . . lest thou, and thy household, and all that thou hast, come to poverty." Verse 11.

There was not a trace of meanness in Joseph's character. He was powerful and wealthy, and in a position to "get even" with these men who had been so cruel to him; but he never once thought of it; his only concern was for their welfare.

"And he fell upon his brother Benjamin's neck, and wept; and Benjamin wept upon his neck. Moreover he kissed all his brethren, and wept upon them." Verse 14.

173

Yes, he kissed them all. Reuben, Simeon, Judah—every one, even those who had actually thrown him into the pit, and who had sold him into slavery. He kissed them! What love! What forgiveness!

"And the fame thereof was heard in Pharaoh's house." And it spread to Canaan, and Jacob heard of it. At first he couldn't believe the good news, but "when he saw the wagons which Joseph had sent to carry him," he knew it must be true. A new light came into the old man's eyes, and a great joy in his heart. "It is enough," he said; "Joseph my son is yet alive: I will go and see him before I die."

Eagerly he set out on the journey to meet his long-lost son, taking his family with him. "And Israel dwelt in the land of Egypt, in the country of Goshen; and they had possessions therein, and grew, and multiplied exceedingly." Genesis 47:27.

Thus by the grace of God and the faithfulness of a noble youth, thousands of people were greatly blessed, the "seed of the woman" was again preserved, and the divine plan of salvation went marching on down the years.

God Plans a Rescue

G REAT and prosperous though he was, enjoying almost unlimited power as governor of Egypt, Joseph was homesick for Canaan. Deep in his heart was a yearning to return to the land from which he had been so cruelly exiled when a boy. Though he lived to be a hundred and ten years old, and a great-grandfather, the thought of the green hills and fertile valleys of his native land made him lonesome.

He wanted so much to go back. Yet he never could. He was always too busy. The burdens of leadership made it impossible. So when the day of his death drew near, he called his brothers to him again, all of them now old men, and said to them, "I die: and God will surely visit you, and bring you out of this land unto the land which He sware to Abraham, to Isaac, and to Jacob. . . . And ye shall carry up my bones from hence." Genesis 50:24, 25.

God's plan for them, he knew, could never come to pass while they lived in the midst of a heathen nation. They would

175

have to return to the land of their fathers, and he wanted to go along.

He remembered, too, God's promise to Abraham: "Know of a surety that thy seed shall be a stranger in a land that is not theirs, and shall serve them; and they shall afflict them four hundred years. . . . But in the fourth generation they shall come hither again." Genesis 15:13-16.

How he must have wondered when the four hundred years would be up, and what would happen then!

Then he died and was buried, probably in a tomb near the pyramids. Yet even in his death he was a blessing to his people, for whenever they would pass his burial place they would say, "Joseph sleeps there, and he promised that we shall return to Canaan some day"—and their hearts would thrill with hope.

Of course, it didn't matter much when things were going well and the Egyptians were friendly, but afterward, when everything went wrong and persecution started, how precious his promise was then!

And things did go wrong. Very wrong. "There arose up a new king over Egypt, which knew not Joseph." Exodus 1:8. This man was shrewd and cruel. Looking over his kingdom, he noted that there were actually more Israelites than Egyptians in the country, so greatly had they multiplied. He saw, too, that they occupied not only the best of the land but many of the best positions in state and city government. Complaints were brought to him by jealous Egyptians about the advantages the Hebrews had gained to the harm of the native people.

Calling his counselors, he said to them, "Behold, the people of the children of Israel are more and mightier than we: come on, let us deal wisely with them; lest they multiply, and it come to pass, that, when there falleth out any war, they join also unto our enemies, and fight against us, and so get them up out of the land."

Then he announced his course of action. The Hebrews henceforth would be slaves. No longer would they be permitted to work for themselves and their own profit. Henceforth they must labor for the state. So he "set over them taskmasters to afflict them with their burdens. And they built for Pharaoh treasure cities, Pithom and Raamses."

After enjoying so much freedom the Hebrews must have felt it very hard to find themselves servants all of a sudden. But there was nothing they could do about it; they could only submit.

Yet if Pharaoh thought he could exterminate the Hebrews by hard work and cruel bondage, he was mistaken. The more he afflicted them, "the more they multiplied and grew."

Then another plan came to the king's mind. Having failed to reduce the Hebrew population by working them to death, he would try more desperate means. He would kill their children! And he would start with their boys.

12

So he gave orders that every baby boy born to a Hebrew mother should be thrown into the river Nile and drowned.

It was a wicked decree, and must have brought great fear and sorrow into every Hebrew home. Instead of looking forward with happiness to the birth of a baby son, many a family must have been well-nigh frightened to death lest Pharaoh's soldiers should find the child and kill it before it had scarcely begun to live.

This was Israel's darkest hour. It made them want to leave Egypt as they had never wanted to leave it before. They remembered Joseph's promise that God would one day deliver them and take them home. And they began to pray for that day to dawn.

At this very moment, when everything seemed at its worst, and the people were too sad for tears, God began to prepare for their rescue. It happened this way:

Walking by the riverside one day, attended by her maids, Pharaoh's daughter suddenly spied a strange object floating

© BY R&H

near the riverbank, partly hidden by bulrushes. It looked like a small, oblong basket which someone had made watertight by coating it with pitch. Curious to know what it might contain, she sent one of her maids to fetch it.

Little did she guess that within this basket lay a bundle of dynamite that would one day blast Pharaoh's power and wrest from his grasp a million slaves. Little did she know that herein was a mighty man of God who would look the tyrant in the face, demand his people's freedom, and lead them in triumph through the Red Sea to Canaan.

If only she had known, she might never have opened that basket.

But she did not know, and she opened it. Inside, warmly wrapped with the infinite care of a heartbroken mother, was a baby boy, just three months old.

"And when she had opened it, she saw the child: and, behold, the babe wept. And she had compassion on him, and said, This is one of the Hebrews' children."

But now what to do? Here was a problem. She dare not take the child to the palace, fearing her father's anger. Yet her tender heart could not leave the poor weeping thing here, hungry, alone, and a prey for crocodiles.

Just then a little girl ran up, with eager face and eyes aglow. Though the princess did not know it, this was Miriam, the child's sister, who loved that baby more than her own life, and who had been watching the basket from a hiding place on the riverside with mingled fear and hope.

"Please," she said to the princess, "shall I go and call a nurse of the Hebrew women, that she may nurse the child for you?"

Glad for a way out, the princess said, "Yes, by all means"; and away went Miriam, running like the wind, her heart pounding fit to burst. I can almost hear her, as she neared home, shrieking at the top of her voice, "Mother, come quick, come quick! The princess has found Baby Brother, and she wants you to nurse him!"

Mother needed no second invitation, but ran as fast as she could to the river. There she found everything just as Miriam had said. There was the princess, and the open basket, and her own precious baby crying piteously as one of the maids sought to comfort it.

"Take this child away," said the princess to Miriam's mother, "and nurse it for me, and I will give thee thy wages."

GOD PLANS A RESCUE

How Mother Jochebed hugged that baby of hers as she hurried back to the house, with Miriam dancing excitedly at her side! Not only was the child alive, but its life was guaranteed by the princess, and money was provided for its keep. Surely the hand of God was in this!

It was. Unknown to all the poor, suffering Hebrews, the life of their future deliverer had been spared.

How much depended upon Jochebed! She must give her baby her best, for she knew she had so little time, only a few short years, before she must hand him over to the princess to be *her* son.

In those precious years she taught the boy to love God. She told him all she knew of the divine plan of salvation, the story of which had been handed down from father to son from the days of Adam. She told him of his own deliverance from death in the river, and her conviction that he was born for some high purpose. She taught him to pray, and kindled in his heart a desire to do good and follow the right.

Then one day, when Moses was only twelve, she had to bid him good-by. I can see the two walking up the palace stairs hand in hand, the boy's heart full of wonder, the mother's full of fears and sadness. And then the last good-by, with mother saying, amid her tears, "Be brave, dear son, be good! Remember, I love you always."

Then he was gone. Lost in the great palace. Yet not lost, for God knew he was there. And God would watch over him and bring him out again in His own good time.

The Great Deliverance

WHEN the palace gates closed behind Moses, leaving his mother outside, the world must have seemed a sad and lonely place to him. But when he was led into the presence of the princess and told to call her "mother," that was harder still. He may well have cried himself to sleep that night, thinking he was forever cut off from his home and his people, and could never return to them.

A lad of fine appearance, "exceeding fair," as the Bible says (Acts 7:20), he was soon a favorite in the court. The best teachers in the land were ordered to tutor him, and as time went by, he became "learned in all the wisdom of the Egyptians, and was mighty in words and in deeds." Verse 22.

Years passed. No longer a boy, Moses was now in the prime of life. Strong of body and keen of mind, he already had the makings of a leader. There was little about the history, geography, and religion of Egypt that he did not know. He had made himself familiar with all the sciences as they were then understood. He had studied all there was to know about military affairs and the art of war.

All the court—indeed, all Egypt—knew that here was a man of unusual gifts, well able to take Pharaoh's place. And Moses himself was not unaware that he was in direct line to the throne. Someday, he knew, if he so desired, he could become ruler of Egypt.

Yet amid all his studies and all his busy life, he never forgot the things his mother had told him in his boyhood. Not a day passed but he thought of God and of what mother had said God wanted him to be and to do. As the years slipped by, he felt more and more out of place in the palace. Deep loyalties, which court life could not change, drew him toward his people, now suffering greater hardships than ever at the hands of their overlords.

Reports of the way the Hebrew slaves were being treated filtered in through the gay, easygoing life of the court. Sometimes Moses wondered if he should go to their aid. He counted the cost, and what it might mean to him of revealing that he was not an Egyptian after all, but belonged to the very people whom the Egyptians despised. He would lose his position. He would lose his chance for the throne. But what else could he do?

When he said his prayers he talked with God about it all. Then one night he made a life-changing decision—as sooner or

later we all must do—"choosing rather to suffer affliction with the people of God, than to enjoy the pleasures of sin for a season; esteeming the reproach of Christ greater riches than the treasures in Egypt." Hebrews 11:25, 26.

That was a great and noble choice to make, and it proved to be a turning point in the history of Israel and of the world.

"And when he was full forty years old, it came into his heart to visit his brethren the children of Israel."

He was deeply moved at their hardships, and "seeing one of them suffer wrong, he defended him, and avenged him that was oppressed, and smote the Egyptian: for he supposed his brethren would have understood how that God by his hand would deliver them: but they understood not." Acts 7:24, 25.

He should have known better. This was no way to begin the deliverance of his people. And as to his expecting them to welcome him, why should they? They knew him only as some great man from Pharaoh's court, someone to be feared, not trusted. So they didn't attempt to keep secret what he had done, and the word swept through the homes of the Hebrews, "Do you know what Moses did? He killed an Egyptian taskmaster." It flashed to every military outpost and into the court itself: Moses had killed an Egyptian!

When Pharaoh heard it he was very angry, and gave orders for Moses' arrest and execution. But someone—perhaps the princess—sent him word just in time, and he made his escape, fleeing across the desert toward the land of Midian.

As he fled it must have seemed to him that his life was a terrible failure; that he had spoiled his one great chance of

184

helping his people. But he need not have been discouraged. God had not forsaken him. Many years passed by. Then, as he wandered over the barren hills one day, he suddenly noticed a strange sight. A bush seemed to be on fire, yet it did not burn. His scientific mind wondered what this could be, and he drew near to watch it. Then he heard someone calling his name. "Moses, Moses!" And he knew it was the voice of God.

How wonderful it was! God had followed him into the wilderness!

Then God told him how concerned He was about the sufferings of His people. "I know their sorrows," He said; "and I am come down to deliver them."

Now Moses realized why God was talking with him. Here was a lesson he needed to learn. Not Moses, but God, would deliver Israel. Once Moses had thought he could do it by himself, in his own way. Now he knew better.

So when God said, "Come now . . . , I will send thee unto Pharaoh, that thou mayest bring forth My people," Moses an-

swered, "Who am I, that I should go?" He was humble now, and God could use him.

Finally, with many misgivings, Moses accepted God's call and started on his way. One bright spot in his journey was his meeting with his brother, Aaron, whom he had not seen for forty years. With what joy they must have greeted each other, and how much they must have had to talk about! Then they went on together, back to Egypt.

As they journeyed they discussed how they would carry out God's commission. As a first step they decided to go to Pharaoh and request permission for the children of Israel to take time off from their work to hold a religious meeting in the desert.

Familiar with the ways of the court, they gained admittance to the king's presence and made their request. It would mean a three-day journey into the desert, they said, and Pharaoh quickly saw that this would consume at least a week's time for all his many slaves. This was too much. He refused the request, then decreed that more work should be laid upon the slaves. If they thought they had time to take a week off, then let them work harder. So word was sent out that the Hebrews must not only make the same number of bricks every day as before, but must gather the straw to put in them—for bricks were made by mixing clay and straw in those days.

At this the people groaned in weariness and disappointment. The new order almost doubled their work. They wished Moses and Aaron had never gone to see Pharaoh. As for Moses, he turned to God and said, "Why is it that Thou hast sent me? . . . Since I came to Pharaoh to speak in Thy name, he hath done evil to this people; neither hast Thou delivered Thy people at all." Exodus 5:22, 23.

"Then the Lord said unto Moses, Now shalt thou see what I will do to Pharaoh." "Wherefore say unto the children of Israel, I am the Lord, and I will bring you out from under the burdens of the Egyptians, and I will rid you out of their bondage, and I will redeem you with a stretched out arm, and with great judgments." Exodus 6:1, 6.

These were great words of hope and encouragement. Moses told them to some of the leaders. The people repeated them to one another as they gathered straw and made bricks and groaned under the lashes of the taskmasters. "I wonder whether they mean anything?" they asked in their agony. "I wonder whether God will help us."

They did not have long to wait. Soon the first of God's ten terrible judgments fell upon the land. First, the river Nile became as blood, so that there was no water for the Egyptians to drink. Then came the frogs, millions upon millions of them, which even entered Pharaoh's bedroom and terrified the royal

© BY RG

family. Then came the lice and the flies. Then the cattle of the Egyptians began to die, and terrible boils broke out on the people. Next there was a frightful storm, with such hail and lightning as Egypt had never seen, leveling all crops. This was followed by a plague of locusts, which ate up every green thing that remained. Then came great darkness, filling every heart with dread as to what other terror might be in store.

The Egyptians were desperate now; Pharaoh himself was frightened; but still he refused to let God's people go.

Then God warned Moses that the last plague was about to fall. It was to be the most terrible of all. The angel of death would pass throughout the land of Egypt, destroying every first-

The night Israel was to leave Egypt every parent sprinkled the blood of a lamb on the doorposts of his house as a sign to God to save his family from the destroying angel.

born son. The Egyptians, who had killed so many of the baby boys belonging to the Hebrews, would now learn what it meant to lose their own.

To make sure that the Hebrews would not suffer from this plague, God told them to take the blood of a lamb and sprinkle it upon the doorposts of their homes. "And when I see the blood," He said, "I will pass over you." Exodus 12:13.

They followed God's word, and their loved ones were spared. That blood upon the doors was a symbol of the blood of Jesus, "the Lamb of God, which taketh away the sin of the world." When we accept Jesus as our Saviour we, as it were, sprinkle His blood upon our hearts, and God forgives us our sins and promises to pass over us in the day of judgment. This is what the apostle meant when he said, "Christ our Passover is sacrificed for us." 1 Corinthians 5:7.

That last awful plague finally brought Pharaoh to his knees. The Bible says he "rose up in the night, he, and all his servants, and all the Egyptians; and there was a great cry in Egypt; for there was not a house where there was not one dead. And he called for Moses and Aaron by night, and said, Rise up, and get you forth . . . ; and go, serve the Lord, as ye have said."

So deliverance came at last. God kept His promise. The four hundred years of oppression were over. His people were free at last.

189

A Path Through the Sea

BEFORE the sun was up next day, all the Israelites were astir. Most of them had been awake all night, too worried to sleep. In the distance they had heard the wails of the Egyptians as their children died, and they had wondered whether the angel of death would see the blood on their own doorposts and spare their first-born. Now, as the news spread that Pharaoh had agreed to let them go, their relief and joy knew no bounds.

But this was no time to celebrate their new freedom. Pharaoh might change his mind. They must leave Egypt at once, without a moment's delay.

A PATH THROUGH THE SEA

So with all speed they gathered up their most precious belongings, packed all the food they could carry, and hastened to the place of meeting that Moses had arranged.

At last came the order to march, and the long column moved slowly but eagerly forward. Altogether there were "six hundred thousand on foot that were men, beside children. . . . And flocks, and herds, even very much cattle." Exodus 12: 37, 38.

Joyfully they pressed on, leaving behind the pyramids and the Sphinx, traveling ever farther and farther from the cities which they had worked so hard to build, out into the desert toward the Red Sea and Canaan.

As they went by Joseph's tomb they remembered his last request that he be buried in his own land. "And Moses took the bones of Joseph with him." Exodus 13:19.

At first nobody felt tired. Not even the children. They were all so happy to be leaving the country where they had suffered so much. All they wanted was to put as many miles as possible between themselves and Pharaoh.

As the great caravan journeyed on, a strange cloud, shaped like a tall pillar, appeared ahead of them. At first many wondered what it might be; then word came from Moses that God was in the cloud and would lead them all the way they had to go.

At night the cloud glowed with such a beautiful light that the people called it a pillar of fire. It was wonderfully comforting—especially that first night they camped in the desert—to know that God was so near.

Presently they came to the shore of the Red Sea and camped again. At once everybody began to ask, "How are we going to get across?" I can imagine the children saying, over and over again, "Daddy, where are the boats?" But there were no boats, and no means of making any.

Then a terrible thing happened that took all the joy out of their hearts.

Someone, looking back across the desert, spied a cloud of dust, far in the distance. Watching more closely, he noticed that it rose from hundreds of galloping horses.

The Egyptians!

It was even so. The very thing that the fleeing Hebrews most feared had happened. Pharaoh had changed his mind. Losing so many slaves all at once had completely upset the business of the country. All building had ceased. Many factories had been forced to close. Without slaves the Egyptians had been compelled to do their own chores, and they didn't like it. Pharaoh, too, wanted revenge for all that he and his people had suffered in the plagues. So he had marshaled his army and set forth in pursuit.

As the awful news spread through the camp, the helpless Hebrews became almost frantic with fear. They felt sure that Pharaoh would punish them dreadfully for running away; they knew how cruel he could be.

192

A PATH THROUGH THE SEA

Forgetting all that God had done for them so far, they turned on Moses and almost shrieked at him that it would have been better to have lived in bondage in Egypt than to die here at the hands of the soldiers.

But Moses, sure that God would not forsake His people now, no matter how dark things looked, answered with great words of faith and courage: "Fear ye not," he said, "stand still, and see the salvation of the Lord. . . . The Lord shall fight for you, and ye shall hold your peace."

At that moment he did not know what God would do, but he felt sure that something very wonderful would happen. And he was right.

As he cried to God to deliver His people, God spoke to him and said, "Wherefore criest thou unto Me? speak unto the children of Israel, that they go forward."

So the command went through the camp: "Go forward!"

"Go forward!" many cried, as they heard the command. "How can we go forward? Can we go through the sea?"

Oh, what a night that was!

Suddenly the people noticed that the pillar of cloud which had been in front of them all the way from Egypt had moved behind them until "it came between the camp of the Egyptians and the camp of Israel; and it was a cloud and darkness to them, but it gave light by night to these."

Then the wind began to blow. And what a wind! It roared in from the east with great fury, throwing up huge clouds of sand in the desert and lashing the sea into white-capped waves.

13

Standing on the shore, with outstretched hand, Moses watched as God wrought one of the greatest miracles of history. Divinely directed, the wind blew in such a way, and with such tremendous force, as to cleave a path through the sea. Down and down went the water in this wind-swept avenue until the sea bottom was uncovered. Soon, straight ahead, lay a wide strip of dry land, stretching clear to the farther shore (Exodus 14:21).

Thousands of Israelites now lined the beach, barely able to stand in the raging wind but held to the spot by sheer wonder at the amazing sight. They could hardly believe their eyes, but there before them the sea had divided, offering a way to safety, the water rising like walls on either side, foam and spray whirling up from

A PATH THROUGH THE SEA

their tossing summits, and the whole scene shimmering like some fairyland in the bright glow from the pillar of fire.

Would the water stay where it was while they crossed? Would the hurricane suddenly subside and bring the whole mighty mass crashing down upon them? But there was no time to think of such dread possibilities. The night was wearing on. Pharaoh's camp would soon be astir. God had provided a way of escape, and they must take it or perish

So they forgot their fears and hastened forward. Anxious mothers urged their children to hurry. Worried fathers drove their cattle as fast as they dared. Old men prayed. Little ones were silent. Girls carrying baby brothers hugged them more tightly. All hearts thrilled at the majesty and wonder of God's power.

Bread From Heaven

HARDLY had the last of the Israelites mounted the farther shore of the Red Sea, barely had the last little boy, lagging behind to gaze at the wonderful walls of water, come running to join his parents, than a great cry of terror arose.

"The Egyptians are following us!"

It was even so.

Already the first of Pharaoh's horsemen were dashing along the path through the sea. Fearfully, Israel watched them coming. Would they get across?

Suddenly the advancing column stopped. Their chariot

wheels had sunk into the soft ground. Horses tugged at them in vain. The wheels came off. Other chariots, crowding in from behind, suffered a similar fate. Soon there was great confusion, with some shouting, "Go on!" and others, "Go back!" But they could neither advance nor retreat. They were stuck in the middle of the channel.

Then, at God's command, Moses stretched forth his hand over the sea "and the waters returned, and covered the chariots, and the horsemen, and all the host of Pharaoh that came into the sea after them; there remained not so much as one of them. . . . Thus the Lord saved Israel that day. . . . And the people feared the Lord, and believed the Lord, and His servant Moses." Exodus 14:28-31.

At last Israel was completely free. All danger from the Egyptians was over. They could banish this fear forever.

Moses, Aaron, and Miriam now led the people in a song of praise to God, saying, "I will sing unto the Lord, for He hath triumphed gloriously: the horse and his rider hath He

thrown into the sea. The Lord is my strength and song, and He is become my salvation." "Who is like unto Thee, O Lord, . . . who is like Thee, glorious in holiness, fearful in praises, doing wonders?" Exodus 15:1, 2, 11.

Everybody was supremely happy and full of faith in God, and it is hard to believe that within three short days they were all miserable again. Yet that is exactly what happened.

Leaving the Red Sea, they journeyed on through the hot, dry wilderness, and it was not long before they had used up all the drinking water they had brought with them. Half a million men, besides women and children, and thousands of cows and sheep, can drink a lot of water, especially in warm weather. So they began to worry about how they were going to get

198

water; and when they came across some pools and found them too bitter to drink, they were very disappointed.

Going to Moses, they grumbled and complained, forgetting that he was much more concerned than they were about the water supply of so large a host. As always, he took his troubles to God, "and the Lord shewed him a tree, which when he had cast into the waters, the waters were made sweet."

So that problem was settled. A few days later, however, the people began to notice that their food was running short. What was left of the bread and other eatables they had brought from Egypt was all dried up and musty. And there wasn't much of that. Children began to cry for food. Everybody was hungry.

Once more they turned on Moses, as though their troubles were all his fault. "Would to God we had died . . . in the land of Egypt," they said, angrily, ". . . for ye have brought us forth into this wilderness, to kill this whole assembly with hunger.

It was very foolish, but people often say stupid things when they are angry.

True, Moses had no food for them, but he trusted God to

© BY R&H

supply it. Again he prayed for help, and the Lord answered him, saying, "Behold, I will rain bread from heaven for you."

Bread from heaven! the people exclaimed. What could that mean? How could bread come down from heaven?

But it did. The very next morning, as they went out of their tents, they saw the ground covered with something white, like frost. The Bible says that "when the dew that lay was gone up, behold, upon the face of the wilderness there lay a small round thing, as small as the hoar frost on the ground. . . . And Moses said unto them, This is the bread which the Lord hath given you to eat." Exodus 16:14, 15.

So they stooped down and picked up some of it and put it into their mouths. To their great surprise it had a very pleasant taste, "like wafers made with honey." How good it must have seemed to those poor, hungry people, and especially to the boys and girls!

They called the food manna, which means, "What is it?" for this was the question they all kept asking but could never answer.

Morning by morning they found the manna there, right at their tent doors. All they had to do was to gather it up and eat it. For the next forty years this was their main source of food.

There was one strange thing about it, however. It appeared on the ground only six days a week. It was never there on the seventh day—not one particle.

Why? Because God wanted to teach these people to keep His Sabbath holy. Adam and Eve had kept the Sabbath in the

201

Food was not easy to find in the wilderness, so God sent manna from heaven every day. But on the sixth day of the week He sent a double portion to last them over the Sabbath.

beginning. So had Abraham, Isaac, and Jacob. When the children of Israel went into Egypt, at Joseph's invitation, they had kept it too; but when they were slaves they were not able to keep it. During that time many came to think it didn't matter; that God didn't require it any more. Some had even forgotten which day it was.

So now, by the miracle of the manna, God sought to bring them back into the right and true way. Every Friday, the sixth day, they were told to go out and gather a double portion, enough to last over the Sabbath. Marvelously, the manna gathered on Friday kept for two days, whereas when it was gathered on other days it quickly spoiled. This, plus the fact that no manna appeared on the seventh day, made it absolutely plain which day God intended to be kept as the Sabbath. There simply couldn't be any doubt about it. It was the seventh day and none other.

At first there were some who didn't believe God meant what He said. These went out "on the seventh day for to gather, and they found none." God was displeased with them, and said, "How long refuse ye to keep My commandments and My laws? See, for that the Lord hath given you the sabbath, therefore He giveth you on the sixth day the bread of two days; abide ye every man in his place, let no man go out of his place on the seventh day."

This lesson, taught once every week—fifty-two times a year—for forty years, forever fixed in the minds of the Israelites the true Sabbath day and God's will concerning it. They have never forgotten that lesson. Nor should we.

They Hear God's Voice

MANY times the children of Israel must have wondered why the pillar of cloud did not lead them due north, straight into the land of Canaan, where they wanted so much to go. The direct route was but a short distance, and they could have arrived there quickly. But instead of going north, the cloud moved south, and the Israelites found themselves, three months after leaving Egypt, far down the peninsula of Sinai.

It seemed a strange thing for God to do, but He had two good reasons for taking them there. First, He knew that His people, just free from years of slavery, were not strong enough to contend with the warlike Philistines who occupied the southern part of Palestine. And, second, He had some important lessons to teach them, and wanted them all to Himself in a quiet and private place. They had learned many wrong things in Egypt which they must unlearn.

So God brought them to Mount Sinai to prepare them for the great future He had planned for them.

And what was the first thing God said to them? Something very beautiful and comforting. "Ye have seen," He said, ". . . how I bare you on eagles' wings, and brought you unto Myself. Now therefore, if ye will obey My voice indeed, and keep My covenant, then ye shall be a peculiar treasure unto Me above all people: for all the earth is Mine: and ye shall be unto Me a kingdom of priests, and an holy nation." Exodus 19:4-6.

"A peculiar treasure unto Me." What a wonderful promise! Another version reads: "You shall be My own prized possession among all nations" (Moffatt). This was what God wanted His people to be—a "peculiar treasure," "a prized possession." For this purpose He had brought them out of Egypt.

But there were conditions. They must obey His voice. They must keep His commandments.

THEY HEAR GOD'S VOICE

But how were they to know what God wanted them to do? Some knowledge of God's laws had been handed down from father to son during the long dark years of slavery, but nothing was very clear to them. Some believed one thing and some another.

So God spoke again, revealing His mind and His will to them in such a way that forever after there could be no mistake or misunderstanding.

That was a great day in the history of Israel and of the world. To mark its importance, "there were thunders and lightnings, and a thick cloud upon the mount. . . . And mount Sinai was altogether on a smoke, because the Lord descended upon it in fire: and the smoke thereof ascended as the smoke of a furnace, and the whole mount quaked greatly."

What an awesome sight it was! The children of Israel, gathered about the base of the mount, were very frightened. Everybody trembled at the fearful scene. Even the boys and girls were silent and still as they watched the mighty spectacle with wide-eyed wonder. They would never forget this; the great God of heaven had come down to earth to speak to them!

Then, far up the mount where Moses had gone, a wondrous sound was heard—deep, rich, melodious. It was the voice of God, so clear and plain that everybody could hear it (Exodus 19:9).

"And God spake all these words, saying, I am the Lord thy God, which have brought thee out of the land of Egypt, out of the house of bondage."

Then God declared His holy will in the Ten Commandments:

1. "Thou shalt have no other gods before Me."

2. "Thou shalt not make unto thee any graven image, or any likeness of any thing that is in heaven above, or that is in the earth beneath, or that is in the water under the earth: thou shalt not bow down thyself to them, nor serve them: for I the Lord thy God am a jealous God, visiting the iniquity of the fathers upon the children unto the third and fourth generation of them that hate Me; and shewing mercy unto thousands of them that love Me, and keep My commandments."

3. "Thou shalt not take the name of the Lord thy God in vain; for the Lord will not hold him guiltless that taketh His name in vain."

4. "Remember the sabbath day, to keep it holy. Six days shalt thou labour, and do all thy work: but the seventh day is the sabbath of the Lord thy God: in it thou shalt not do any work, thou, nor thy son, nor thy daughter, thy manservant, nor thy maidservant, nor thy cattle, nor thy stranger that is within thy gates: for in six days the Lord made heaven and earth, the sea, and all that in them is, and rested the seventh day: wherefore the Lord blessed the sabbath day, and hallowed it."

5. "Honour thy father and thy mother: that thy days may be long upon the land which the Lord thy God giveth thee."

6. "Thou shalt not kill."

7. "Thou shalt not commit adultery."

8. "Thou shalt not steal."

206

During the journey of the children of Israel through the wilderness, God called Moses to the top of Mount Sinai and gave him the Ten Commandments, written on tables of stone.

9. "Thou shalt not bear false witness against thy neighbour."

10. "Thou shalt not covet thy neighbour's house, thou shalt not covet thy neighbour's wife, nor his manservant, nor his maidservant, nor his ox, nor his ass, nor any thing that is thy neighbour's."

As the people listened they were greatly moved. That lovely voice, speaking with such majesty and power, yet with a tenderness they had never heard before, touched every heart. It made them want to be good. If this was the will of God, then they wanted to do it. So they "answered together, and said, All that the Lord hath spoken we will do." Three times they said it, and I believe they meant it.

But God knew how soon they would forget, and that some would begin to question what it was He had said. So, because these commandments were His will not only for the Israelites but for all mankind, and in order that men should know that they are unchangeable, He wrote them on two slabs of stone. The Bible says that "He gave unto Moses, when He had made an end of communing with him upon mount Sinai, two tables of testimony, tables of stone, written with the finger of God." Exodus 31:18.

God wrote them Himself, with His own finger! How very important they must be!

Jesus thought so too. When, long years after that wonderful scene at Sinai, our loving Saviour came to teach us how to live, and once again revealed the mind and will of God, He said, "Till heaven and earth pass, one jot or one tittle shall in

14

The first four commandments of the Decalogue teach us our duty to God, and the last six our duty to men. This wonderful law given to us through Moses has never been changed.

no wise pass from the law, till all be fulfilled." Matthew 5:18.

And He added these solemn words: "Whosoever therefore shall break one of these least commandments, and shall teach men so, he shall be called the least in the kingdom of heaven: but whosoever shall do and teach them, the same shall be called great in the kingdom of heaven." Verses 18, 19.

Today these Ten Commandments are still God's will for us, and all who love Him truly will say with gladness, like the Israelites of old, "All that the Lord hath said will we do, and be obedient."

So every night, as you say your prayers, remember to add this earnest, sweet petition: "Incline my heart to keep Thy law."

> Lord of the earth, the sky, the sea,
>   Help me Thy child, Thine own, to be;
> My heart incline Thy law to keep
>   As now I lay me down to sleep.
>
> Lord of all life, all time, all space,
>   Help me to run a noble race;
> My heart incline to go Thy way
>   When dawn shall bring another day.
>
> A. S. M.

STORY 31

Lessons in Love

~~~~~~

TO TEACH His people the Ten Commandments was
not the only reason God brought them into the wilderness of Sinai. More important still, He wanted to tell
them what to do when they should break these commandments,
as He knew they would. They must learn of His plan of salvation. They must know of His willingness to forgive them and
to release them from the penalty of sin. Yet how to tell them?
How to make it plain?

As a first step God called Moses to the top of Mount Sinai
again, so that He might talk to him alone about it. "And Moses
went up into the mount, and a cloud covered the mount. And
the glory of the Lord abode upon mount Sinai, and the cloud
covered it six days: and the seventh day He called unto Moses
out of the midst of the cloud. And the sight of the glory of the
Lord was like devouring fire on the top of the mount in the eyes
of the children of Israel."

So on that wonderful Sabbath in the long ago the children

211

of Israel, looking up toward the top of the mount, saw their leader disappear into the fiery cloud to be with God.

There God told Moses what He had in mind, how He intended to make His people understand, in a clear and simple way, His great plan for the redemption of the world.

"Let them make Me a sanctuary," He began; "that I may dwell among them." Then He described in detail how it was to be built, showing him a plan of the heavenly sanctuary, and saying, "See . . . that thou make all things according to the pattern shewed to thee." Hebrews 8:5.

Of course God didn't mean that Moses should make anything so big and glorious as the sanctuary in heaven, but that he should follow the same general plan. In other words, the earthly sanctuary was to be a miniature of the heavenly sanctuary. And the reason Moses was to be so careful to follow the pattern was that every part had some important meaning. Every board, every covering, every piece of furniture, every service, was to help the people understand how much God loved them and how great a sacrifice He planned for their salvation.

212

LESSONS IN LOVE

The sanctuary, or tabernacle as it was sometimes called, was not to be a large building, for it was to be moved from place to place. Yet God said it was to be very beautiful inside, lined with pure gold. There were to be lovely curtains of blue, purple, and scarlet, with figures of angels worked upon them. The furniture was to be of gold, and the high priest's robes were to be adorned with precious stones.

As God continued to outline His plan, Moses may well have exclaimed, Where shall we obtain all these things out here in this wilderness? But God knew how much the people had brought out of Egypt, and He said, "Speak unto the children of Israel, that they bring Me an offering: of every man that giveth it willingly with his heart ye shall take My offering."

After Moses finally came down from the mount, he told the people what God desired, and at once they responded.

"And they came, every one whose heart stirred him up, and every one whom his spirit made willing, and they brought the Lord's offering to the work of the tabernacle. . . . And they came, both men and women, as many as were willing hearted, and brought bracelets, and earrings, and rings, and tablets, all jewels of gold." Exodus 35:21, 22.

It must have been a wonderful sight to see so many happy, smiling people coming to Moses from all over the camp, each one willingly, joyfully, bringing some prized possession to give to the Lord. And I like to think that the boys and girls had a part too. They didn't have much to bring, perhaps just some little toys or trinkets the Egyptians had given them, but I am sure they brought what they could.

Then the most skilled men in the camp were chosen to build the tabernacle and to make the various articles of furniture to go inside it, while the women set to work to make the curtains and coverings.

The tabernacle was fifty-five feet long, by eighteen feet wide, by eighteen feet high, shaped like an oblong box, but divided into two compartments: first the "holy place," then the "most holy place." There was very little inside. In the holy place were just the table of showbread, the altar of incense, and the seven-branched candlestick.

The showbread was to remind the people that God would supply all their needs. It pointed forward to Jesus, the Bread of Life. The candlestick, too, whose light never went out, also pointed to Jesus, the light of the world. And the smoke rising from the altar of incense told the people that their prayers, mingled with the fragrance of Jesus' love, would always be heard by God.

Inside the Holy of Holies was a golden box known as the ark, in which the two tables of stone bearing the Ten Commandments were placed. Above this was a slab of pure gold called the "mercy seat," with golden angels looking down upon it. Here the glory of God appeared in a holy light known as the Shekinah. What a beautiful thought it is that God placed a "mercy seat" between Himself and His law! This was the greatest "lesson in love" in the whole sanctuary. God wanted His people to know that, though they might break His law, if they would repent and ask His forgiveness, He would have mercy upon them and pardon them.

All the services in the sanctuary revolved around this

215

lovely thought. When a man broke God's law he had to show his sorrow by bringing a lamb and killing it. It was a terrible thing to have to do. But God wanted the people to realize that all sin is terrible—that it is utterly hateful to Him. For this reason He had said, "The soul that sinneth, it shall die." This is why the sinner had to kill the lamb—to show that he knew he deserved to die, but was offering the lamb in his stead, if God would be pleased to accept it.

And God did accept it, for in that slain lamb He saw Jesus, who one day would die on Calvary, "the Lamb of God, which taketh away the sin of the world."

Today when we sin we do not need to kill a lamb and have its blood carried into the old tabernacle. All we need to do is fall on our knees before God and claim Jesus' sacrifice, "who died for us." And God will hear and forgive us, for "the blood of Jesus Christ His Son cleanseth us from all sin." 1 John 1:7.

STORY 32

The Price of Rebellion

≈≈≈≈≈≈≈≈≈≈≈≈≈≈≈≈≈

I T TOOK about six months for the children of Israel to make the tabernacle, and it was finished just one year to the day after they left Egypt. If you think that was a long time, remember that they did all the work in a wilderness, without any modern tools. The golden candlestick and the golden cherubim over the mercy seat each had to be beaten out of one piece of gold by hand, and the yards and yards of colored curtains had to be stitched without a single sewing machine.

When the work was all completed, "the glory of the Lord filled the tabernacle." Everyone knew then that their great labor of love had been accepted. From this moment "the cloud of the Lord" was upon it by day, "and fire was on it by night." Thus all Israel was to know that God was there; that He was dwelling with them, as He had promised; and that by day and night He was ready to forgive all who were truly sorry for their sins and who came to Him offering the proper sacrifice.

217

When the building of the tabernacle was completed, everyone knew that his labor of love was accepted, for the "cloud of the Lord" was on it by day, "and fire was on it by night."

Then one day, about seven weeks after the tabernacle had been completed, someone noticed that the cloud was rising and moving away. Word swept through the camp that this was the signal to march. At once Levites began to take the tabernacle apart, while the people packed their tents and other belongings, ready to go.

It was a great day. Everybody was cheerful. They hadn't been so happy since that wonderful night they left Egypt. Soon they would be in Canaan, the land of their dreams.

But it did not turn out that way. They did not realize it, of course, but they were not ready for Canaan. Their hearts were not right before God. They had seen His great miracle at the Red Sea. They had heard His voice on Mount Sinai. They had eaten His manna every day for many months. Yet they did not truly love Him. Their faith in Him was very weak.

Not far from Sinai they began to grumble again. This time it was about the manna. They were tired of it. They wanted meat to eat. "Who shall give us flesh to eat?" they cried. "We remember the fish, which we did eat in Egypt freely; the cucumbers, and the melons, and the leeks, and the onions, and the

218

garlick: but now our soul is dried away: there is nothing at all, beside this manna." Numbers 11:4-6.

There was a sneer in their voices as they said, "This manna," and God did not like it. The Bible says: "When the people complained, it displeased the Lord."

It is not good to find fault with God's gifts. Especially we should not complain about our food, which really comes from Him. Grumbling displeases Him today as it did in the wilderness of old.

To satisfy the people, yet teach them another lesson, God said that He would give them flesh to eat, and so much that they would grow weary of it. It would become loathsome to them.

Moses wondered how this could happen, and asked, "Shall the flocks and the herds be slain?" But God said, No; He would bring them meat in another way. "And there went forth a wind from the Lord, and brought quails from the sea."

The birds came in flying very low—about three feet above the ground—and the people just stood there and knocked them down, hundreds and thousands of them. Then they had one huge feast, and paid for it. Many ate too much,

became sick, and died. If only they had been content with God's pure, wholesome manna, this would not have happened.

When this sad experience was over, Israel moved on again and found themselves once more in the wilderness of Paran, through which they had passed on their way to Sinai. Here they were quite close to Canaan, only a few days' march away. Everybody must have thought that their wanderings were almost over.

Fresh excitement came when Moses announced that twelve men—one from each of the twelve tribes of Israel—were to go into Canaan to find out present conditions, and report. They were to spread out all over the country and learn how many people lived there, how strongly their cities were fortified, what sort of food they were growing, and whether there were any trees for lumber.

It was a great honor to be chosen for this mission. Each tribe sent its best man. All were "heads of the children of Israel." Much depended upon them. Indeed, much more than they knew!

Caleb was sent by the tribe of Judah, and Joshua by the tribe of Ephraim. There were ten others, whose names nobody remembers today.

As the twelve set forth there were many good-by's and lots of good wishes from the thousands who gathered to see them off. Then, when the last had disappeared from view, the rest went back to their tents to await the spies' return.

A week passed. Two weeks. Three weeks. Still there was no word. What could have happened? They wondered whether or not all the twelve spies had been slain by the Canaanites.

Four weeks. Five weeks. How long the waiting time seemed! Then on the fortieth day they came back.

All were loaded down with various kinds of fruit. And how good it looked to people who had lived in a wilderness so long! The object that caught everybody's eye was a huge bunch of grapes—so large that it took two men to carry it. If this was the produce of Canaan, what a wonderful place it must be!

As for the spies, they said they had never seen such a country. "We came unto the land whither thou sentest us, and surely it floweth with milk and honey; and this is the fruit of it."

Up to that point everybody was happy. Everybody wanted to go to Canaan at once. Then came the bad news.

"Nevertheless the people be strong that dwell in the land, and the cities are walled, and very great: and moreover we saw the children of Anak there."

As some of the spies continued to describe how strong the people of Canaan were, and how difficult it would be to take the land away from them, the hearts of the Israelites sank. This

221

was a terrible blow. They had thought everything was going to be easy, just like the manna falling and the quails being blown in by the wind. But this was terrible. Again they complained.

But "Caleb stilled the people before Moses, and said, Let us go up at once, and possess it; for we are well able to overcome it." Numbers 13:30.

It was a brave thing to say at such a time; for all the rest—almost all—were against him. Ten of the men who went with him cried out, "We be not able to go up against the people; for they are stronger than we."

It was two against ten—for Joshua stood with Caleb—and the people took the word of the ten. Their hopes were dashed, and they gave way to despair. "And all the congregation lifted up their voice, and cried; and the people wept that night." Numbers 14:1.

Next morning they were all in an ugly mood, seething with rebellion against Moses and against God.

"Would God that we had died in the land of Egypt!" they cried, and "Would God we had died in this wilderness!" Then someone raised the cry, "Let us make a captain, and let us return into Egypt."

That was a terrible moment in Israel's history. Then it was that Caleb and Joshua stood before the raging throng and cried, "The land, which we passed through to search it, is an exceeding good land. If the Lord delight in us, then He will bring us into this land, and give it us. . . . Only rebel not ye against the Lord, . . . the Lord is with us: fear them not." Numbers 14:7-9.

← PAINTING BY FRANK FORD   © BY REVIEW AND HERALD

The twelve spies sent to spy out the land of Canaan came back after a long time with wonderful samples of the fruit they had found there. All the people rejoiced at their story.

"Stone them! Stone them!" cried the people.

But there were no stones thrown. Suddenly the glory of the Lord appeared in the tabernacle, and the angry crowd was hushed. Israel waited, ashamed and afraid, to hear what God would say.

They had not long to wait. But when God spoke, they realized what an awful mistake they had made.

They had said they wished they had died in the wilderness. All right, said God, they should have their wish. "All those men which have seen My glory, and My miracles, which I did in Egypt and in the wilderness, and have tempted Me now these ten times, and have not hearkened to My voice; surely they shall not see the land which I sware unto their fathers." "In this wilderness they shall be consumed, and there they shall die." Numbers 14:22, 23, 35.

Back to the wilderness! Shut out of Canaan forever! The heartbreak of it! What a terrible price they paid for rebelling against God!

STORY 33

Victory and Defeat

~~~~~~~~~~~~~~~~~~~~~~~~~~~~~~~~

FOR forty years the children of Israel wandered in the wilderness. "And the soul of the people was much discouraged because of the way." Numbers 21:4. There was but one gleam of comfort: their boys and girls would see Canaan. Grown to manhood, they would enter the Promised Land.

Slowly, wearily, the years rolled by. One by one, all who had taken part in the great rebellion passed away. Six hundred thousand graves dotted the lonely desert. The three great leaders died also—first Miriam, then Aaron, then Moses.

By and by Caleb and Joshua were the only ones left of all their generation. Of these two brave and noble men Joshua was chosen the new leader. The Bible says he was "full of the spirit of wisdom," which is no doubt why God laid so great a responsibility upon him. God is always looking for young people who are wise and good, that He may give them great tasks to do for Him.

"Now after the death of Moses . . . the Lord spake unto

Joshua the son of Nun, Moses' minister, saying, Moses My servant is dead; now therefore arise, go over this Jordan." Joshua 1:1, 2.

No one knew the difficulties and dangers of such an expedition better than Joshua, for he had been one of the twelve men who had spied out the land. And now the people of Canaan had had forty years to grow in numbers, and to make their cities stronger than ever. No wonder he had some misgivings. But God reassured him. "As I was with Moses," He said, "so I will be with thee: I will not fail thee, nor forsake thee.

"Be strong and of a good courage. . . . Only be thou strong and very courageous. . . . Have not I commanded thee? Be strong and of a good courage; be not afraid, neither be thou dismayed: for the Lord thy God is with thee whithersoever thou goest."

Wonderful promise! Who would not be encouraged with such words as these? Immediately Joshua commanded the officers of the people, saying, "Pass through the host, and command the people, saying, Prepare you victuals [food]; for within three days ye shall pass over this Jordan, to go in to possess the land."

What excitement there was then! This was the day of which their fathers and mothers had talked so many times, and which had seemed to them only a beautiful dream. Now it was about to come true. They would see the Promised Land after all.

On the third day came the command to march. And the whole mighty company moved straight down toward the river.

226

VICTORY AND DEFEAT

The priests bearing the ark went ahead, and as their feet "were dipped in the brim of the water," the river was mysteriously blocked, and "the waters which came down from above stood and rose up upon an heap." Quickly the rest of the water drained away toward the Dead Sea, leaving the riverbed exposed.

The priests now moved to the middle of the riverbed and stayed there till everyone else had crossed. This took great faith, for none of them knew when the waters would flow again. However, all believed that as long as the ark was there, they were safe.

At last the crossing was completed. The impossible had happened again. How wonderfully God had helped them, in spite of all the bad things they had said and done in the wilderness!

Now they were in Canaan, but the task of taking the country was still ahead. Right before them was their first problem—

the city of Jericho, key fortress of the fruitful Jordan Valley.

The people on the city walls had watched the Israelites cross the Jordan on dry land, and were filled with wonder and fear. They closed their gates and waited to be attacked.

But the attack never came—at least not in the way they expected, with battering-rams and scaling ladders. Instead they saw the Israelites form into one long line and march clear round the city, then go back to their camp.

The next day it happened again. Not a spear was thrown, not an arrow was shot; indeed, not a sound was heard save the blowing of the priests' trumpets and the constant tramp, tramp of the marching host. It was most uncanny.

So it was each day for six days, and the people questioned one another what it was all about. At last, on the seventh day they learned. On that day the armies of Israel marched round the city in the same manner, not once, but seven times. The seventh time, as the priests blew their trumpets, "Joshua said unto the people, Shout; for the Lord hath given you the city." So they shouted, and lo the walls of Jericho fell flat, and the Israelites ran in and captured it.

Everybody was thrilled at the victory. "If it is all going to be this easy," they said to one another, "we shall soon take the whole country."

But they were mistaken. A few days later they went to attack a much smaller city and met with a severe defeat. "And they fled before the men of Ai."

This was hard to bear. They couldn't understand it. But

there were two reasons for their failure. First, they had become too self-confident, and had begun to believe they could take all Canaan themselves without God; and second, someone had sinned in the camp and God could no longer bless them.

"There is an accursed thing in the midst of thee, O Israel," said the Lord: "thou canst not stand before thine enemies, until ye take away the accursed thing from among you." Joshua 7:13. The "accursed thing" proved to be a wedge of gold and a Babylonish garment which a man called Achan had looted from Jericho and hidden in his tent. Such looting had been expressly forbidden, and Achan had deliberately disobeyed the order.

So great was this sin in God's sight that the punishment decreed was death, for himself, his wife, his children, his livestock, "and all that he had."

It was a sad fate for this poor family, just as they had entered the Promised Land, too; but Israel had to learn how serious is disobedience to the will of God. We too must learn this important lesson; and remember that we can never enjoy His blessing while an "accursed thing" lies hidden in our homes or hearts.

Two Strong Men

~~~~~~

AFTER Achan had been put to death, and the camp had
been cleansed of his sin, the city of Ai was easily taken,
and Israel marched on from victory to victory.

Several of the rulers of the cities of Canaan banded themselves together to resist the invaders, but to no purpose. Every
time they did so they were defeated. Even the giants of Anak,
who once had so frightened the ten spies, were killed. "There
was none of the Anakims left." Joshua 11:22.

"So Joshua took the whole land, according to all that the
Lord said unto Moses." Verse 23.

After that came years of peace. Canaan, with its vineyards,
olive groves, and farms, was divided among the tribes of Israel.
Their years of wandering were over at last.

"There failed not ought of any good thing which the Lord
had spoken unto the house of Israel; all came to pass." Joshua
21:45.

His lifework ended, Joshua passed to his rest. After that

came many years of trial and struggle. The Israelites, in their desire to settle down too soon, failed to drive out all the Canaanites, and before long these people turned against them, trying to regain some of the land they had lost.

Sad to say, Israel forgot the lessons learned in the wilderness, and God's wonderful deliverances at the Red Sea and the Jordan. They turned away from serving Him to worship idols. This was the real cause of all their defeats and sorrows.

Now and then some good man would arise and call the people back to God. Then for a time their fortunes would change. Everything would look bright again—until they weakened in their faith and turned from God once more.

This was the period of the judges, when there was no king over Israel. How they must have missed the strong leadership of Moses and Joshua!

A hundred years passed. Two hundred years. Then, almost at the same time, two strong men were born.

Both became great leaders, one strong in spirit, the other strong in muscle.

Strangely enough, their names were very similar. One was called Samuel; the other, Samson.

Both were born of godly parents. Both were dedicated to God before they were born; both were blessed of God in their childhood; yet how differently both grew up!

Samuel, who was born just ten years before Samson, was the son of Elkanah and Hannah. They wanted this baby so much that they called him "Asked of God," which is the meaning of Samuel.

232

TWO STRONG MEN

So thankful was Hannah that God had given her Samuel that she said, "I have lent him to the Lord; as long as he liveth he shall be lent to the Lord."

Remembering her promise, she took Samuel to the temple while he was still a little lad, leaving him there to be a page to Eli, the high priest, to run errands for him and help in every way a little boy could.

Living in the temple, watching the priests at their work, asking questions about the meaning of all the services and sacrifices, Samuel came to know much about God and His plans for the children of Israel.

One night, "ere the lamp of God went out in the temple of the Lord, where the ark of God was, and Samuel was laid

down to sleep; . . . the Lord called Samuel: and he answered, Here am I." 1 Samuel 3:3, 4.

As Samuel rose from his bed, half asleep and rubbing his eyes, he thought Eli had called him. So "he ran unto Eli, and said, Here am I; for thou calledst me."

But Eli answered, "I called not; lie down again. And he went and lay down."

Again the voice spoke and again the boy thought it was Eli who had called him. So once more he "arose and went to Eli, and said, Here am I; for thou didst call me. And he answered, I called not, my son; lie down again."

TWO STRONG MEN

Then "the Lord called Samuel again the third time. And he arose and went to Eli, and said, Here am I; for thou didst call me. And Eli perceived that the Lord had called the child. Therefore Eli said unto Samuel, Go, lie down: and it shall be, if He call thee, that thou shalt say, Speak, Lord; for thy servant heareth. So Samuel went and lay down in his place."

How Samuel's heart must have beat with wonder and fear! The great God of heaven had spoken to him, a little boy! God had even called him by his name! It was too wonderful!

As Samuel lay there, tense and excited, listening amid the stillness of the night, he heard the voice again, tender, gentle, melodious. "Samuel, Samuel!"

Looking up with wide-open eyes, the boy whispered, trembling, "Speak; for Thy servant heareth."

That experience was the beginning of a great ministry in God's cause, a life of noble service among God's people. The Bible says, "And Samuel grew, and the Lord was with him, and did let none of his words fall to the ground. And all Israel from Dan even to Beer-sheba knew that Samuel was established to be a prophet of the Lord." 1 Samuel 3:19, 20.

There is no limit to the possibilities of the boy or girl who will listen to the voice of God. Should you ever hear Him speak to you—for God still speaks to His children today—remember Samuel, and reply, "Speak, Lord; for Thy servant heareth." It will be the beginning of great things for you.

As for the other boy, what happened to him? Like Samuel, his mother and father wanted him very much, and dedicated him to God. But as he grew up he became willful and disobedi-

235

ent. He made friends among the heathen boys and girls, and was always getting into lots of trouble.

Oh, yes, he was strong. Very strong. Once, meeting a lion, he tore it to pieces with his bare hands. Another time, finding himself caught in the city of Gaza, he picked up the gates of the city, posts and all, and carried them to the top of a nearby hill. Even after he had been made prisoner by the Philistines, he seized hold of the pillars of their stadium and brought the roof crashing down, killing three thousand people.

Oh, yes, he was strong—one of the strongest men of all time. But he was not strong toward God. How much better to be like Samuel, strong in the Spirit, a man of great goodness and truth!

From Shepherd Boy to King

~~~~~~

LONG after Samson died among the ruins of the building which he pulled down upon himself, Samuel, the man of God, continued to minister to Israel. They honored him as a prophet and he became their king-maker.

Up to that time Israel had had no king. Indeed, since the death of Joshua they had had no great leader at all; at least, not one whom all the people would obey. Now they came to Samuel and asked him to choose one of their number and anoint him as king.

Samuel prayed about their request, and God said, "Hearken unto their voice, and make them a king." But upon whom, of all the hundreds of thousands of Israelites, should this great honor be bestowed? Presently Samuel was led to think of Saul, "a choice young man, and a goodly: and there was not among the children of Israel a goodlier person than he: from his shoulders and upward he was higher than any of the people." 1 Samuel 9:2.

Feeling sure that this was the man of God's choice, Samuel anointed him. Then he called the people together and said, "See ye him whom the Lord hath chosen, that there is none like him among all the people? And all the people shouted, and said, God save the king."

But Saul was a failure. Outwardly he had all the qualities of a king, but he wasn't a king inside. He was tall and handsome and, in his armor, must have looked a giant of a man, but in his heart he was small, peevish, jealous, and obstinate.

True, he started well, and God was with him at first and blessed him; but he made so many mistakes and was such a wretched example to the people he ruled that God finally rejected him.

While all this was going on, God was looking for someone who might one day take Saul's place. His eyes roamed through all the cities and villages of Israel, out upon the lonely moun-

238

tainsides and moorlands, seeking a boy good enough and great enough to be a king.

And what a wonderful thought it is that the eyes of God do "run to and fro throughout the whole earth, to shew Himself strong in the behalf of them whose heart is perfect toward Him"! 2 Chronicles 16:9.

God is constantly looking for boys and girls who think of Him and love Him, for He has great plans for every one of them.

So God searched for a boy through all the land of Canaan, one who might become king of Israel when Saul should come to his unhappy end.

And God found His boy. Not in a city or a village, but out on the hills, alone with the sheep for which he was caring. There was a struggle going on at the time, for a lion had crept out of the underbrush and seized a lamb in its powerful jaws; but the shepherd boy, unafraid, set upon the lion and killed it and rescued the lamb.

"What a boy!" God must have said to Himself.

David was surely a boy to watch, for when, later, a bear attacked his sheep, instead of running away, he fought and killed it.

Most of his time David spent out of doors, minding his sheep, seeing to it that they had plenty to eat, keeping them from danger, and caring for the lambs. Alone for many hours at a stretch, he would make up little songs about the trees, the wildflowers, and the animals, the beauty of nature and the goodness of God, singing them aloud as he led his sheep in

239

The Lord is my shepherd; I shall not want. He maketh me to lie down in green pastures: he leadeth me beside the still waters. He restoreth my soul: he leadeth me in the paths of righteousness for his name's sake. Yea, though I walk through the valley of the shadow of death, I will fear no evil: for thou art with me; thy rod and thy staff they comfort me. Thou preparest a table before me in the presence of mine enemies: thou anointest my head with oil; my cup runneth over. Surely goodness and mercy shall follow me all the days of my life: and I will dwell in the house of the Lord for ever. — Psalm 23.

green pastures and by still waters. Some of his songs have lasted three thousand years and may be read today in the book of Psalms. He was quite a musician, too, and played on his harp for hours.

One day a messenger came to him and told him that the prophet Samuel was at his home and had asked to see him.

"To see me!" David must have exclaimed. "Why should he want to see me?" But he ran home, his heart aflutter, wondering what the great prophet could want with him.

Meanwhile Samuel had been talking to David's father, Jesse. One by one he had looked carefully at all the other boys in the family, but though they were all tall, strong, and healthy, he knew they were not God's choice for king.

Anxious that Samuel's experience with Saul should not be repeated, God had said to him, as each of the boys had passed by: "Look not on his countenance, or on the height of his stature: . . . for the Lord seeth not as man seeth; for man looketh on the outward appearance, but the Lord looketh on the heart." 1 Samuel 16:7.

So the seven older sons of Jesse had been passed by. Then Samuel had said to him, "Are here all thy children?" And Jesse had replied, "There remaineth yet the youngest, and, behold, he keepeth the sheep."

"Send and fetch him," Samuel had said.

So David was brought in, all out of breath with running. The Bible says that at that moment "he was ruddy, and withal of a beautiful countenance, and goodly to look to. And the Lord said, Arise, anoint him: for this is he."

16

As a shepherd boy, David faithfully tended his father's sheep. Alone with his flocks in the fields he learned lessons of God's watchcare and later wrote the beautiful shepherd psalm.

The brief ceremony over, David returned to his work of minding sheep. He didn't dare discuss what had happened with anybody, for his brothers would have been jealous and Saul would have killed him. All he could do was talk to God about it; and I like to think that there on the mountainside, minding his sheep, he gave his heart to God as he never had done before, and pledged that he would try to be a good king if that was what God wanted him to be.

One day his father asked him to take some food to three of his brothers who were with the army of Israel, now fighting the Philistines in the valley of Elah. As he drew near to the battleground he saw that the soldiers of Israel were on one hill and the Philistines on another, some distance away. Suddenly a huge man, clad in shining armor, strode out of the camp of the Philistines and shouted taunts and challenges at the Israelites. "Choose you a man . . . , let him come down to me!" he bawled. But no one accepted the challenge. Instead, the Israelites fled as he approached.

This was too much for David. "Who is this uncircumcised Philistine," he cried, "that he should defy the armies of the living God?"

Jealous for the honor of Israel he couldn't understand why no one would go and fight the Philistine; so he offered to go himself.

Just then his eldest brother heard about it and, like so many other elder brothers, felt it his duty to put the youngest in his place. "Why cameth thou down hither?" he asked, "and with whom hast thou left those few sheep in the wilderness? I

242

know thy pride, and the naughtiness of thine heart; for thou art come down that thou mightest see the battle."

But David was not to be discouraged or turned aside from the great purpose that was now in his heart. He would fight that Philistine or else!

King Saul was told of David's courageous words, and sent for him.

"Thou art not able to go against this Philistine . . . ," he said kindly, "for thou art but a youth."

Then David told Saul how he had killed the lion and the bear, "and this uncircumcised Philistine," he added vigorously, "shall be as one of them, seeing he hath defied the armies of the living God."

"The Lord that delivered me out of the paw of the lion, and out of the paw of the bear," he added, "He will deliver me out of the hand of this Philistine."

David was so brave and earnest that Saul became convinced the boy should have his chance. "Go," he said, "and the Lord be with thee."

Putting aside Saul's armor, which the king offered him, David went forth with his shepherd's staff, a sling, and five small stones.

At first Goliath refused to notice the boy. He "looked about," this way and that, as if nobody were there. Then he cursed David by his gods. And David replied in these glorious, ever memorable words: "Thou comest to me with a sword, and with a spear, and with a shield: but I come to thee in the name of the Lord of hosts, the God of the armies of Israel, whom thou hast defied."

As Goliath, in great fury, strode forward to cut David in pieces, the boy placed a stone in his sling and sent it spinning toward the Philistine. It was a perfect shot. Hitting Goliath in the forehead, it brought him crashing to the ground.

That was a great day for David. From that moment he was a national hero. Saul could not do enough for him. And God was well pleased too. "He is a boy after My own heart," He said. So He led David on, step by step, from shepherd boy to king.

A Mighty Man of God

≈≈≈≈≈≈≈≈≈≈≈≈≈≈≈≈≈≈≈≈≈≈≈≈≈≈≈≈≈≈

DAVID did not come easily to the throne of Israel. Saul became jealous of him and drove him from the court, then chased him from place to place, ever threatening to kill him.

The Bible says, "There was long war between the house of Saul and the house of David: but David waxed stronger and stronger, and the house of Saul waxed weaker and weaker."

At last Saul died and David was crowned king of Israel. He was only thirty years old at the time, but he reigned forty years. "And David went on, and grew great, and the Lord God of hosts was with him." 2 Samuel 5:10.

He made many mistakes, some of them very serious ones, but he had a tender heart and repented of his sins. Once, after doing something very wrong, he cried out brokenheartedly: "Have mercy upon me, O God, according to Thy lovingkindness: according unto the multitude of Thy tender mercies blot out my transgressions." "Create in me a clean heart,

O God; and renew a right spirit within me." Psalm 51:1, 10.

God never turns away from such a prayer as that. He forgave David, even as He will forgive us if we repent of our sins with equal sincerity.

When David died, his son Solomon ascended the throne and did great things for Israel. He built the most beautiful temple men had ever seen, and greatly strengthened the defenses of Jerusalem. He became very rich and powerful, and many famous people, like the Queen of Sheba, traveled far to visit him.

Solomon's reign was the most glorious period in Israel's history. This was because as a youth he had asked God not for riches and fame, but for wisdom.

"Ask what I shall give thee," God said, and Solomon replied, "I am but a little child: I know not how to go out or come in. . . . Give therefore Thy servant an understanding heart to judge Thy people, that I may discern between good and bad. . . .

At the dedication of the temple Solomon prayed: "I am but a little child: I know not how to go out or come in."

A MIGHTY MAN OF GOD

"And the speech pleased the Lord. . . . And God said unto him, Because thou hast asked this thing, and hast not asked for thyself long life; neither hast asked riches for thyself, nor hast asked the life of thine enemies; but hast asked for thyself understanding to discern judgment; behold, I have done according to thy words: lo, I have given thee a wise and an understanding heart; so that there was none like thee before thee, neither after thee shall any arise like unto thee. And I have also given thee that which thou hast not asked, both riches, and honour."

Solomon was richly rewarded for his humble prayer. God loved him for it, and gave him all that a boy's heart could desire. His experience shows that it is far better to seek God for wisdom that we may bless others than for riches to benefit ourselves.

But alas, even Solomon, with all his wisdom and all his possessions, turned away from God and did many foolish things. It is said of him that "his heart was not perfect with the Lord

his God, as was the heart of David his father." He "did evil in the sight of the Lord," and so much so that at last God said to him, "I will surely rend the kingdom from thee."

What a pity! Such a good start and such a sad finish! But things happen like this when people who have loved God as boys or girls forget Him when they grow up. God help us to be true to Him always!

After Solomon's death, as God had warned him, great trouble came to the nation. The kingdom was divided into two parts, with Israel in the north and Judah in the south. There was constant strife between the rulers of these two kingdoms. Many of them were bad men who led their people into idolatry and other sins.

God must have been terribly disappointed as He thought of the way He had brought His people out of Egypt, through the Red Sea and the Jordan, into the Promised Land, only to see them fighting each other and worshiping other gods. Well might He have decided to leave them forever. But He did not. He loved them still and sent prophet after prophet to bring them back to the right and true way.

One of His messengers, a mighty man of God, appeared on the scene about fifty years after the death of Solomon. Already, in so short a time, the northern kingdom of Israel had turned almost completely to the worship of Baal, the sun god. King, court, and people were as wicked as the heathen about them. They had forgotten completely that God had once chosen them to be the light of the world, to witness for righteousness and truth in an evil generation. They neither knew

248

nor cared what God wanted them to be or do. Then Elijah came.

He was a man of prayer and had great faith in God. Grieved that so many of the people had begun to worship idols, he believed that nothing would bring them to their senses but some great tragedy, like a famine. So he prayed earnestly that there should be no rain for three and a half years. It was a strange prayer, but it was for the people's good, and God heard it.

Then to Ahab, king of Israel, Elijah sent this message: "As the Lord God of Israel liveth, before whom I stand, there shall not be dew nor rain these years, but according to my word."

Ahab no doubt laughed at Elijah. Who was this queer old man who thought he could turn the rain on and off?

But strangely enough, no rain fell. Day after day, week after week, the skies were clear and the hot sun blazed down on the countryside. Fields turned brown. Trees shriveled and died. Corn was stunted, and the harvest failed. Cattle, finding little to eat, grew thin and died. The people cried to their idols for rain, but no rain came.

Ahab became anxious now, and sent for Elijah. But Elijah was nowhere to be found. Actually the prophet was hiding by the brook Cherith, which was still running, despite the drought. Here, by a miracle, ravens brought him food every morning and evening.

When at last this brook dried up, God sent him to a village called Zarephath, where a widow cared for him. This kind lady gave up her last handful of meal and her last little drop of oil to make a cake for the hungry man of God, and Elijah said to her, "Thus saith the Lord God of Israel, The barrel of meal shall not waste, neither shall the cruse of oil fail, until the day that the Lord sendeth rain upon the earth."

And that is exactly what happened. Because of this widow's kindness, God saw to it that she never lacked food all through that dreadful famine.

A MIGHTY MAN OF GOD

Meanwhile Ahab was getting desperate. Ruin stared him in the face. His best animals were dying. Now, more than anything in the world, he wanted to find Elijah and force him to make it rain again.

Three years passed. Three years without rain. Three years without a harvest. Everybody was hungry and thirsty. Many realized that all this had happened as a punishment for their sin in turning away from the God of heaven.

"And it came to pass after many days, that the word of the Lord came to Elijah in the third year, saying, Go, shew thyself unto Ahab."

So he went, and the two men met for the first time since the rain ceased.

"Art thou he that troubleth Israel?" cried the angry king.

"I have not troubled Israel," said Elijah; "but thou, and thy father's house, in that ye have forsaken the commandments of the Lord, and thou hast followed Baalim."

Elijah was right. He knew that God would never have permitted such terrible suffering to come to the people if they had remained loyal and true to Him. He knew, too, that the time had come for the lesson to be driven home to them in a still stronger way. So he said to Ahab: "Gather to me all Israel unto mount Carmel, and the prophets of Baal four hundred and fifty, and the prophets of the groves four hundred, which eat at Jezebel's table."

Ahab agreed. Perhaps he thought it would be a good chance to kill the man who had caused the famine. Anyhow, he sent word that the whole nation should assemble, with all the

251

During the time of terrible famine in Israel a poor widow shared her last loaf of bread with the prophet Elijah and God honored her faith by keeping her jars full of oil and meal.

priests of Baal. It was a hungry and sober company that turned up.

"And Elijah came unto all the people, and said, How long halt ye between two opinions? if the Lord be God, follow Him: but if Baal, then follow him."

No one replied. No doubt the consciences of many troubled them, and they did not know what to say. Perhaps, too, they were afraid of what Ahab and the priests of Baal would do to them if they spoke up for God.

Then Elijah suggested that a test should be made to demonstrate which was the true God. Let two sacrifices be prepared, he said, "and the God that answereth by fire, let him be God."

This pleased the people, and they answered, "It is well spoken."

So the prophets of Baal went to work. First they killed a bullock and put it on an altar of wood, quite confident that fire would fall from heaven and consume it. Then they called on the name of Baal "from morning even until noon, saying, O Baal, hear us. But there was no voice, nor any that answered."

At noon Elijah, who knew no fire would come at their call,

mocked them and said, "Cry aloud: for he is a god; either he is talking, or he is pursuing, or he is in a journey, or peradventure he sleepeth, and must be awaked."

This made them angrier than ever. In their frenzy they leaped on the altar and cut themselves with knives. All afternoon they kept up their screaming and crying till they must have been completely worn out. But "there was neither voice, nor any to answer, nor any that regarded."

When everyone saw that it was hopeless, and that Baal had been completely discredited, "Elijah said unto all the people, Come near unto me. And all the people came near unto him. And he repaired the altar of the Lord that was broken down."

What a lesson was that! All over the country were altars of the Lord which had broken down through neglect, and the people knew it.

To repair this altar, Elijah took twelve stones, one for each of the tribes of Israel—a reminder that Israel was still one nation to God.

Then he dug a trench all round the altar, and the watching thousands must have wondered why; but they soon found out. For when he had put the wood in place, and the bullock on the wood, Elijah commanded that both sacrifice and altar should be drenched with twelve barrels of water—probably sea water, for Carmel was on the coast. "And the water ran round about the altar; and he filled the trench also with water." He was determined that no one should say he lighted the fire himself.

The light was fading now. It was time for the offering of

253

the evening sacrifice under God's appointed plan—the sacrifice that was to point the world to Jesus, God's sacrifice on Calvary. Then it was that Elijah, looking heavenward, cried out, so that all could hear, "Lord God of Abraham, Isaac, and of Israel, let it be known this day that Thou art God in Israel, and that I am Thy servant, and that I have done all these things at Thy word. Hear me, O Lord, hear me, that this people may know that Thou art the Lord God, and that Thou hast turned their heart back again." 1 Kings 18:36, 37.

With bated breath the people watched and listened. Would God answer? Was Jehovah greater than Baal?

"Then the fire of the Lord fell." Suddenly out of the darkening sky came a stream of light, a roaring flame. Unerringly it rushed straight for Elijah's altar and engulfed it in a blaze of glory. With an intensity of heat men had never felt before, it "consumed the burnt sacrifice, and the wood, and the stones, and the dust, and licked up the water that was in the trench."

A moment later nothing was left save the charred soil and the billows of smoke rolling majestically heavenward.

"And when all the people saw it, they fell on their faces: and they said, The Lord, He is the God; the Lord, He is the God."

That night the prophets of Baal were slain, and the way was opened for Israel to worship the Lord once more. Then Elijah prayed again, the rain fell, and the famine was ended.

Thus by much pleading and many mighty wonders God sought to bring His people back to Him.

255

As Elijah prayed, a brilliant, roaring flame flashed from the sky, consuming the sacrifice and the stones of the altar, completely licking dry the trench that had been filled with water.

STORY 37

The Maid Who Saved
Her Master

~~~~~~~~~~

YEARS passed by. Elijah, that mighty man of God who brought fire down from heaven, went up to heaven himself in a chariot of fire (2 Kings 2:11).

Elisha, his servant and companion, took his place as the prophet of the Lord. He, too, worked many wonderful miracles to help the people remember the power of God and to keep the knowledge of Him alive in their hearts.

256

THE MAID WHO SAVED HER MASTER

Strong men were needed in those days to champion God's cause, for so many of the rulers and the people were very wicked and hated anyone who told them to be good. Despite all the warnings God sent them, they continued to worship idols and to follow the evil ways of the heathen about them.

Nevertheless, not everybody was bad. Scattered among the cities and villages of Israel were people who loved the Lord; fathers and mothers who tried to bring up their children to love and serve Him. Though sometimes it seemed as if the whole kingdom had gone after false gods, the Lord, who knows all hearts, could say, "I have left Me seven thousand in Israel, all the knees which have not bowed unto Baal, and every mouth which hath not kissed him." 1 Kings 19:18.

Always there was this holy remnant, the truly good people, men and women, boys and girls, who in their own quiet way were trying to do right. They said their prayers morning and evening, and often repeated the commandments of God, so that they should never forget them.

It was hard to be good in those days— as hard then as now, perhaps even harder. The times were harsh and cruel, and life was cheap. Invading armies would break into homes, kill the men, and carry the women and children away as captives. It was all very wicked and heartless, and brought great sorrow to many.

During one such raid a little girl was snatched up by a soldier and carried away into the land of Syria. How she must have cried for her mother, whom she knew she would never see again!

17

She was a good little girl, for her mother had brought her up to love the Lord. Young as she was, she knew all the great stories of what God had done for Israel at the Red Sea and in the wilderness. She knew about Elijah, and how he had brought fire from heaven at Carmel. And she knew about Elisha, too, and the miracles he had wrought to help the sick and the poor in Israel.

Because she was such a good girl, God watched over her in captivity and opened the way for her to become a maid in the home of Naaman, captain of the king of Syria's armies. Here she was safe with a kind mistress.

Naaman, however, though he held such a high position and was a close friend of the king, was a very sick man. He had caught that dreadful disease known as leprosy, for which, in those days, there was no cure. Naturally he was very worried about it, and afraid that his wife would catch it too.

So kind had both of them been to the little maid that she was sorry for them. One day she said to her mistress, "Would God my lord were with the prophet that is in Samaria! for he would recover him of his leprosy."

The mistress smiled. "But that isn't possible," she said; "nobody can ever be cured of leprosy."

"But it's true; I know it's true," said the little girl eagerly. "You see, he is a prophet of the true God, and he can work miracles. Oh, if only my master would go and see him! I know he would get better right away!"

So she pleaded with her mistress, telling her all she knew of the wonderful power of the living God. Impressed by her

258

earnest little face and eager words, the mistress told her husband, and he told the king.

And it must have been a great story the little girl told, for the Bible says, "And one went in, and told his lord, saying, Thus and thus said the maid that is of the land of Israel." What a lot is wrapped up in those three words, "thus and thus"!

The king listened, and he was impressed too; so much so that he told Naaman to follow her advice and go to Samaria.

So Naaman went, and his confidence in the little girl's story is revealed by the fact that he took with him "ten talents of silver, and six thousand pieces of gold, and ten changes of raiment."

But when the king of Israel saw Naaman and read the letter which the king of Syria had sent with him, saying that his chief captain had come to be healed of leprosy, he was terribly

shocked. "Am I God," he cried, ". . . that this man doth send unto me to recover a man of his leprosy?"

Naaman was shocked too. He had not expected this. Could it be that the little girl had not told the truth? Fortunately the story of Naaman's visit, and what the king of Israel had said to him, spread through the court and out among the people. Someone brought the news to Elisha. To the king's great relief, Elisha sent a message saying, "Let him come now to me, and he shall know that there is a prophet in Israel."

So Naaman came "with his horses and with his chariot," and all his presents of gold and silver and beautiful clothing, "and stood at the door of the house of Elisha." Perhaps, he thought, all will be well now. But not yet. For Elisha did a

strange thing. Instead of going out to see Naaman himself, he sent a messenger to him with these instructions: "Go and wash in Jordan seven times, and thy flesh shall come again to thee, and thou shalt be clean."

This was too much for Naaman. Now he was sure he had been deceived. Angrily he rode away, muttering, "I thought, He will surely come out to me, and stand, and call on the name of the Lord his God, and strike his hand over the place, and recover the leper."

But being angry didn't help matters. It never does. Luckily for him, he began to calm down after a while. Then his servants reasoned with him and said, "If the prophet had bid thee do some great thing, wouldest thou not have done it? how much rather then, when he saith to thee, Wash, and be clean?"

At last, reluctantly, he decided to obey the word of God's prophet, and turned his chariot toward the Jordan, thirty miles or so away.

Again and again, as his chariot rolled and bumped over that rocky road through the mountains, he wondered why he had ever listened to that little maid of his. What good could possibly come from bathing in the Jordan?

The same thought struck him again as he removed his uniform and waded into the river. What a strange thing to do! He dipped himself in the water. Nothing happened. He did it again, without result. He looked at his poor, leprous skin, and it was as white as ever.

Three, four, five, six times Naaman dipped in the water. Still there was no change. He felt the same as before.

261

THE MAID WHO SAVED HER MASTER

Then he went under the seventh time. Suddenly he felt a surge of new life flowing through him. Wiping the water from his eyes, he looked at his hands. They were clean! Not a trace of the dread disease was to be seen. But how about his face, his poor, leprous face? O for a mirror! Then he looked down at the water, now calm and still, and there before him was a reflection of himself. His skin was clear as a child's! The dread leprosy had completely gone! He was healed!

Rushing from the water, he put on his clothes, and drove at full speed to Samaria. What a ride that was! How he must have sung and shouted for joy as his chariot raced over that wild mountain trail!

At last he came again to Elisha's house, "he and all his company." With heart overflowing with thankfulness he cried out to the prophet, "Now I know that there is no God in all the earth, but in Israel." 2 Kings 5:15.

For a time he had doubted. He had thought the little maid's story had been only make-believe; now he knew that every word she had said was true. There *was* a God in Israel who could help a man in need and cure the worst of diseases. And this wonderful God was willing to heal even a Syrian.

So Naaman returned home. And what a story he had to tell his wife and the king! No doubt he did something very special for his little maid, but her greatest reward, I am sure, was the knowledge that her witness for God in a heathen land had brought such happy results.

You never can tell how much good will come from speaking a word for the Lord.

263

The leprosy of Naaman, captain of the host of the king of Syria, was cured when he obeyed the word of the Lord through Elisha and washed himself seven times in the Jordan.

Window of the Future

THERE was so much war and bloodshed in those olden times, and so many people were carried away as slaves by cruel conquerors, that there must have been many boys and girls who witnessed for God in heathen lands, like Naaman's little maid. Fortunately the Bible has preserved the story of a very brave boy who followed her example.

Because God's people refused to keep His commandments, and would not listen to the warnings of His prophets, the Lord finally permitted a terrible punishment to come upon them.

The Bible says: "All the chief of the priests, and the people, transgressed very much after all the abominations of the heathen. . . . And the Lord God of their fathers sent to them by His messengers, rising up betimes, and sending; because He had compassion on His people, and on His dwelling place: but they mocked the messengers of God, and despised His words, and misused His prophets, until the wrath of the Lord arose against His people, till there was no remedy. Therefore He brought upon them the king of the Chaldees." 2 Chronicles 36:14-17.

So it was that when Nebuchadnezzar laid siege to Jerusalem, God did not go to the rescue of His people, as He had so many times before. Instead, He let the Babylonian soldiers break down the walls of the city, destroy the beautiful Temple Solomon had built, and lead tens of thousands of the people into captivity.

Among the great company of Israelites captured by Nebuchadnezzar was a boy named Daniel. He was a good-looking lad, and well brought up. His mother had taught him to honor God's commandments, and had told him all she knew of His plan of salvation—those great stories of divine love which had come down from Adam and Enoch and Noah, and, after the Flood, had been passed on by Abraham, Isaac, and Jacob, then by Joseph, Moses, and Joshua. All this precious knowledge Daniel carried with him in his mind and heart as he trudged

the weary miles to Babylon; and he made up his mind that come what might he would be true to his God.

There was something about the boy that appealed to his captors. He was clean and honest and truthful. Before long he was given special favors above the other prisoners.

In Babylon he went to school and proved to be one of the brightest students his teachers had ever known. Always he tried to set a good example so that others would think well of his religion. The officer who had special charge of him came to like him very much. With "favour and tender love," the Bible says.

Then one day word came to Daniel that he was in great danger. King Nebuchadnezzar had gone into one of his wild rages and had decreed that all the "wise men" of Babylon should be slain. Apparently this included even young people with higher education.

Alarmed, as well he might have been, Daniel went to see Arioch, the king's captain, who had been ordered to carry out the execution.

"Why is the decree so hasty from the king?" he asked. "What has happened? What is it all about?"

Then Arioch, who also loved Daniel, told him the story of what had taken place in the palace. While asleep, Nebuchadnezzar had had a dream which had made a great impression on him, but when he had awakened he could not remember anything about it. So he had sent for his magicians, astrologers, and others who claimed they had special knowledge of such things, and demanded that they tell him his dream.

266

WINDOW OF THE FUTURE

Of course they could not do it. So Nebuchadnezzar, becoming very angry, had said they should all be killed—they and everybody associated with them. It was very rash, said Arioch, but—well, there was nothing to do but carry out his orders. After all, the king had spoken.

Then Daniel went in to see the king himself. It was very brave of him, knowing the king was so angry. But he went, and spoke kindly to him, and Nebuchadnezzar agreed to postpone the execution.

Daniel now sought out his special friends and told them what had happened, and of the great peril in which they all stood.

"Our only hope is in prayer," he said. "Let us ask God to show us the dream."

So they all knelt in prayer. And what a wonderful prayer meeting it was! God heard them.

That night Daniel was given the very same dream that

Nebuchadnezzar had had a little while before. But it was more than a dream to him. For the meaning of it flashed into his mind, and he knew that God had spoken to him in a vision.

In the morning, deeply thankful, he fell on his knees again and said, "Blessed be the name of God for ever and ever: for wisdom and might are His: and He changeth the times and the seasons: He removeth kings, and setteth up kings: . . . He revealeth the deep and secret things: He knoweth what is in the darkness, and the light dwelleth with Him.

"I thank Thee, and praise Thee, O Thou God of my fathers, who hast given me wisdom and might, and hast made known unto me now what we desired of Thee: for Thou hast now made known unto us the king's matter." Daniel 2:20-23.

Then Daniel went to Arioch and let him know that the king would be told his dream, and that the wise men need not be destroyed. In haste, for there was but little time left, Arioch hurried with Daniel into the presence of Nebuchadnezzar.

"Are you able to tell me my dream?" asked the king.

"Not I," said Daniel, "but there is a God in heaven that revealeth secrets, and maketh known to the king Nebuchadnezzar what shall be in the latter days."

So Daniel gave all the glory to God, and God drew near to help him.

"Thy dream," he went on, "and the visions of thy head upon thy bed, are these; . . . thy thoughts came into thy mind upon thy bed, what should come to pass hereafter."

"That's right," said Nebuchadnezzar to himself. "Now I remember. I was thinking about the hereafter, and what will

268

happen to my kingdom after I am dead." He leaned forward on his throne, gazing intently at the lad before him.

"He that revealeth secrets," Daniel continued, "maketh known to thee what shall come to pass."

"Good!" muttered the king to himself. "That is what I want to know—what is going to happen in the future."

Very calmly and respectfully, Daniel spoke again.

"Thou, O king, sawest, and behold a great image. This great image, whose brightness was excellent, stood before thee; and the form thereof was terrible."

The king's eyes glistened with excitement. Yes! This was it! Just what he had seen in his dream! A great image of many colors. Exactly! How wonderful that this boy should know it!

"This image's head," said Daniel, "was of fine gold, his breast and his arms of silver, his belly and his thighs of brass, his legs of iron, his feet part of iron and part of clay.

"Thou sawest till that a stone was cut out without hands, which smote the image upon his feet that were of iron and clay, and brake them to pieces.

WINDOW OF THE FUTURE

"Then was the iron, the clay, the brass, the silver, and the gold, broken to pieces together, and became like the chaff of the summer threshingfloors; and the wind carried them away, that no place was found for them: and the stone that smote the image became a great mountain, and filled the whole earth."

Nebuchadnezzar was overcome with amazement. Every detail was correct! It was marvelous. But what did it mean? How did it reveal the future, as Daniel had said?

Then Daniel told him. The head of gold stood for Nebuchadnezzar himself and his rich and powerful empire of Babylon. The king was greatly flattered as Daniel said, "Thou art this head of gold."

But Babylon would not continue forever. "After thee shall arise another kingdom," said Daniel, a kingdom represented by the breast and arms of silver. Then a third world empire would arise, represented by the belly and thighs of brass. This in turn would be overthrown by a fourth kingdom, strong as iron, like the legs of the image. Then as the feet and toes of the image were made of a mixture of iron and clay, so this fourth kingdom would be divided, and remain divided, until God, the King of kings, should come to set up His everlasting kingdom.

"Whereas thou sawest the feet and toes," said Daniel, "part of potters' clay, and part of iron, the kingdom shall be divided; but there shall be in it of the strength of the iron, forasmuch as thou sawest the iron mixed with miry clay.

"And as the toes of the feet were part of iron, and part of clay, so the kingdom shall be partly strong, and partly broken.

"And whereas thou sawest iron mixed with miry clay, they

271

In the dream that God sent him, Nebuchadnezzar saw a great image with a head of gold. Its breast was of silver, its thighs of brass, its legs of iron, and its toes part iron, part clay.

shall mingle themselves with the seed of men: but they shall not cleave one to another, even as iron is not mixed with clay.

"And in the days of these kings shall the God of heaven set up a kingdom, which shall never be destroyed: and the kingdom shall not be left to other people, but it shall break in pieces and consume all these kingdoms, and it shall stand for ever.

"Forasmuch as thou sawest that the stone was cut out of the mountain without hands, and that it brake in pieces the iron, the brass, the clay, the silver, and the gold; the great God hath made known to the king what shall come to pass hereafter: and the dream is certain, and the interpretation thereof sure."

As Daniel talked on, Nebuchadnezzar forgot that he was sitting in the throne room of Babylon. It seemed to him that he was standing at a window, with the curtains drawn, looking down the ages upon the great events of history to be.

WINDOW OF THE FUTURE

And he was. In fact, both king and prophet, lord and slave, were looking through the mystic window of the future. Before them stretched the mighty panorama of all the years to come. Close by them they saw the golden temples of Babylon, but beyond were the silver minarets of Medo-Persia, the brazen towers of Grecia, and the iron domes of Rome.

On, on down the ages they peered, till they saw the mighty Roman Empire divided into the nations of modern Europe. They saw these nations fighting one another in great and terrible wars, as strong leaders tried in vain to unite them into one great empire again. Then, "in the days of these kings"—the nations of our day—they saw something new in history. Sud-

denly their eyes were drawn from earth to heaven, and there in the sky they beheld a great fiery glow as the King of kings descended in glory to bring all earthly empires to an end.

Wonderful vision! How their hearts must have thrilled at the sight! When it was over, the king bowed low before this lad whom God had so wonderfully used to reveal the future to him, saying, "Of a truth it is, that your God is a God of gods, and a Lord of kings, and a revealer of secrets, seeing thou couldest reveal this secret."

PAINTING BY HERBERT RUDEEN   © BY REVIEW AND HERALD

"Then the king made Daniel a great man, and gave him many great gifts, and made him ruler over the whole province of Babylon, and chief of the governors over all the wise men of Babylon."

Thus yet another boy, like Joseph and David before him, was honored and rewarded because he was faithful in witnessing for God. Not all who are loyal to Him will become princes and rulers in this world, but all will be greatly blessed in God's own wonderful way, both here and hereafter.

As for the dream, what a lesson it has for us today! For we are living in the very time that Daniel described—the days just before the coming of the Lord in glory to set up His own eternal kingdom.

Daniel and Nebuchadnezzar saw this climax of history in vision; but we shall see it in reality. To them it was far in the future; but to us it is close at hand.

Let this be our prayer:

"Then, O my Lord, prepare
My soul for that great day;
O wash me in Thy precious blood,
And take my sins away!"

© BY RGH

Faithful Unto Death

~~~~~~

ALL through Nebuchadnezzar's long reign Daniel held his high office in Babylon. His wisdom and his friendly spirit won the respect of all.

The memory of the great dream never left him, and he saw the beginning of its fulfillment in his day. After Nebuchadnezzar died, Babylon grew weaker and weaker in the hands of unworthy kings, and Daniel lived to see the city fall to the Medo-Persians.

Belshazzar was king then. Careless of the fact that the enemy was already at his gates, he was holding a great feast for a thousand of his lords. Suddenly, as the drunken revelers raised to their lips the gold and silver vessels taken from the Temple at Jerusalem, the fingers of a man's hand appeared writing on the wall of the banquet room. The king saw the mysterious fingers, and turned pale as death, his knees knocking together in fright. Then he pointed to the strange writing and demanded that someone tell him what it said. But no one

277

could read it. Then the queen remembered Daniel, and how, nearly seventy years before, he had interpreted Nebuchadnezzar's dream. So Belshazzar sent for him.

Though he was an old man now, Daniel's mind was clear, his bearing noble. To those trembling, drunken men in the banquet hall, he must have seemed like a man from another world.

Boldly he addressed Belshazzar, reminding him of all God's goodness to Nebuchadnezzar, and saying, "And thou . . . hast not humbled thine heart, though thou knewest all this; but hast lifted up thyself against the Lord of heaven; . . . and the God in whose hand thy breath is, and whose are all thy ways, hast thou not glorified."

Because the king had not recognized the hand of God in his life, that hand had now written his doom upon the wall before him.

"This is the writing that was written," said Daniel, "MENE, MENE, TEKEL, UPHARSIN." Which meant: "God hath numbered thy kingdom, and finished it. . . . Thou art weighed in the balances, and art found wanting. . . . Thy kingdom is divided, and given to the Medes and Persians."

Even as Daniel spoke, the enemy soldiers were already pouring through the gates of the city, rushing with swords and torches toward the banquet hall.

© BY R&H

"In that night was Belshazzar the king of the Chaldeans slain. And Darius the Median took the kingdom."

The new king, sensing the nobility of Daniel's character, and his great experience and wisdom, appointed him chief president of all the princes of his kingdom. The Bible says, "This Daniel was preferred above the presidents and princes, because an excellent spirit was in him; and the king thought to set him over the whole realm."

But the princes of Medo-Persia did not approve the king's choice. They could see no reason why Darius should give him such high honors.

Becoming more and more jealous, as they saw how wise and capable Daniel really was, they began to plot his overthrow. But they could find nothing against him. "Forasmuch as he was faithful, neither was there any error or fault found in him.

"Then said these men, We shall not find any occasion against this Daniel, except we find it against him concerning the law of his God."

Knowing that Daniel never failed to say his prayers three times a day—morning, noon, and night—they agreed together to persuade King Darius to issue a decree that no one should ask a petition "of any God or man" save himself, for the next thirty days, the penalty being death in the den of lions.

Darius the king, highly flattered by the suggestion, signed the decree.

Then someone told Daniel what had been done. He saw through the plot at once, and realized that he was in a very difficult place. But did he alter his lifelong plan of daily worship? Did he decide to give up saying his prayers, or to whisper them secretly, out of sight? No, not he! He had witnessed for God all his life in this heathen city, and he was not going to give up now. If it meant dying in the den of lions, all right, let it be so. He would be faithful unto death.

So "when Daniel knew that the writing was signed, he went into his house; and his windows being open in his chamber toward Jerusalem, he kneeled upon his knees three times a day, and prayed, and gave thanks before his God, as he did aforetime."

People were used to seeing Daniel praying at that window, but now they crowded the street before his house to witness his quiet defiance of the new law.

"Look at him!" they cried. "Doesn't he know about the king's decree?"

"He'll know when he finds himself in the den of lions," said others.

Meanwhile the jealous princes hurried to Darius with the story. The king then realized what they had been up to. They had not wanted to flatter him but to destroy Daniel. He was angry, and he was sorry, but, having made the decree, there was nothing he could do but order that Daniel be thrown to the lions.

So the cruel order was given, and Daniel was taken and led through the streets to the den.

What a procession that must have been! The aged prophet out in front, then the soldiers and the princes, while thousands of common people looked on, wondering whether to be sorry or glad that this brave old man was going to be killed. But Daniel strode on unmoved, his trust in God unshaken.

The den was opened. Daniel was thrown in. But the lions never touched him. Instead, they slunk away, as though afraid of him. All that night, while Daniel prayed, they paced to and fro, growling now and then, but never venturing to attack him.

Early in the morning Daniel heard a familiar voice calling to him from outside the den. It was the king!

"Daniel, Daniel," cried Darius, "servant of the living God, is thy God, whom thou servest continually, able to deliver thee from the lions?"

Oh, yes, indeed. Abundantly able.

Daniel joyfully cried, "My God hath sent His angel, and

281

hath shut the lions' mouths, that they have not hurt me. . . .

"Then was the king exceeding glad for him, and commanded that they should take Daniel up out of the den. . . . And no manner of hurt was found upon him, *because he believed in his God.*"

Brave Daniel! May we trust God with like devotion today. Let us resolve that we too will be faithful unto death. Then one day the King of kings will come to seek us in the morning, and call us by name, and deliver us, and rejoice over us "with exceeding joy" through all eternity.

STORY 40

Great Expectations

HAVE you ever looked forward to something you wanted to happen and hardly known how to wait for it? Perhaps it was a long-promised trip to the seaside, or a visit from a dear friend, or the arrival of a baby brother. How you counted the weeks, the days, the hours! How you reminded father and mother of their promises! And how you dreamed of the good time you would have!

And so it was in those far-off days before Jesus was born in Bethlehem. For thousands of years, even from the beginning of the world, people had looked forward to His coming. They had cherished the promise that had been made to Adam and Eve in the Garden of Eden about the "seed of the woman" bruising, or crushing, the serpent's head, believing it to mean that sometime, somehow, God would send someone to make an end of all evil and bring back the happy Eden days again. Every fresh hint or suggestion made by God's prophets as to how and when the promised Deliverer would come was greatly prized.

283

Because Daniel continued to pray to the true God, whom he had worshiped all his life, he was thrown into a den of lions, but an angel protected him by shutting the lions' mouths.

There was the promise God had made through Moses: "The Lord thy God will raise up unto thee a Prophet from the midst of thee, of thy brethren, like unto me; unto Him ye shall hearken." Deuteronomy 18:15. So they looked for a prophet like Moses.

There was the prophecy Balaam had made to Balak: "There shall come a Star out of Jacob, and a Sceptre shall rise out of Israel." Numbers 24:17. So they had looked for a star and a king, but didn't think they could be related.

There were the beautiful words of the prophet Isaiah: "Unto us a child is born, unto us a son is given: and the government shall be upon His shoulder." Isaiah 9:6. So many believed that their Deliverer must come as a little boy and grow up to kingship.

Then there was the prophecy about the place of His birth: "But thou, Bethlehem Ephratah, though thou be little among the thousands of Judah, yet out of thee shall He come forth unto Me that is to be ruler in Israel." Micah 5:2. So naturally all eyes turned expectantly to Bethlehem, confident that someday something wonderful would happen there.

All down the centuries people talked of these things in their homes and told them as stories to their children until they, too, were looking forward to the coming of the Messiah, or "Anointed One," for whom all longed so eagerly. (The Hebrews called Him Messiah because only their kings and

Genesis 3:15

Deuteronomy 18:15

Numbers 24:17

© BY RGH

GREAT EXPECTATIONS

Isaiah 7:14

priests were anointed, and they were sure their Deliverer would be both king and priest. The word *Christ* has the same thought behind it.)

Over and over again the question was asked, "But when will He come?" Children must have asked it of their parents a thousand times. Then mother or father would tell about the book of Daniel—the book that tells of the fiery furnace, the lions' den, and Nebuchadnezzar's wonderful dream—and how an angel said to Daniel, "From the going forth of the commandment to restore and to build Jerusalem unto the Messiah the Prince shall be seven weeks, and threescore and two weeks." Daniel 9:25. And then, I suppose, they would take their writing materials and try to work out just when this would be.

Everybody knew when the commandment went forth to restore and build Jerusalem (457 B.C.). Everybody knew also that in prophecy a day stands for a year (Ezekiel 4:6), and that therefore "seven weeks, and threescore and two weeks" should be understood as 483 years (69 multiplied by 7). So they must have come very close to the right date for Messiah to appear.

If there had been newspapers in those days—say about 10 B.C.—there would no doubt have been banner headlines on them, such as HIGH PRIEST BELIEVES MESSIAH COMING SOON, or, MESSIAH EXPECTED AT BETHLEHEM WITHIN 25 YEARS, or, DANIEL SAYS MESSIAH DUE NOW.

Micah 5:2

Daniel 9:25

Of course there were no newspapers then, and therefore no such headlines. Nevertheless, news got around just the same, and the idea that the Messiah might soon appear spread all over Palestine and, in fact, all over the world, wherever Jews were living. Some, no doubt, laughed at the story and said it was impossible, but others believed it. Many a mother wondered whether her own baby boy might be the son mentioned in prophecy who should become the governor of Israel.

Far to the east of Palestine, possibly in Persia or Arabia, a group of Wise Men gathered to study the prophecies of the Holy Scriptures, and became more and more convinced that the hour was at hand for the Messiah to appear. They were known as Magi, and were learned men such as philosophers and astronomers. As they sat together in the gathering dusk one evening and read again the words, "There shall come a Star out of Jacob," suddenly one of them, pointing upward into the darkening heavens, cried, "Look! Look at that star!"

And there *was* a star, brighter and more beautiful than any ever seen before. And it was moving toward Palestine. Somehow it seemed to be beckoning them to follow. What could they do but mount their camels and make off across the desert? Surely the time had come. The promised star had appeared. Messiah was at hand! They were so sure of it that they prepared rich gifts of "gold, frankincense, and myrrh," and took them as presents for Him, to show how glad they were.

In the Temple in Jerusalem there were others with great expectations in their hearts. Old Simeon was sure the time was

© BY RGH

HERBERT
RUDEEN

near for Messiah to appear. All his life he had hoped that he would see Him, and now, as he studied the prophecies anew, he became more and more certain that his dearest wish would come true. One day the Holy Spirit spoke to him and told him that "he should not see death, before he had seen the Lord's Christ." Luke 2:26.

Now he knew for sure Messiah must be near, very near. But how would He appear, and when? Every morning Simeon must have wakened with the thought, "Will He come to the Temple today?" How he must have peered into the face of every visitor, wondering, "Can this be He?"

Simeon talked with Anna about it—dear old Anna, eighty-four years of age. She spent her time at the Temple and was also looking for the Messiah, hoping she would see Him before she died. How glad she was when Simeon told her that he had been assured by God that "the Lord's Christ" would soon appear! Perhaps, then, she would see Him too! Eagerly she talked about it to her friends; in fact, to "all them that looked for redemption in Jerusalem," and excitement continued to mount from day to day.

There were great expectations in heaven, too, for the angels knew that the time was near for their Lord and Master to go down to the earth to live as a man among men. One of their number, Gabriel, was appointed to visit Mary and tell her that she had been chosen to be the mother of Jesus. He, by the way, was the very one who had been sent to the prophet Daniel to explain about the time when the Messiah should come (Daniel 9:25). Now, at just the right time, he sped from heaven to earth to make the word of God come true.

"Hail, thou that art highly favoured," he said to Mary, "the Lord is with thee: blessed art thou among women. . . . Fear not, Mary: for thou hast found favour with God. And, behold, thou shalt conceive in thy womb, and bring forth a son, and shalt call His name JESUS. He shall be great, and shall be called the Son of the Highest: and the Lord God shall give unto Him the throne of His father David: and He shall reign over the house of Jacob for ever; and of His kingdom there shall be no end." Luke 1:28-33.

"How shall this be?" asked Mary, greatly surprised and wondering whether she was dreaming. Gabriel answered, "The Holy Ghost shall come upon thee, and the power of the Highest shall overshadow thee: therefore also that holy thing which shall be born of thee shall be called the Son of God." Verse 35.

Great expectations now came into the heart of this pure, sweet girl as she thought of what the angel had said to her. How she wondered what would happen when her babe was born! She had always believed that the Messiah would come—and soon—but had never dared to hope He would come through her!

Now only months remained. Then weeks; then days. Never was heaven so near to earth as then. Angels pressed close to witness the great event. It could well be that some were sent to form the star to lead the Wise Men to Bethlehem. All were told to be present to herald the birth of the Saviour of men.

Hearts beat high with excitement. In Jerusalem, in Nazareth, in many a humble home throughout the land of Israel, far off across the desert where the Wise Men lived, the conviction grew that the hour of destiny had arrived, that the most wonderful event of the ages was about to happen. Angels and men were already moving toward the sacred spot where the Messiah would appear. The great hope of God's people was about to be realized!

19

The Miracle of Bethlehem

EVERY road in Palestine was crowded. Not in a long while had there been so much traffic. Families living in the south were moving north, and others living in the north were going south. Clouds of dust rose from the rough dirt roads as people in oxcarts, on horseback, on donkeyback, and on foot went by on their various ways.

The reason for all the disturbance was that there had gone out a decree from Caesar Augustus "that all the world should be taxed." "Enrolled" is the word in the margin of Luke 2:1. The emperor of Rome wanted money, and he wanted also to find out how many people there were in his empire. So everyone had to return to his home town to be taxed and counted. If you belonged to Jerusalem and were living in Jericho, you had to go back to Jerusalem. If you had been born, say, in Capernaum, and were living in Joppa, you had to take the long, dusty trip back to Capernaum, or perhaps get into trouble with the Roman soldiers, who were everywhere. So

"all went to be taxed, every one into his own city." Verse 3.

If you had been standing somewhere on the main north-south highway at that time—say a mile or so out of Jerusalem—you would have seen a sight to make your heart ache. Riding on a donkey was a girl, young and beautiful, but very tired. The shawl about her face was dusty, as was all her clothing. You could see by the weary look on her face that she longed for a place where she could stop and rest. But there could be no stopping, for the hour was late, and they had to reach Bethlehem before nightfall. With so many people traveling, the inn might be full and then what would happen? There was the Baby to think of. He might be born that very night. And He was the most important Baby in the world!

291

Joseph, walking at her side, was worried too. He was afraid the gates of Bethlehem might be closed before they got there. He wanted to hurry, but he dared not. There was nothing he could do but trudge on patiently, speaking a word of courage to Mary now and then.

Though the two tired travelers did not realize it, angels were watching them every step of the way. And if angels ever get anxious, they were worried too. They were thinking of the motion of the donkey, the ruts in the road, and the constant danger of a fall. If that Baby should be born too soon! That was unthinkable. He just *had* to be born in Bethlehem! So they watched and hoped and hovered over the humble little procession as it moved, oh, so slowly, on its weary way.

They had passed Jerusalem now. Only six miles more! How long seemed the last lap of the journey!

Presently, in the gathering dusk they could see a group of

flat-topped houses built on a hillside, and Joseph no doubt cried out with relief, "There it is! That's Bethlehem! Just a little farther. Soon we'll be at the inn, and then you can rest all night in comfort."

New strength came to both of them as they moved on up the hill. They were so happy that the long, tedious journey was almost over that they scarcely noticed all the other people hurrying past them with the same thought in mind of finding a place to stay before nightfall.

Darkness was upon them, and little oil lamps were burning in many a house when, at long last, they entered the village and made their way toward the inn. Now they were delayed by the people, the animals, and the carts that thronged the narrow streets. Finally, however, they reached the inn and knocked on the door.

The innkeeper appeared. "Sorry, no vacancy. Every room was booked long ago."

"But the girl and the Baby! The Baby might be born any time now. Surely you could find a corner for them somewhere?"

"Sorry, but there isn't a place anywhere—at least not in the inn."

"Well, is there anywhere else?"

"Every place in town is crowded."

"But, sir, the Baby——"

"Well, there's the stable. You may take shelter there if you care to."

The stable! They had so hoped for a bed in the inn. All the way Mary had been wondering just where "the Son of the

Highest" might be born. Perhaps in the inn. Perhaps in somebody's home. But never in a stable. Not there, of all places. But a stable it had to be.

As the door creaked on its hinges, they caught the first smell of the cows and the dung. What a place to sleep! What a place for a baby to be born! What a place for the Messiah to appear!

Of course, if the innkeeper had known what Mary knew, he would have made room for her somewhere. Certainly he would not have sent her to the stable. What a blessing he lost that night! If he had given up his own room for the Saviour's birth it would have been a source of joy and holy pride to him the rest of his life. He would have been able to talk about it to his friends and his customers, his children and his grandchildren. Thousands upon thousands would have trekked to his door just to see the place and hear his story. In his heart and in his pocketbook he would have been blessed beyond all imagining. By failing to be kind to a poor, needy girl he missed the greatest opportunity of his life. Perhaps he is one of those who will one day hear Jesus say, "Inasmuch as ye did it not to one of the least of these, ye did it not to Me." Matthew 25:45.

What a lesson to us to be kind to everyone in need! We can never be quite sure who the needy one is, or what the consequences of our good deed may be.

Now Joseph is lighting the wick of a little oil lamp. Its feeble, flickering rays reveal what a dank, gloomy place the stable is, with its low roof, its rough beams, and its mud-and-straw-covered floor. Cows turn their heads and moo as the strangers enter. Rats scurry away to their holes.

Where to go? Down at the end there is an empty stall, and they go there. Joseph gathers straw to make a bed for Mary. But she is thinking only of the Baby. Where shall she put the Baby when He comes?

She spies the manger, half filled with hay for the cows to eat. The very thing! Not very beautiful, but soft and cozy, and at least He will be safe in it. He couldn't fall out.

Sinking gently upon the straw to rest, and looking out in the shadows all about her, Mary may well have thought to herself, Too bad that He should have to be born here! What was it that the angel had said? How well she remembered! "The Holy Ghost shall come upon thee, and the power of the Highest shall overshadow thee: therefore also that holy thing which shall be born of thee shall be called the Son of God."

The Son of God! To be born in a stable!

"Thou shalt call His name JESUS," the angel had also said: "for He shall save His people from their sins." Matthew 1:21.

It was hard to understand. How could it be that God would permit His Son, the Saviour of the world, to be born in a cow barn? Surely there must be some mistake.

But no. It was all in the divine plan in order that the lowest and humblest of the people of earth might know that Jesus cares for them and came to save them. If He had been born in Herod's palace, He would have been thought of as the Saviour of the rich and the powerful. The poor would never have dared to claim Him. But He was born in a stable, and nobody could ever feel left out.

Perhaps Mary thought of the words of the psalmist: "Who is like unto the Lord our God, who dwelleth on high, who humbleth Himself to behold the things that are in heaven, and in the earth! He raiseth up the poor out of the dust, and lifteth the needy out of the dunghill; that He may set him with princes, even with the princes of His people." Psalm 113:5-8. How appropriate these words must have seemed to her now.

One thing she could not know, and that was that within sixty years one of the greatest Jews of his day would write of her Baby, "Though He was rich, yet for your sakes He became poor, that ye through His poverty might be rich." 2 Corinthians 8:9.

Another thing she did not know was the excitement outside the stable at that moment. Not in the village, for the people of Bethlehem were all asleep by now, but in the sky above.

Within the stable all was dark, save for the feeble rays of the little oil lamp. But above, directly overhead, a wondrous light was shining as all the hosts of heaven waited eagerly to sing the glory song when the Son of God should be born.

This Day a Saviour

SUPPOSE you had been living in Bethlehem the night that Jesus was born—"the night before Christmas," the first Christmas—wouldn't that have been wonderful! Of course, you might have been so tired that night you would have slept through everything that happened. Most people did.

But suppose some children, just one or two maybe, *were* awake that night. What did they see? What did they hear?

Ben and his little sister Ruth loved to sleep on the roof of their flat-topped house—that is, when father and mother gave them permission to do so. They liked to feel the cool breeze blowing over them and to lie on their backs, looking up into the sky, trying to count the stars.

298

THIS DAY A SAVIOUR

This night was just like any other night except that there was something new to talk about. There was Caesar's decree about the taxing that had brought so many people to town.

"I never saw so many people in all my life," said Ben.

"Nor I," said Ruth. "Nor so many horses and oxen. The place is full of them. I wonder how long everybody will stay?"

"Only till the taxing is over, I suppose."

There was silence for a while.

"I've been wondering and wondering," said Ben.

"Wondering what?" asked Ruth. "About how long the people will stay?"

"No, no," said Ben. "Not that. But about what father has been telling us lately. You know, about the Messiah's coming. He says that the old prophecies must be fulfilled soon."

"Isn't it true that He is to come to Bethlehem?"

"Yes," said Ben. "He's coming to our town. The prophet Micah says so. I wonder when."

"Won't it be marvelous!" murmured Ruth, lying back on her bed of rushes. "Aren't we lucky that He's coming here!"

"I should say we are," said Ben. "I hope we don't miss Him. Let's go to sleep."

There was a pause.

"Ben! Look up there in the sky!"

"What at?"

"Look, look! That light! What can it be?"

"Oh my!" cried Ben. "Whatever is it? And it's almost over-head! Now it's coming low. It's right over the old inn. No, it isn't. It's over the stable behind the inn. I wonder what's hap-

299

pening? Let's go see! Quietly! Careful! Everybody's asleep."

Silently they slipped downstairs, across the road, and over toward the inn. Then they stopped, for the light now seemed to be outside the village.

"Look over there!" cried Ben. "Is it a fire?"

"Let's go see!" cried Ruth.

They ran on through the empty streets, then out across the fields to the place where shepherds brought their sheep at night for safety. The shepherds were standing in a group gazing at a beautiful being standing close beside them.

Could this be the promised Messiah everybody was expecting? No, not the Messiah, but an angel; and he was saying, "Fear not: for, behold, I bring you good tidings of great joy, which shall be to all people. For unto you is born this day in the city of David a Saviour, which is Christ the Lord." Luke 2:9-11.

Ben squeezed Ruth's hand.

"Did you hear that?" he whispered. "This is the night! Messiah has come! And He has come to Bethlehem!"

"S-sh!" whispered Ruth, entranced. "Listen! The beautiful angel is speaking again."

"And this shall be a sign unto you," said the angel. "Ye shall find the Babe wrapped in swaddling clothes, lying in a manger."

"Swaddling clothes!" whispered Ruth. "Then the Babe is just born. They only put newborn babies in swaddling clothes. I wonder where He is?"

Both were hushed to silence by what happened next; for "suddenly there was with the angel a multitude of the heavenly host praising God, and saying, Glory to God in the highest, and on earth peace, good will toward men." Verses 13, 14.

All heaven seemed flooded with light. Indeed, everywhere it was light as day. They could see the rugged mountains, the awestruck shepherds, the trembling sheep, and the white-walled houses and synagogues of Bethlehem. But what gripped them most was the vision of the angels. It was wonderful beyond words. So many angels! All of them singing as though

302

their very lives depended on it, as though they had waited for ages and ages to sing this song.

"Glory to God! Glory to God! Glory to God in the highest!" The majestic music seemed to roll around the world and out toward the stars to the farthest reaches of infinite space. "Glory to God in the highest!"

Then in softer cadences, "On earth peace, good will toward men." How tenderly and hopefully they sang these closing words of their hymn of praise! It was as if they longed to see men everywhere welcome the Saviour with open arms and open hearts, and make the Son of God the Lord of their lives. Then, they knew, there would be peace on earth and good will among men.

As suddenly as they had come, the angels vanished. Darkness settled again over the hills and fields.

"And it came to pass, as the angels were gone away from them into heaven, the shepherds said one to another, Let us now go even unto Bethlehem, and see this thing which is come to pass, which the Lord hath made known unto us. And they came with haste." Verses 15, 16.

What haste! Can't you see them running as fast as their old legs would carry them, stumbling over holes and rocks and

briers, but getting up and hurrying on, bursting with the great news they had heard? And I like to think that maybe there were a couple of children there—for there are always some children about when something special is happening—running along behind, eager to see the wonderful Baby for which all Israel had been waiting so long.

In through the gates they clattered, down the cobbled streets. "Anybody know if a baby has been born in town tonight?" "Yes, down there, in the stable behind the inn."

It is still dark, but there is a light in the stable, and listen!

There is a faint cry of a tiny baby inside! This, then, must be the place!

One of the shepherds opens the old door. It creaks back on its hinges. They all step in. At first they see only the cattle in the stalls. Then, at the farther end, they make out a man standing, and a young woman resting on a pile of straw. Beside her, in the manger, is a baby. Obviously newborn, it is wrapped in swaddling clothes, just as the angel said.

Surely this *must* be the Saviour, the Messiah, Christ the Lord!

Reverently, but excitedly, the shepherds file down through the barn. Joseph and Mary look up startled, wondering what these strange men might want. Had they come to turn them out of the stable? No, indeed. They had come with news. Great news. One of them begins to explain. He tells how they were all there in the fields, just outside the village, keeping watch as usual over their flocks by night. Then how, of a sudden, an angel appeared and told them that this was the very night Messiah was to be born, and how they would find Him lying in a manger.

Mary's eyes glow. So she had not been mistaken! God had not forgotten her! He knew that she couldn't get into the inn that night. He knew His Son had had to be born in a stable and cradled in a manger. How comforting! God was watching over them, even though everything had seemed to go wrong. And if the angels had appeared to these shepherds, how near must they be to her!

Over and over the shepherds tell their story, with one or another breaking in every now and then to add some fresh detail about what happened on the hillside. And all the while they keep looking at the Babe, remarking on His beauty and loveliness. Then, as it dawns upon them ever more clearly that this is the Child of promise and prophecy, the long-looked-for Messiah, the Son of the living God, they kneel before Him in adoration.

By and by the shepherds leave. A new day is dawning—a new day for Bethlehem and for the world. People are waking up and getting breakfast. Some are already out of doors tending their animals. Imagine their amazement as they see the shepherds, whom they supposed to be out in the fields minding their sheep, "glorifying and praising God" in the main street of the village—stopping passers-by and telling them in excited voices of all the marvelous things they had seen and heard that night.

"You mean you saw angels? Angels here in Bethlehem?"

"Yes, indeed, a multitude of the heavenly host, praising God and saying——"

"Impossible!"

"But we did. And they said Messiah was born."

"Messiah born here last night! Oh, no. That couldn't be."

"Yes indeed. It's true! He's in the stable over there behind the inn."

THIS DAY A SAVIOUR

"And all they that heard it wondered at those things which were told them by the shepherds."

The whole town was stunned.

Some believed their story, and some did not. Some went to the stable to see the Child. Some didn't bother to go. They let the greatest event of the ages go right past them without a thought. They busied themselves with their daily chores— washing dishes, cleaning house, feeding animals, making money —while the very One they said they wanted so much was right in their midst. How careful we need to be lest we get so burdened with cares that we do not realize when Jesus is near!'

Of those who went to the stable that morning, some saw just another baby, and some saw God. It has been that way ever since. It is that way still. As you look at Him today, whom do *you* see?

Dangerous Days

~~~~~~~~~~~~~~~~~~~~~~~~

NEWS about the Baby in the stable, and the shepherds' story of the angels they had seen, gave Bethlehem something to talk about for a day or two; but with all the rush and bother and business connected with the taxing, most people soon forgot all about it.

So there were no bands playing and no procession when Mary took her little Son to the Temple in Jerusalem to present Him to the Lord. Nobody in the jostling crowd pointed to her and said, "There is the mother of the Messiah!" or "That Baby she is carrying in her arms is the Son of God." Nobody, that is, until they came into the Temple. Then it was that old Simeon, to whom the Holy Spirit had spoken, saying that "he should not see death, before he had seen the Lord's Christ," suddenly recognized the Child. What a thrill of happiness surged through his dear old heart!

"Then took he Him up in his arms, and blessed God, and said, Lord, now lettest Thou Thy servant depart in peace, ac-

309

As Mary looked upon this lovely Babe in her arms, and pondered the far-reaching prophecy of Simeon, she was full of grateful joy and hope that here at last was Israel's Deliverer.

cording to Thy word: for mine eyes have seen Thy salvation, which Thou hast prepared before the face of all people; a light to lighten the Gentiles, and the glory of Thy people Israel."

Anna came in at that moment, and, beaming with joy as she looked at the Baby, "gave thanks likewise unto the Lord."

The service over, Mary and Joseph returned quietly to Bethlehem, marveling at all that had happened that day and "at those things which were spoken of Him."

Much greater excitement came to Jerusalem with the arrival of the Wise Men from the East. As they rode in on their camels through the city gate, everybody recognized them at once as men of wealth and position. Their fine clothes and stately appearance told that they were not of the common people. But the greatest interest was aroused by the question which they kept asking, "Where is He that is born King of the Jews? for we have seen His star in the east, and are come to worship Him." Matthew 2:2.

This set everybody talking. Some who had mocked at the story told by the poor shepherds were thrilled as these rich

strangers from the East spoke of following a star to find the King of the Jews. Others asked, "How could the King of the Jews be just born? The only king we know is Herod."

Soon all Jerusalem was agitated. The subject was even discussed in Herod's palace. When the king heard of it he became worried. Had a child really been born who would one day take his place as king of Israel? He sent for the chief priests and "demanded of them where Christ should be born." As king of the Jews he should have known without asking, but he had been too busy or too careless to find out.

"In Bethlehem of Judaea," replied the priests, quoting the prophecy of Micah 5:2.

So! thought Herod. Then I must find out if a child has been born in Bethlehem who might possibly become king. If so, I shall know what to do with him.

But how to find out? Possibly these Wise Men from the East would know. He sent for them and listened to their story. Particularly was he interested in the star which they said they had seen. The Bible says he "enquired of them diligently what time the star appeared." No doubt this was to find out how old the child might be.

Then he sent the Wise Men on to Bethlehem, saying, "Go and search diligently for the young child; and when ye have found Him, bring me word again, that I may come and worship Him also."

The old rascal! He had no thought of worshiping Jesus. He was planning to kill Him. But it sounded well, and the Wise Men no doubt thought what a good, kind king he was.

As they left the city gates, lo, there in the sky they saw the star again. Why they had lost sight of it, nobody knows. But whatever the reason, the star was there now, ready to guide them again.

And "when they saw the star, they rejoiced with exceeding great joy." Now they would keep their eyes fixed on it, no matter where it should lead them.

It did not take them far. Only six miles. Then it stopped, seeming to hover over a house in the village. Through the dark streets they hurried toward it, and knocked on the door.

Imagine the astonishment on Joseph's face as he opened the door and saw the Wise Men standing there in their rich robes! How he must have wondered who they were and why they had come! A moment later they were looking eagerly toward Mary and the Child they had come so far to see.

The Bible says, "When they were come into the house, they saw the young child with Mary His mother, and fell down, and worshipped Him."

As they rose from their knees they took packages from the folds of their long cloaks and unwrapped them. Mary's eyes opened in astonishment.

Gold! Jewels! Priceless treasures! To poor people like herself and Joseph, it was a fortune. She did not realize then that God had sent all this wealth to provide for the long journey they would soon have to take into Egypt.

There was frankincense and myrrh too—rich offerings usually reserved for princes, kings, and gods. Mary understood. It fitted in with all that the angel had said to her, and the shepherds, and Simeon and Anna in the Temple.

Having presented their gifts, the Wise Men prepared to leave and return to Jerusalem. They were eager to tell the king of their good fortune in finding the Child they had sought so long. But that night God warned them in a dream that they should not return to Herod. At once they saw through the king's wicked plan, and "they departed into their own country another way." Matthew 2:12.

As a result of the visit of the Wise Men, Jesus was, of course, in great danger. In Jerusalem, Herod waited for them to return and report the result of their search. How long he waited we do not know, but it could not have been more than a few days at most. Then, when they did not come, and he was told that they had disappeared, he was furious. His pride was hurt. He thought he had deceived *them,* and now, lo, they had deceived *him!* Now he would never know for sure about that Child they were seeking. Did they find Him, or not? Had a king been born in Bethlehem?

If Herod had not been so angry, he could have found out easily enough. Surely somebody in Bethlehem must have known about the visit of the Wise Men and just which house they had visited. But rage always makes people blind and foolish.

So, partly in anger because his wicked plan had failed, and partly to make sure that no king would come out of Bethlehem if he could help it, he ordered his soldiers to go to the village and kill every child "from two years old and under." That, he thought, would settle the matter.

But it didn't. God knew his thoughts, and planned a rescue. Even as Herod was giving his cruel order to his soldiers, the angel of the Lord appeared to Joseph in a dream, saying, "Arise, and take the young child and His mother, and flee into Egypt, and be thou there until I bring thee word: for Herod will seek the young child to destroy Him."

Joseph now saw the peril they were all in. Of course, if Herod should hear that the Wise Men had offered Jesus frankincense and myrrh, he would be very jealous. Perhaps his soldiers were on their way at this very moment. They must leave at once.

Mary was awakened. Together they packed their few belongings, not forgetting, of course, the precious treasures which the Wise Men had brought. These they hid where no prying eyes would find them. Then Joseph saddled the donkey, put Mary and the Child upon it, and set off.

Just in time! Hardly were they a safe distance from the village than Herod's soldiers arrived to do their murderous work. Perhaps upon the ears of the Baby Jesus—one day to be the comforter and burden bearer of His people—fell the cries of the poor little baby boys who died that night in Bethlehem.

STORY 44

The Best Boy Who Ever Lived

I T WAS not so very far from Bethlehem into Egypt, not more than a hundred miles at the most. Today you could cover that distance by car in two hours. At the pace a donkey travels, however, it may well have taken Joseph and Mary four or five days. How glad they must have been when at last they crossed the border into Egypt and felt safe from Herod's soldiers!

Just where they lived in Egypt no one knows, nor how long they stayed there. Probably Jesus was between two and three years old before they heard that Herod was dead and that it was now safe for them to return to their homeland.

At the time they left Bethlehem, the angel had said, "Be thou there until I bring thee word." So they had waited patiently for God's leading. At last the angel came. Once more he appeared to Joseph in a dream, saying, "Arise, and take the young child and His mother, and go into the land of Israel: for they are dead which sought the young child's life."

What a happy day that was! In Egypt, with the money the Wise Men had given them, they had been able to live in comfort; but it was not home. They knew they were strangers and foreigners there. Now they could go back and see their friends and loved ones again. So one day they left Egypt and came once more into the land of Israel.

Their first thought was to return to Bethlehem; but they were afraid to do that, for Herod's son, Archelaus, cruel as his father, was ruling there. So they journeyed north toward Nazareth, the place they had left at the time of the taxing by Caesar Augustus.

Back at last in their old home town, they started life anew, and lived peacefully there for many years. As for Jesus, we are told that "the child grew, and waxed strong in spirit, filled with wisdom: and the grace of God was upon Him." Luke 2:40.

These words suggest that He was a very good boy. And He was—the best boy who ever lived. It is a pity that we do not know more about His early days; how He helped Mary in the home and Joseph in his workshop. It must have been wonderful to have such a boy about the place, so kind, so thoughtful, so loving, so considerate of others.

The words "strong in spirit" would suggest that He was no

sissy. He had a mind of His own. He had opinions and a will. Brave and fearless, He refused to go with the other boys of the village when they were up to mischief. He was always ready to stand alone for right, even though it meant being laughed at by His friends.

From His earliest days He studied the Bible with His mother. Of course, they had only the Old Testament then, but Jesus learned all its greatest passages by heart. He could recite many of the psalms of David, the prophecies of Isaiah, and, of course, the Ten Commandments.

Remembering what the angel Gabriel had said to her before her Baby was born, and all that had happened at Bethlehem at the time of His birth, Mary led Jesus to study especially the chapters that mention the Messiah. Soon He knew where to find them all. One day—we know not when—the Spirit of

319

God revealed to Him that they were all to be fulfilled by Him.

Every Friday evening the little family would kneel together to welcome the holy Sabbath. Every Saturday morning they would go to the synagogue for worship. It was their custom to do so (Luke 4:16). They never missed. The preacher could always be sure that Joseph, Mary, and that wonderful little Boy of theirs would be in their places in the house of God. What a privilege it must have been for the minister to preach to a Boy like that in church, so attentive and interested, always looking up with such keen, wide-open eyes!

Many times Joseph and Mary talked with Jesus about the yearly Passover services in Jerusalem. "Someday," they told Him, "when You are old enough, we will take You to see them."

Poor people, and poor people's children, did not get many treats those days, and a trip to Jerusalem must have seemed very wonderful to the son of a carpenter in Nazareth. No doubt

Jesus looked forward with great eagerness to the time when He would be twelve years of age and so could go to the big city.

At last, however, the longed-for day arrived, and the family set off on their journey. How interested Jesus must have been in everything and everybody—in the people who were thronging the roads to the holy city, in the things they talked about, in the animals on which they rode, but most of all in the great historical ceremony He was going to attend, and of which He had read so often in the books of Moses! All the way He asked questions about it. What would it be like? What did each part of the service mean?

The first sight of Jerusalem, with the Temple gleaming in the sunlight, must have brought a great thrill to His heart. Any boy of twelve would have been excited. Joyfully He entered the city gate and climbed the Temple steps. His sharp eyes took in everything—the priests offering a sacrifice, the dying

lamb, and the smoke of the altar fire spiraling up to heaven.

Mary had told Him much about all these things before, but now, as He saw them for Himself, they made a deep impression upon Him. If they pointed forward to the Messiah, then would Messiah have to die, Himself a sacrifice? Thus the mystery of His own mission gradually opened before Him.

There was a school attached to the Temple, and Jesus went in to see it. Here it was that He began asking questions of the priests, and they, amazed at His knowledge of the Scriptures, began asking questions of Him. So interested did they become that they did not want the Boy to leave.

Hours slipped by, and meanwhile the people who had attended the Passover began to leave. Joseph and Mary went with them. Having learned to have perfect trust in their Son, and knowing that He would never do anything wrong, they went on their way without a worry, even though He was not with them. Jesus was always so trustworthy, so reliable. They supposed He was with friends and would catch up with them in a little while. But when several hours had passed and He did not appear, they began to fear that some harm might have come to Him. So they started back to the city, asking everyone they met, "Have you seen Jesus? Our little Boy, you know. He's just twelve. Can you tell us where He is?"

Some said they had seen Him during the Passover, but nobody knew where He was now. So Joseph and Mary went all the way back to Jerusalem, getting more and more anxious every minute.

Now where to go? In her heart Mary knew there was only

323

← PAINTING BY WILLIAM HUTCHINSON   © BY REVIEW AND HERALD

After the Passover services had come to an end Jesus slipped away from His parents and went to the Temple to reason with the rabbis. They marveled at His knowledge of the Scriptures.

one place Jesus was likely to be. And it wasn't some place of amusement. It was the Temple.

So they made for the Temple.

"Is our Jesus here?" they asked.

Yes, He was there all right. Not just playing, as other boys of His age might have been, but "sitting in the midst of the doctors, both hearing them, and asking them questions." And the doctors seemed to be enjoying themselves most of all, for "all that heard Him were astonished at His understanding and answers." Never had they met a boy who knew the Scriptures so well and who understood their meaning so perfectly. And His questions! The wisest men there found them very hard to answer.

As Mary looked in on the scene she was amazed, as well she might have been. But she was so glad to find her Son that she forgot all about the learned doctors and ran right over to Him with outstretched arms.

"Son, why hast Thou thus dealt with us?" she said to Him in tender rebuke. "Behold, Thy father and I have sought Thee sorrowing."

Jesus was equally surprised to see His mother, and perhaps just a little sorry that this wonderful meeting with the
doctors should have to come to an end.

"How is it that ye sought Me?" He asked. "Wist ye not
that I must be about My Father's business?"

"My Father's business." That was a strange thing for a boy
to say.

The doctors heard Him say it, and wondered what He
meant. How could this man Joseph, they thought, a mere
carpenter of Nazareth, have any business in the Temple? But
Mary knew what He meant. Jesus was not thinking of Joseph.
He was thinking of God. He believed that in learning more of
the Scriptures, and storing up their wonderful truths in His
mind, He was doing God's business, preparing Himself for what
God would call Him to do when He was grown up.

This is still God's business today, for you and for me.
Some people think that to spend time studying the Bible or
going to church to hear someone preach the Word of God is
wasting time. It isn't. It is the most important thing we can do.
It is our Father's business, and in doing it we are helping to
make ourselves strong and wise for the tasks that God will call
us to do for Him in days to come.

Amid the friendly farewells of the doctors, Jesus left the
Temple with Mary and Joseph. Then together they made their
way back to Nazareth, where for many years more He lived
with them and "was subject unto them." That is, He honored
them and obeyed them, as all children should honor and obey
their parents today.

He worked with Joseph in the carpenter's shop, and learned what it meant to labor long and hard. He learned a trade, too, which is a good thing for every boy and girl to do. He learned how to make tables and chairs and windows and other useful things. And He learned to make them well. No shoddy work for Him. Every job He turned out was the best He could do. When people came to buy something at the carpenter's shop, they may well have asked first if Jesus had made it. If so, they knew the workmanship would be faultless.

What a pity we do not have just one thing He made in that carpenter's shop! What an example it would be for all the boys of the world today! How square the saw cuts! How perfect the mitering! How smooth the edges! How invisible the joints!

By doing this perfect work in the carpenter's shop Jesus was preparing Himself for His future ministry just as much as when He was studying with the doctors in the Temple in Jerusalem. He could not afford to leave a poor record anywhere. He had to be faithful and true in everything, that He might be the perfect example for every boy and girl in the world. He is still our example now. Let us keep our eyes on Him.

Called to Service

≈≈≈≈≈≈≈≈≈

SLOWLY the happy, carefree years in Nazareth passed away—the years of daily duties in the old home, of labor in the carpenter's shop, of Bible study and prayer with Mary and Joseph. Now the years of larger service were at hand.

One day news came to Jesus at Nazareth that His cousin John had begun to preach with great power down by the Jordan River. Thousands of people were flocking to hear him.

"He preaches like one of the ancient prophets," says one excited messenger. "He says he is 'the voice of one crying in the wilderness, Prepare ye the way of the Lord.' Some people are wondering whether he might be the promised Messiah, but he says, No, but He will appear soon. 'I indeed baptize you with water,' John says; 'but one mightier than I cometh, the latchet of whose shoes I am not worthy to unloose: He shall baptize you with the Holy Ghost and with fire.'"

"He's a powerful preacher and no doubt about it," reports another. "He's afraid of nobody. You should have heard him talk to the Pharisees and Sadducees when they came to hear him. 'O generation of vipers,' he said to them, 'who hath warned you to flee from the wrath to come? Bring forth therefore fruits meet for repentance: and think not to say within yourselves, We have Abraham to our father: for I say unto you, that God is able of these stones to raise up children unto Abraham.' What a sermon was that! Israel has heard nothing like it since the days of Elijah."

Jesus was deeply moved by the reports that reached Him about His cousin, and at last He decided to go down to the Jordan and hear John Himself. In His heart He felt sure that the way John was stirring up the people and calling the whole nation to prepare for the appearance of the Messiah was all part of God's plan and a clear sign that His own great mission must soon begin.

Bidding farewell to His mother, to the old carpenter shop, and to everything around that was so familiar and dear to Him, He strode down the hill to the Jordan—and the new life He now must lead.

It was not hard to find the way to the place where John was preaching, for it seemed as though all the inhabitants of Jerusalem and Judea had left their homes and were headed in the same direction.

Jesus mingled with the crowd. Then, when John called for men and women to turn again to God and show their repentance by being baptized in the Jordan, Jesus went forward with the rest and humbly waited His turn. Scores of people were baptized. It must have been a wonderful sight. Presently

John came to where Jesus was standing. For a moment he did not know what to do. He knew that Jesus was the One about whom he was preaching—the Messiah for whom all were waiting. So he said, "I have need to be baptized of Thee, and comest Thou to me?"

Humbly Jesus answered, "Suffer it to be so now: for thus it becometh us to fulfil all righteousness."

If it was right for the people to be baptized, then Jesus wanted to be baptized too. Thus He would be an example for all who should afterward believe in Him. So John gently lowered Him into the waters of the Jordan and lifted Him up again. Then Jesus "went up straightway out of the water: and, lo, the heavens were opened unto Him, and He saw the Spirit of God descending like a dove, and lighting upon Him: and lo a voice from heaven, saying, This is My beloved Son, in whom I am well pleased." Matthew 3:16, 17.

What a moment was that! It marked the end of all the years of training and preparation that Jesus had had in Nazareth. He had been a dutiful son of His father and mother. He had been an example of kindness and purity to His brothers. He had mingled with His townsmen as a common carpenter, doing His work with efficiency and faithfulness. He was now to begin the great work for which God had sent Him into the world. Now He was indeed the Messiah, the Anointed One —anointed by the Holy Spirit and approved by His Father.

Was Jesus happy when He heard God say, "This is My beloved Son, in whom I am well pleased"? I think He must have been very, very happy for this evidence of God's approval.

330

How much these sweet words tell us of the character of Jesus! What a good boy He must have been! What a noble, straightforward youth! Day by day, week by week, month by month, year by year, God had been watching His growth and development. Angels had hovered near Him from Bethlehem to Nazareth, and now to Jordan. Never had they seen one failure, never a deed or a word of which they had felt ashamed. Never had Jesus disappointed them. He "was in all points tempted like as we are, yet without sin."

Now as God looked back upon the boyhood of Jesus, upon His youth and early manhood, He was justly proud of Him.

331

Gladly He recognized Him as His own. The very words "This is My beloved Son" suggest that He wanted everybody to know how very satisfied He was.

"In whom I am well pleased." What a beautiful commendation! Would you like your father to say this about you? I know you would. But *could* he say it? Could your mother? Could God?

God wants us all to live so like Jesus that He may be able to use these very words about us. Yes, about you and me. Let us ask Him now to help us to be so good and kind and true and faithful that someday we too may hear Him say, "This is My beloved son—My beloved daughter—in whom I am well pleased."

STORY 46

Victory Over Temptation

HAVE you noticed how often, right after you have had some very happy experience, everything seems to go wrong? Just when the sun is shining its brightest, a cloud comes up and covers it. Just when you have made up your mind to be very, very good, the devil seems to try especially hard to make you do wrong. Isn't that true?

That's how life is. And that is exactly what happened to Jesus. Down by the Jordan He had had the most wonderful experience of His life. He had seen heaven open and the Holy Spirit descend upon Him in the form of a dove. He had heard the voice of God saying to Him, "This is My beloved Son, in whom I am well pleased." His heart had thrilled with holy joy. Everything had seemed to be going so well. Then, all of a sudden, the scene changed. The sun went behind the clouds. "Then was Jesus led up of the Spirit into the wilderness to be tempted of the devil." Matthew 4:1.

That must have been a very lonely journey. The great

333

Bidding His mother farewell, Jesus went out from His quiet home at Nazareth to three and a half years of ministry, preaching to the poor, teaching the people, and healing the sick.

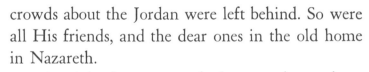

crowds about the Jordan were left behind. So were all His friends, and the dear ones in the old home in Nazareth.

At night there was no bed except the sand, no shelter save a rock, and no food. How often must He have thought of the meals His mother Mary had prepared for Him! But there was no Mary here. Only He—and God. And here He prayed, hour by hour and day by day. The Holy Spirit had warned Him that temptation was coming, so He prepared for it by talking with His heavenly Father, thinking of the Scriptures He had learned so well, and praying for strength and victory in the trying days which were to follow.

What thoughts must have come to Him in the dark, lonely evenings under the silent stars! What memories of all that Mary had told Him of His birth, of His visit with the doctors in the Temple, of the prophecies He believed He was to fulfill.

It is a wonderful thing to know in your heart that God has accepted you as His child and wants you to do something very special for Him. It gives you a lovely feeling inside, doesn't it? When Somebody has a plan for your life, you need not worry.

Perhaps you have had thoughts like these already. If not, you will someday, if you love God and truly want to do His will.

As the days passed and Jesus became hungrier and hungrier, He grew weaker and weaker. How He lived without food for forty days and forty nights, we cannot tell. It is hard enough for us to go without food for one day, let alone forty. Fancy hav-

VICTORY OVER TEMPTATION

ing no breakfast, no lunch, no supper, for nearly six long weeks!

Each day He waited for the great temptation to come. Each day He sought to make Himself more ready to meet it when it should come. Then at last it came. And the devil struck where He was weakest. Said the tempter, "If Thou be the Son of God, command that these stones be made bread." Matthew 4:3.

It appeared so innocent, as temptations often do. Jesus was hungry—terribly hungry. I imagine He had looked at the stones that covered so much of this wilderness and wished He could eat them. Now the thought came, "Why not?" What wrong would there be in making just one stone into bread? Surely it would be better than dying of hunger. Surely, too, if He were indeed the Son of God, He would have but to speak the word and it would happen.

But no; Jesus would not do it. He saw the danger in that ugly *if*. Should He work this miracle, it would mean He had a doubt in His own mind about His relation to God. And how could He doubt the words that God had spoken: "This is My beloved Son"?

Jesus recognized, too, that, should He yield to this temptation, He would spoil the whole purpose for which He had come into the world. If He used His power to turn stones into bread, then people would come to Him, not for the spiritual help He could give them, but for material things, like food and clothes and houses and money. It would be easy to gather a great following this way; but it would not be God's way. Thus, this seemingly simple temptation was designed by the devil to wreck the whole plan of salvation.

Jesus saw through it and, desperately hungry though He was, refused, saying to the tempter, "It is written, Man shall not live by bread alone, but by every word that proceedeth out of the mouth of God."

His long study of the Scriptures helped Him to find the right text with which to answer the devil. And so it was when the second temptation came.

Now the devil led Him to Jerusalem, and they stood together on a high part of the Temple, perhaps where the wall was built on the very edge of a precipice. Then the devil said, quoting Scripture himself this time, to make this temptation seem more innocent than the first: "If Thou be the Son of God, cast Thyself down: for it is written, He shall give His angels charge concerning thee: and in their hands they shall bear thee up, lest at any time thou dash thy foot against a stone."

What was wrong with the devil's suggestion? Had not God promised that the angels would look after Him? Then why not put His promise to the test? If He were indeed the Son of God, surely God would save Him if He jumped off the wall.

336

Jesus refused to do it, saying, "It is written again, Thou shalt not tempt the Lord thy God." In other words, we are not to expect God to use His power to protect us when we take un necessary risks or embark on foolhardy enterprises. When we go where He sends us, we can always count on His promise to send His angels to take care of us; but we are not to expect divine help when we do something utterly foolish, like jumping off a church steeple.

With His clear mind Jesus saw a yet deadlier peril in this temptation. Like the first, this too was designed to ruin His mission. He saw that if He jumped and was miraculously saved from death, people would flock to Him as to a magician. They would point to Him as "the man who jumped from the Temple wall." He wanted no such cheap advertisement. He had come to save people by love, not by acrobatics and circus stunts. The devil's suggestion was opposed to every principle of His kingdom.

Defeated again, the devil tried a new approach. He led Jesus to a mountaintop—of which there are many in Palestine —where they could see for a great distance. There he showed

22

Him "all the kingdoms of the world, and the glory of them; and saith unto Him, All these things will I give Thee, if Thou wilt fall down and worship me."

The devil knew that Jesus was interested in setting up a kingdom; that He was planning to do it the hard way, by sacrifice and suffering, by persuasion and love; so he offered Him a kingdom the easy way. It was as though he said to Jesus, "I know You want to set up a kingdom, but it is going to cost You a lot. You don't need to pay the price. You don't need to pay anything. Here are all the kingdoms of the world, free for the asking. Just bow to me, and they will all be Yours—all the power and the glory a man could want. No suffering, no opposition, no crucifixion."

It was the easy way, but it was not God's way. Nor was Jesus interested in setting up a kingdom like those of the world, full of vice and wickedness. His plan was far different. He sought a kingdom of converted people, in which the inhabitants would be all righteous. As for falling down before Satan for any glory he could give, Jesus rejected it. "Get thee hence, Satan," He said sternly: "for it is written, Thou shalt worship the Lord thy God, and Him only shalt thou serve." Verse 10.

In that great crisis of His life, what a blessing was His knowledge of the Scriptures! The right words came to His mind just when they were needed. Even so will our study of the Bible help us meet the devil's temptations today. However deceitful the temptations may be, the words of God will be our wisdom and strength. They will help us to make right decisions and give right answers.

It is possible that we may even have to meet the same temptations Jesus did. He was tempted first through His appetite, then through His pride, and finally through His ambition. We may be attacked from the same three quarters. But we do not need to fail. We can resist the devil and win the battle against him every time if we know the Bible and walk with God as Jesus did.

When the devil saw that he could make no headway at all with Jesus—when he saw that though Jesus was weak and starving He could not be moved in the least from His loyalty to God, he went away. So will he leave us when he sees that we are determined at all costs to be true to God.

Then, the Bible says, "Behold, angels came and ministered unto Him." They had been watching the struggle with bated breath. Would Jesus stand against "the wiles of the devil"? Would He win this great battle with the prince of darkness?

As the devil slunk away defeated and Jesus' victory was no longer in doubt, they pressed close and in ways unknown to us brought Him food and comfort.

Now we see Him coming back from the wilderness. There is a new light in His eye, a new confidence in His step and in His bearing. He has won the fight with His archenemy. He has proved that the worst temptations can be met and conquered. Tested, tried, and triumphant, He strides victoriously toward the Jordan, back to the cities and villages of Israel, to begin the great work He came to the world to do.

STORY 47

Good Deeds Every Day

≈≈≈≈≈≈≈≈≈≈≈≈≈≈≈≈≈≈≈≈≈≈≈≈≈≈≈≈≈≈≈≈

SOON after Jesus returned from the wilderness, bad news reached Him. His cousin John, who had been doing such a wonderful work for God by the Jordan, had been arrested by Herod's soldiers and cast into prison. John had rebuked the king for his wicked deeds, and this was the result.

Such news was enough to make most men stop and ask whether it was wise to preach at such a time. But nothing could stop Jesus now. The Bible says that He "returned in the power of the Spirit into Galilee: and there went out a fame of Him through all the region round about. And He taught in their synagogues, being glorified of all." Luke 4:14, 15.

What sermons were those! How I wish I could have listened to just one of them! Just to hear His melodious voice, to see His flashing eyes, to note the certainty with which He turned from text to text and made plain the great prophecies about the Messiah and the kingdom of God. How the people's hearts must have thrilled as they listened to Him! How they

341

must have wondered at His amazing knowledge and power!

What did He preach about? Mark tells us. "Jesus came into Galilee," he says, "preaching the gospel of the kingdom of God, and saying, The time is fulfilled, and the kingdom of God is at hand: repent ye, and believe the gospel." Mark 1:14, 15.

When He said, "The time is fulfilled," He was, of course, referring to the time prophecy in the ninth chapter of the book of Daniel, which told when Messiah was to come—the same prophecy so many people had been talking about at the time the star appeared and the Wise Men came from the East. It was the one that Simeon and Anna knew so well, and that the priests and rabbis had argued about so long. "Now," Jesus said with great certainty, "it is fulfilled. Messiah has come at the time appointed." And He preached so well and with such authority, that a great many believed Him.

But He did not spend all His time preaching. Once, coming to a village called Cana, He was invited to a wedding. His mother was there, and how pleased He must have been to see her again! While she busied herself with the refreshments, He talked with the guests. Presently she came to Him and said, "They have no wine." Just like any other mother, she thought her big Son should be able to help her out. Certainly she expected Him to, for she turned to the servants and said, "Whatsoever He saith unto you, do it."

Jesus did not fail her. Noticing six large stone waterpots standing in the yard, He said to the servants, "Fill the waterpots with water. And they filled them up to the brim."

As soon as the last waterpot was full He said,

342

"Draw out now, and bear unto the governor of the feast."

They might well have replied, "What, take the governor water to drink?" But they did not. They did what Jesus said, and lo, as the water came out of the waterpots it was the color of wine! They carried it to the governor, wondering what he would say when he tasted it. But it tasted so good that the governor called the bridegroom and exclaimed on its high quality. "Most people bring out the good wine first," he said, "but you have kept it till the last!" No doubt the bridegroom smiled and nodded, wondering what the man meant. But he soon found out, for the servants couldn't keep such a story to themselves. Soon everybody was talking about it. "It's a miracle!" they said. And it was.

"This beginning of miracles did Jesus in Cana of Galilee, and manifested forth His glory; and His disciples believed on Him." John 2:11.

From now on Jesus revealed His power in many wonderful ways, healing the sick, casting out devils, opening the eyes of the blind. Today all Boy Scouts and Girl Guides have as their motto, "A Good Deed Every Day," but Jesus was not content with one good deed a day; He tried to bring joy and comfort to others all the time.

One day while He was preaching in the synagogue in Capernaum, a poor man cried out and made a great disturbance. Jesus saw that he was possessed with an evil spirit, and said in a tone of command, "Hold thy peace, and come out of him!"

GOOD DEEDS EVERY DAY

Everybody turned toward the poor crazy man to see what would happen. "And when the unclean spirit had torn him, and cried with a loud voice, he came out of him."

Then there was a great silence and the astonished people whispered to one another, "What thing is this? What new doctrine is this? for with authority He commandeth the unclean spirits, and they come out."

Like the miracle of the wine, the story of the healing of the man with the evil spirit—right in church too—made a great sensation. "Immediately His fame spread abroad throughout all the region round about Galilee." Mark 1:28.

Visiting in Peter's home, Jesus found a sick woman lying there. Peter's mother-in-law was in bed with a fever, so He came to her, "and took her by the hand, and lifted her up; and immediately the fever left her."

News of this new miracle spread quickly, and soon the whole town was stirred. The people were sure now that a great healer was among them, and everybody with an ache or pain of any sort set out for Peter's house. What a sight it must have been—all those poor sick people waiting for help! Some were groaning in pain, some crying out in agony, some shrieking in madness.

Perhaps Jesus planned it this way so that Peter would catch a glimpse of the great need of the world about him. Anyway, "at even, when the sun did set, they brought unto Him all that were diseased, and them that were possessed with devils. And all the city was gathered together at the door."

What would Jesus do? Everybody waited to see. He had healed one person in the synagogue and an elderly woman in Peter's house, but could He heal all these? There were so many. And some of them had such terrible sicknesses. As for the maniacs, what could He do for them?

While all looked on in amazement, Jesus began His work of healing. Gradually the groaning ceased, the cries of agony were stilled, the shouts of the devil-possessed were silenced. Soon a hush came over the whole crowd. Never had Capernaum seen anything like this.

As those who had been healed hurried back to their homes and told the wonderful story of what had happened to them, the excitement must have been intense. Other sick people, who had refused to go to Jesus because they felt timid or afraid, wished they had gone with the others. They wanted to go *now,* and made up their minds to find Him.

346

GOOD DEEDS EVERY DAY

News of these miracles of healing was carried to the next town, and the next, and the next. It spread over the whole countryside until everybody wanted to see the great new Teacher.

"And Jesus went about all Galilee, teaching in their synagogues, and preaching the gospel of the kingdom, and healing all manner of sickness and all manner of disease among the people.

"And His fame went throughout all Syria: and they brought unto Him all sick people that were taken with divers diseases and torments, and those which were possessed with devils, and those which were lunatick, and those that had the palsy; and He healed them." Matthew 4:23, 24.

I can imagine some children talking about Him, maybe in a little back street in Jerusalem.

"If only we could take

mother to see this kind Man, perhaps she would get well again. Perhaps He could do something for her eyes, so she could see properly. And dad, poor old dad, with his backache and that sore on his leg, perhaps he could be cured too. Somehow we must take them both to the great Healer."

In thousands of homes children and parents and older people were talking like this about the Miracle Worker and His marvelous power, all wondering how they could find Jesus, then sitting out along the roadside with their sick folk hoping to meet Him.

"And there followed Him great multitudes of people from Galilee, and from Decapolis, and from Jerusalem, and from Judaea, and from beyond Jordan."

The Bible does not begin to tell in detail about all the people who were healed. If it did, it would be such a big Book that nobody could pick it up to read it. Instead, it describes some special cases, like the story of the leper who called out to Jesus, "Lord, if Thou wilt, Thou canst make me clean." People were afraid of lepers, because the disease is so terrible. They wouldn't go near them, let alone touch them. But "Jesus put forth His hand, and touched him, saying, I will; be thou clean. And immediately his leprosy was cleansed."

There was the Roman officer, a centurion, who came to Jesus not for himself but for his servant. "My servant lieth at home sick of the palsy, grievously tormented," he said.

"I will come and heal him," said Jesus.

Then the soldier, in words that deeply moved the Master, said, "Lord, I am not worthy that Thou shouldest come under

349

The fame of Jesus as a great healer went through all Judea and Syria. As parents led their sick children to Him, He was never too busy to turn aside to heal and bless them.

my roof: but speak the word only, and my servant shall be healed."

Such faith and humility, coming from a Roman centurion, was most unusual. Jesus marveled at it, saying to those about Him, "I have not found so great faith, no, not in Israel." Then to the centurion He said, "Go thy way; and as thou hast believed, so be it done unto thee. And his servant was healed in the selfsame hour."

Then there was the woman who had been sick for many years, and who had spent every penny she had on doctors' bills. Hoping she wouldn't be seen, she pressed through the crowd and managed to touch only the hem of His garment, but was healed immediately.

There was the poor widow of Nain, walking tearfully beside the coffin of her only son. When the Lord saw her, "He had compassion on her, and said unto her, Weep not." His tender heart could not bear the sight of this poor, heartbroken woman. Then He spoke to the dead boy. "Young man, I say unto thee, Arise. And he that was dead sat up, and began to speak. And He delivered him to his mother."

No wonder "there came a fear on all: and they glorified God, saying, That a great prophet is risen up among us; and, That God hath visited His people." Luke 7:11-16.

Then there was the rich nobleman whose son was healed, and blind Bartimaeus, whose eyes were opened, and the man with the palsy who was let down through a roof on a bed and went away walking. There was the man with the withered hand whom Jesus healed on the Sabbath day, and Jairus'

350

twelve-year-old daughter, whom He awakened from the sleep of death.

So many stories! Beautiful stories. The Gospels are full of them. You must read them all for yourself. And as you read you will come to see what a wonderful person Jesus was. Your heart will be touched with His thoughtfulness, His kindness, His willingness to help anybody and everybody in need. You will come to love Him more and more for His sweet, gentle nature. And you will say to yourself at last, "Surely this must be the Christ, the Son of the living God. I will love Him and serve Him all my life."

A New Way to Live

AS JESUS saw all the poor sick people coming to Him—many of them diseased, crippled, lame, and deformed—He was very, very sorry for them. He had compassion on them, the Bible says, not only because they were sick, but because they did not have anyone to help them. They were as sheep without a shepherd. They had lost their way—the way which God had shown to Adam and Eve in the Garden. And in losing it they had lost health and happiness and peace of mind and everything that makes life worth living.

So while He healed their bodies He tried also to heal their minds. Without this He knew they would soon return to their old ways and be as sick as they were before. Their minds and hearts must be changed if any lasting good were to be done for them. But could He do it? And how could He convince them it needed to be done?

One night while Jesus was alone in a quiet place where He loved to go and pray, He heard footsteps approaching in

the darkness. Looking up, whom should He see but one of the most important men in Jerusalem. It was Nicodemus, a ruler of the Jews. Why had he come? Because he had heard much about Jesus and wondered whether He might indeed be the Messiah, come to set up the kingdom of God. He wanted to find out.

Respectfully he began, "Rabbi, we know that Thou art a teacher come from God: for no man can do these miracles that Thou doest, except God be with him."

Knowing the thoughts that were running through his mind, Jesus said to him, "Except a man be born again, he cannot see the kingdom of God."

This was a shock to Nicodemus. Like most people of his day, he thought that Israel could have the kingdom of God without a change of heart. But Jesus knew this could not be.

Nicodemus tried to argue, foolishly, that it was impossible for anyone to be born twice. But Jesus was firm. It was the only way to the kingdom He said. Unless a man is reborn, or "born again," he cannot "enter into the kingdom of God."

23

Then He told Nicodemus about God's plan to save men from sin and all its evil results, and how He wanted to help them find a better way of living so that they might enter His kingdom and live with Him forever. In the most beautiful words ever uttered Jesus said: "God so loved the world, that He gave His only begotten Son, that whosoever believeth in Him should not perish, but have everlasting life. For God sent not His Son into the world to condemn the world; but that the world through Him might be saved." John 3:16, 17.

Nicodemus listened, deeply moved. He had never thought of God like this. He had never imagined God could love man

so much. Though he may not have realized it at the moment, his own heart was being changed while Jesus spoke to him. He was being "born again" even while he sat there in the dark.

It was just such a change as this that Jesus longed to work in the minds and hearts of all the people. He knew that without it they would never be happy, nor would they ever see the kingdom of God for which they longed. So He preached about it and talked about it, and tried the best He could to help everybody see His new and better way to live.

One day, "seeing the multitudes, He went up into a mountain: and when He was set, His disciples came unto Him: and He opened His mouth, and taught them, saying,

"Blessed are the poor in spirit: for their's is the kingdom of heaven.

"Blessed are they that mourn: for they shall be comforted.

"Blessed are the meek: for they shall inherit the earth.

"Blessed are they which do hunger and thirst after righteousness: for they shall be filled.

"Blessed are the merciful: for they shall obtain mercy.

"Blessed are the pure in heart: for they shall see God.

"Blessed are the peacemakers: for they shall be called the children of God.

"Blessed are they which are persecuted for righteousness' sake: for their's is the kingdom of heaven.

"Blessed are ye, when men shall revile you, and perse-

A NEW WAY TO LIVE

cute you, and shall say all manner of evil against you falsely, for My sake. Rejoice, and be exceeding glad: for great is your reward in heaven: for so persecuted they the prophets which were before you." Matthew 5:1-12.

These nine teachings of Jesus are known as the Beatitudes, because they tell how people can be made happy. They might be called His "Rules for Happiness."

Many of those who heard Him say these things didn't understand them. They had always thought it was the rich and powerful—kings, priests, army officers, and the like—who were most fortunate in this life; that the people with the big names and the loud voices would get all the "plums" in God's kingdom. "No," said Jesus. "That is all wrong. It is the 'poor in spirit'—the humble, kindly folk—for whom the kingdom of God is reserved. The meek, not the proud, shall inherit the earth.

"Those who would enter God's kingdom must be pure in heart; they must be merciful; they must be peacemakers; they must hunger and thirst after righteousness. Otherwise they will not see the kingdom."

Thus Jesus tried again and again to help the people see that the way to the kingdom, to a better, happier life, is by a change of heart. The way they had been living was not good enough. It had brought them only sorrow and suffering. They must find a new way—His new way.

"Ye have heard," said Jesus, "that it hath been said, An

eye for an eye, and a tooth for a tooth: but I say unto you, That ye resist not evil: but whosoever shall smite thee on thy right cheek, turn to him the other also."

Again: "Ye have heard that it hath been said, Thou shalt love thy neighbour, and hate thine enemy. But I say unto you, Love your enemies, bless them that curse you, do good to them that hate you, and pray for them which despitefully use you, and persecute you; that ye may be the children of your Father which is in heaven."

This was His way, and it was the way to a new life, the way to the kingdom of God. It was the way of love, kindness, and forgiveness.

It is still His way today. If we want to be His children, we must follow it. We shall never see His kingdom or be truly happy unless we do.

But how? Jesus could not have made it plainer. "Except a man be born again, he cannot see the kingdom of God." And that goes for boys and girls too. The same wonderful change must happen in all our hearts.

Has it happened in yours?

"How can I know?" you say.

Jesus made that clear. To Nicodemus, who wondered about the same question, Jesus said, "The wind bloweth where it listeth, and thou hearest the sound thereof, but canst not tell whence it cometh, and whither it goeth: so is every one that is born of the Spirit." John 3:8.

Can you see the wind? Of course not. But you know when it is blowing. How? By what the wind does. When you

358

see a windmill turning, trees bending, or papers flying about the school playground, you know that the wind is blowing.

So it is with the Spirit of God. Nobody can see Him, yet everybody knows when He is at work. When a boy or a girl who has been grumpy and bossy and rude and quarrelsome suddenly becomes pleasant and humble and polite and peace loving, it is clear that something has happened. The Holy Spirit has come into his heart. Like a rushing mighty wind, He has swept out all that is ugly, unclean, and ungodlike, and in its place has brought all the noble and beautiful qualities that God loves.

Have you been born again? Has this change been seen in you? If not, why not ask Jesus now to send His Holy Spirit into your heart? Only so can you be His child. Only so can you enter His kingdom. Only so can you be truly happy, here and hereafter.

The Children's Friend

BUSY as He was with all His preaching, teaching, and healing, Jesus still found time to be kind to children. He loved them, and they knew it. Children always know who loves them, don't they?

Whenever a crowd of people gathered to listen to Jesus and watch His miracles of healing, there were children about. There were the very little ones in their mothers' arms, looking at Him with great big eyes. There were the toddlers, peering shyly from behind trees or from between big people's legs. There were the boys and girls of primary age, standing quietly and obediently as their parents told them to be good. There were the junior boys and girls, listening now and then, but too full of life and energy to stand still very long. All of them, from the youngest to the oldest, loved to be where Jesus was. His kind smile and gentle words were like a magnet to them.

THE CHILDREN'S FRIEND

Sometimes grownups thought He gave too much of His time to children. Once, when some mothers came to Him asking that He would put His hands on their children and bless them, His disciples told them to go away and not bother the Master. They thought that He would be glad they had saved Him so much trouble, but they were mistaken. Jesus was not pleased.

He knew how those children had looked forward to meeting Him. He knew, too, how much time their mothers had spent washing their faces, fixing their clothes, tidying their hair. And He was not going to disappoint them.

"Suffer little children," He said, "and forbid them not, to come unto Me: for of such is the kingdom of heaven." Matthew 19:14.

"Let the children alone, do not stop them from coming to Me," is the way another translation reads. I would love to have heard Jesus say that. "Don't stop the children from coming to Me." It was such a nice, kind thing for Him to say.

And just as He said it then, so He says it still today. "Don't stop the children from coming to Me." He wants all boys and girls to come to Him. He never turns one away.

Now think for a moment of His words: "For of such is the kingdom of heaven." What did He mean? I can think of some children who are so naughty and rude and disobedient that they would turn heaven into a madhouse if they were ever to get there. Others I know are so destructive that they would tear the New Jerusalem to pieces in no time if Jesus were to let them in. No, He was not thinking of children such as these. He was thinking of sweet, innocent, unspoiled children; of children who love their parents and are eager to obey them. The kingdom of heaven will be made up of people like these.

One day, when the disciples of Jesus were arguing among

themselves as to who should be the greatest in the kingdom of heaven, "Jesus called a little child unto Him, and set him in the midst of them, and said, Verily I say unto you, Except ye be converted, and become as little children, ye shall not enter into the kingdom of heaven." Matthew 18:2, 3.

Many people—yes, and many children too—are forever striving to be the greatest, to get the biggest and the best of everything for themselves. This is not good, says Jesus. Those who do so will never see His kingdom. They would spoil it for everybody else. "I'll tell you who will be the greatest in My kingdom," He said. "Whosoever therefore shall humble himself as this little child, the same is greatest in the kingdom of heaven." That is hard for some to understand, but it's the truth just the same. We must be humble and kind and unselfish if we would be great in the sight of God.

The Bible does not say so, but I like to think that at this moment the little child which Jesus was gently holding in His arms looked up into His face and smiled. Why? Because of what Jesus said next: "Whoso shall receive one such little child in My name receiveth Me. But whoso shall offend one of these little ones which believe in Me, it were better for him that a millstone were hanged about his neck, and that he were drowned in the depth of the sea."

Jesus loved that little child. That is easy to see. His words were just like those of a big brother, weren't they? If anybody hurts my little brother, or my little sister, he had better look out! Just so Jesus cares for boys and girls who believe in Him.

That the children returned the love which Jesus showed to them is very clear. Remember the story of the little boy's lunch? I think it is one of the loveliest in all the Bible.

Jesus had gone up into a mountain with His disciples, and the people, always eager to be with Him, "because they saw His miracles which He did for them that were diseased," had followed Him there. In little groups and big groups they had flowed out from the cities and villages until they covered the mountainside. Presently, as Jesus turned from talking with His disciples, He "lifted up His eyes, and saw a great company come unto Him." John 6:5. There were at least five thousand, besides women and children. It was evening and the people were tired and hungry.

The worried disciples cried, "Send them away."

"They need not depart," said Jesus. "Give ye them to eat." Matthew 14:16.

What? Feed this great multitude? Impossible! Philip spoke up and said, "Two hundred pennyworth of bread is not sufficient for them, that every one of them may take a little."

Today, if you were suddenly asked to feed five thousand

364

people, you would probably say, "Five hundred dollars would not be sufficient." Two hundred pence in those days was as hard to get as five hundred dollars now, and Philip was scared at the thought of spending all that money for just one meal.

Only Jesus was not disturbed. "He . . . knew what He would do." Meanwhile the disciples had been looking around to see if they could find any food. Perhaps some of the people had brought a quantity that could be shared. Presently Andrew called out, "There is a lad here, which hath five barley loaves, and two small fishes: but what are they among so many?"

What indeed! It was only a little boy's lunch, and how could that help in feeding five thousand people?

I like to think that this lad had set out this day especially to see Jesus. His mother had packed this lunch for him so he wouldn't be hungry. Like any other boy, he had looked forward eagerly to eating it; but as he stood near the front row of people he had heard Jesus say that He wanted food. Then he had seen the worried look on the faces of the disciples, and had

heard them asking one another what to do. Sidling up to Andrew, he had nudged him until he got his attention. Then I like to think he said, "You may have my lunch, sir, if it would help. I shall be glad for Jesus to have it."

As the boy came face to face with Jesus, and placed his precious lunch in the Master's hands, what a thrill must have come to him! To think that he, a little unknown lad, could do something for the Great Teacher! He would talk about this moment the rest of his life.

As Jesus took the five little barley buns and two small fishes from the boy's hands, there may well have been tears in His eyes, for He knew how great a sacrifice it was for a boy to give up his lunch. And I am sure that He loved that boy very, very much, as He loves all boys and girls today who give up something that they prize for Him.

The best of it was, of course, that though the boy gave up

his lunch he did not lose it. He got it all back, and more be-sides—all he could eat. And as he ate he watched his lunch growing more and more, until Jesus had multiplied it five thousand times and fed the whole great multitude!

So it is with all that we give to Jesus. It comes back to us "pressed down . . . and running over," and at the same time becomes a mighty blessing to others.

But now look back at those six little words, "He . . . knew what He would do." Did you notice them? They mean so much. You see, Jesus never intended to buy any bread that day, or to have His disciples do so. Why? *Because He had had His eye on that little boy all the time!* He had read his thoughts. He knew that that boy was longing to do something for Him, and was willing to give up his lunch if need be. So Jesus planned the whole wonderful miracle with that little boy in mind.

Perhaps, who can tell, He is planning to do some great thing now with YOU in mind. He knows what He would do—if you would let Him.

Even at this moment the children's Friend stands waiting for all boys and girls who love Him to place in His hands their talents and their gifts—as the little lad gave his lunch in the long ago. He is waiting to bless and multiply their humble offerings beyond their wildest dreams. Give Him your best today!

HERBERT RUDEEN

Wonders Jesus Wrought

THE story of Jesus is one of wonder after wonder. As He went on His way through Galilee and Judea, He left a trail of miracles never seen before or since. Again and again He amazed the people by all the marvelous things that He did.

You remember how He touched the leper and healed him; how He took Peter's wife's mother by the hand and the fever left her; how He opened the eyes of blind Bartimaeus. These and a thousand other miracles like them proved His *power over disease*. Jesus showed that He is stronger than the worst sickness anybody ever had, or could have.

Then there was the very special healing of the centurion's servant. You remember how, when the centurion said, "I am not worthy that Thou shouldest come under my roof: but speak the word only, and my servant shall be healed," Jesus spoke the word, and the servant was healed "in the selfsame hour." That proved His *power over space*. Jesus did not have

368

to be present to heal sick people. He could heal them, if necessary, at a distance, and that was very wonderful indeed. Doctors would like to know how to do that today. We have found out how to talk to people at a distance by radio; we can send signals to the moon and back by radar; but we have yet to learn how to heal a sick person miles away as Jesus did.

One evening Jesus got into a fishing boat with His disciples, and, tired out, promptly fell asleep. By the time they had reached the middle of the lake a storm had sprung up. The disciples were used to storms, but this one was different. It became a great tempest "insomuch that the ship was covered with the waves." Even those tough fishermen became afraid. They felt sure their boat was going to sink. In

© BY R&H

their terror they decided to awaken Jesus and ask His help. This they did, crying, "Lord, save us: we perish."

Opening His eyes without a trace of worry, Jesus smiled at them. "Why are ye fearful, O ye of little faith?" He asked. Then, standing up in the tossing boat, He cried to the winds and waves, "Peace, be still!" And immediately the winds ceased, and there was a great calm.

This proved His *power over nature*. It showed that He who had created the world in the beginning was still its master and had it under His control.

The storm over and the sea calm again, the disciples rowed easily to the other side. There, as they got out of the boat, two wild men ran toward them. They were quite mad, possessed with devils. Most people would have run away from them, but again Jesus was unafraid. He just stood there, looking on them with great sorrow for their sad condition. Then He commanded the devils to come out of the fierce-looking creatures, and they came out, leaving them quiet, gentle, and in their right mind. As for the devils, they entered into a herd of swine nearby, and made them so mad that they rushed over a precipice into the lake and were drowned.

By this miracle Jesus proved that He has *power over devils;* that He is stronger than Satan.

His greatest miracle, however, was wrought toward the close of His life on earth. Word reached Him that His friend Lazarus, the brother of Mary and Martha, was very sick and likely to die. By the time He reached their home in Bethany, Lazarus was already dead and buried.

371

← PAINTING BY WILLIAM HUTCHINSON   © BY REVIEW AND HERALD

As the great storm swept over the Sea of Galilee, and threatened to capsize the boat, the disciples cried out in fear. Then Jesus calmed the tempest with the words, "Peace, be still."

He found the two sisters very sad, but grieving most of all because He had not come in time to save their brother from dying. Said Martha, "Lord, if Thou hadst been here, my brother had not died." When Mary met Him a little later, she said the same thing. How those two poor women must have longed and prayed for Him to come! Now, it seemed, He had come too late.

Yet He was not too late. It is never too late for Jesus.

"Thy brother shall rise again," He said.

"I know," said Martha, "that he shall rise again in the resurrection at the last day."

But Jesus did not mean that, not just then. "I am the resurrection, and the life," He said. "He that believeth in Me, though he were dead, yet shall he live. . . . Believest thou this?" He asked.

Martha wasn't quite sure she understood what He meant, but she was sure about Him and His mission. "I believe," she said, "that Thou art the Christ, the Son of God, which should come into the world."

Jesus was pleased at that.

Then Mary came. She was weeping. So were the people who came with her. It was all very, very sad. As Jesus saw them crying He began to cry too. "Jesus wept," the Bible says. His tender heart was touched by so much sorrow, even as it is touched today when we are sad.

But Jesus had come not to weep but to act. He had come, as He always comes, to help.

"Where have ye laid him?" He asked.

Someone pointed out the tomb, and they all went over to it. All the way Jesus prayed to His Father for strength to do what to others seemed impossible.

At last they were there. Mary and Martha stood bowed in grief while the other mourners wailed loudly. Presently all were startled as they heard Jesus say, "Take ye away the stone"!

Take away the stone! Surely not. That would open the grave. Jesus couldn't mean that.

Martha spoke up and said, "Lord, by this time he stinketh: for he hath been dead four days." Better not open it; it wouldn't be nice.

But Jesus replied, "Did I not tell you, if you will only believe, you shall see the glory of God?" (Moffatt).

At this someone rolled the stone away. "And Jesus lifted up His eyes, and said, Father, I thank Thee that Thou hast heard Me." Then in a loud voice He cried, "Lazarus, come forth"!

Everybody looked anxiously toward the tomb. Yes! Something was happening inside! The corpse was moving. It was standing up! It was walking toward the opening! Could this be a living man? Could it be Lazarus?

"And he that was dead came forth, bound hand and foot with graveclothes: and his face was bound about with a napkin."

Then Jesus said calmly, "Loose him, and let him go."

What a stir this made! Immediately people began running to Jerusalem and all over the countryside, crying, "Jesus raised a man from the dead! We saw it with our own eyes!"

In this, the greatest of His miracles, Jesus proved His *power over death*. As the Son of the *living* God He wanted all to know that He is stronger than death. And one day, because of His love for us, because of all He came to earth to do for us, "there shall be no more death, neither sorrow, nor crying, neither shall there be any more pain." Revelation 21:4.

Wonderful Saviour! With power over disease, over space, over nature, over devils, over death, is there anything He cannot do? Nothing! Nor is there anything He will not do for those who love Him and believe in Him with all their hearts today.

STORY 51

Stories Jesus Told

〰〰〰〰〰〰〰〰〰〰〰〰〰〰〰〰

ONE big reason why children loved to stay with Jesus was that He was always telling stories. He didn't preach long sermons that tired people out. Instead He told stories about people and things everybody understood.

Once He told a story about a sower. As the man sowed, said Jesus, some of the seed fell on the roadway instead of on the field, and the birds came and ate it up. Some seed fell where the land was rocky and the soil shallow. When the sun came up, it dried the land and the little plants died. Other seed fell among weeds, and the weeds spread and choked them.

But other seed fell on good ground. This sprang up and bore a fine crop.

Such a simple story! Why did Jesus tell it? Because of the lesson He wanted to teach. The seed is the Word of God. Jesus sows this seed.

Some of this seed falls by the wayside. Some people don't take any notice of it. They don't care.

377

Seeing a sower, Jesus taught the disciples a parable: "A sower went forth to sow," He said; "and when he sowed, some seeds fell by the way side, and the fowls . . . devoured them."

Some of it falls into the hearts of people who decide to be good and follow God's way; but when trials come, they get discouraged and give up.

Sometimes the seed of the Word leads people to start out toward the kingdom of God, but wrong thoughts like weeds come into their minds. Evil chokes the good, and they give up.

But some seed falls into "good ground"—the people who receive it gladly and turn to God with all their hearts. These are the ones who are "born again" by the Holy Spirit. By living good lives and telling other people about Jesus, they produce a great harvest for God.

So, simple as the story of the sower was, it had a deep meaning. It makes everybody who hears it ask, What kind of soil am I? Is my heart hard as a rock, or choked with weeds, or is it good soil where the love of God can do its wonderful work?

Buried Treasure

Jesus also told about a man who found a rich treasure buried in a field. No doubt all the children sat up to listen to this one! We all like stories of buried treasure. Well, the man didn't own the field, and he was afraid that someone else would

© BY R&H

find the treasure and carry it away. What to do? There was only one thing he could do. He must buy the field. When he heard the price he was frightened: it would take all he had in the world. But he wanted that treasure so much he sold all his possessions and bought the field.

What does this story mean? Just this: If we want the treasure to be found in the kingdom of God, we must be willing to give up all we have to get it. We cannot use some talents for the devil and some for God. We must be all for God—always.

Hidden Pearls

Next Jesus told about a merchant "seeking goodly pearls" who, "when he had found one pearl of great price, went and sold all that he had, and bought it."

By the merchant, Jesus meant Himself. He gave up all He had in heaven to come down to earth to seek and save the lost.

So in one story Jesus showed how we must give up all for Him; in the other, that He had already given up all for us.

Highway Robbers

Another story the children loved was about highway robbers. Once upon a time, Jesus said, a man started out to travel from Jerusalem to Jericho, down a rough, steep, dangerous road. On the way he was set upon by highway robbers, and badly beaten up. They took all his money and left him lying on the road half dead.

By and by a priest came along, took one glance at the wounded man, and passed by on the other side. Then a Levite came along and did the same. Both men were in too much of a hurry, or too afraid, to stop.

Then along came a Samaritan. When he saw the poor wounded man he ran over to care for him. First he bound up his wounds, then put him on his own donkey and took him to the nearest inn. There he paid the owner to look after the man till he should get well.

This is known as the story of the good Samaritan, and Jesus told it so that we all might know how God expects us to treat people in need. We are not to pass by on the other side but to give them all the help we can. Jesus finished this story by saying, "Go, and do thou likewise." That is for you and me today.

STORIES JESUS TOLD

The Lost Sheep

Another time Jesus told about a man who owned a hundred sheep, and lost one. Instead of saying to himself, "That's too bad; let it go; I have ninety-nine others anyway," he left the ninety-nine and went out to seek the lost sheep until he found it.

Everybody who heard this story knew that that was exactly what any good shepherd would do. He would not rest till the lost sheep was found. They knew too that when he had found it he would bring it back with great joy and say to the neighbors, "Rejoice with me; for I have found my sheep which was lost."

Who was the good shepherd of this story? Jesus, of course. And the lost sheep? First, the world—the one world in all God's universe that was lost—then everyone who has lost the way to God. Remember, whenever a boy is lost, Jesus is looking for him. Whenever a girl is lost, Jesus is looking for her.

The Lost Coin

So that there would be no doubt about this, Jesus told another story, this time about a lost coin. A woman, He said, had ten coins and lost one. Instead of saying, "Oh well, I've nine others; I won't worry about the lost one," she lit a candle and swept the house from top to bottom till she found it.

Every woman who heard Him tell that story must have smiled and said to herself, "That's just what I would do if I lost a coin!" But Jesus wanted all to see that that is how anxious He is to find, not lost coins, but lost *people,* and bring them back to God.

383

Jesus likened Himself to a faithful shepherd who, although he had ninety-nine sheep safe in the fold, would go out into the mountains to find the one lost sheep that had gone astray.

The Lost Boy

Next He told the most beautiful and touching story of all. This time it was about a lost boy.

A certain man, said Jesus, had two sons. The older one was content to stay at home and help his father on the farm. But the younger one was restless. He wanted to go to the city and have a good time. So he asked his father for his share of the family property, and the kindhearted father gave it to him.

A few days later this boy "gathered all together, and took his journey into a far country, and there wasted his substance with riotous living." He had the good time he wanted—lots of parties, lots of shows, lots of eating and drinking. But after a while he discovered that his money was running low and his new friends were beginning to leave him. Then when a famine came, and prices went up, he found he had neither money nor friends nor food. To get food he had to work, and the only work he could find was in a pigsty, feeding swine. So low were his wages that he could hardly get enough to eat, and he often looked hungrily at the garbage the pigs were eating.

By and by he began to think of the good old days at home. He pictured all the old farm hands he knew so well, eating their fill three times a day while he was starving.

Then he thought of his father. Dear old dad! How kind he had been—giving him so much money when he could easily have refused it! What would he say when he heard that it had all been wasted? Would he forgive? Could he?

"And when he came to himself, he said, . . . I perish with hunger! I will arise and go to my father, and will say unto him,

384

Father, I have sinned against heaven, and before thee, and am no more worthy to be called thy son: make me as one of thy hired servants."

Hungry and weary, but repentant, the boy started for home, wondering all the way how his father would receive him. He did not know that his father had been waiting for him ever since he had gone away. Each morning the old man watched the road, hoping to see the lad coming back.

At last the father's dream came true. Far in the distance he saw a lonely figure trudging wearily toward him. Love told him that this was his son. Forgetting all else, he ran to meet him.

"When he was yet a great way off, his father saw him, and had compassion, and ran, and fell on his neck, and kissed him."

What a welcome!

Then the son began to speak. With tears in his voice he said, "Father, I have sinned against heaven, and in thy sight, and am no more worthy to be called thy son."

386

He was about to add, "Make me as one of thy hired servants," but he never said it. Overcome with joy and excitement, his father interrupted him, giving orders right and left to the servants who had hurried to the scene. "Bring forth the best robe, and put it on him," he cried; "and put a ring on his hand, and shoes on his feet: and bring hither the fatted calf, and kill it; and let us eat, and be merry: for this my son was dead, and is alive again; he was lost, and is found."

Thus did Jesus try to reveal how great is God's love for sinners. No matter how much wrong they may have done, no matter how unkind and ungrateful they may have been, if they will but repent and say to God, "Father, I have sinned," He will receive them with open arms.

This story, like all the others, was not meant just for those who heard it long ago. It is for you and me and everybody today. We are to remember that God loves us with an everlasting love, a love that never dies. Though we leave Him and go far away, if we will but repent and turn again to Him, He will accept us. Even while we are "yet a great way off," He will come running to meet us. For every repentant boy or girl a royal welcome is waiting.

If perchance you feel that you are lost; if you feel like that poor boy as he ate husks among the swine, think again of the Father's house and the love that awaits you there. Don't let pride keep you back. Just say to yourself, "I will arise and go to my Father."

This is the first step back to God, the first step toward the kingdom of heaven, and to happiness. Why not take it now?

387

Lessons Jesus Taught

J ESUS is often called the Great Teacher, and He was, of course, the greatest teacher who ever lived. But did you ever stop to think that He never taught most of the subjects you learn in school? So far as we know He never gave any lessons in reading, writing, or arithmetic. He didn't teach geography or geometry or algebra or physical education. How, then, was He the greatest teacher?

Partly because of the way He taught, which was so simple that everyone could understand Him, and partly because of the kind of lessons He tried to teach. He was always seeking to make people good, not just fill their minds with facts.

As we have seen, Jesus came to change lives; to show people a new and better way to live so that they could live forever in His kingdom. To Him this was more important than teaching them history or how to multiply and divide.

One of the lessons He taught was *How Not to Quarrel*— and we all need that, don't we?

LESSONS JESUS TAUGHT

It happened this way:

The mother of James and John had come to Jesus and asked Him to arrange for her two boys to have the best places in His kingdom. She wanted to make sure that when Jesus became king her boys would sit on either side of His throne. Like any other mother, she wanted the best for her children!

But when the other disciples heard about it, they were very angry. The Bible says that they were "moved with indignation against the two brethren." They thought James and John had stolen a march on them. All of them had been secretly hoping for one of these important places, and they were not going to stand for any tricks like this.

Then Jesus called them together and told them how wrong they were to quarrel over such a matter as this. "Ye know," He said, "that the princes of the Gentiles exercise do-

minion over them, and they that are great exercise authority upon them. *But it shall not be so among you:* but whosoever will be great among you, let him be your minister; and whosoever will be chief among you, let him be your servant: even as the Son of man came not to be ministered unto, but to minister, and to give His life a ransom for many." Matthew 20:25-28.

Notice that Jesus not only told them to stop quarreling but He told them *how*. The way to do it was to stop thinking about themselves and start thinking of others. Each one must stop saying, "How can I get something for myself?" and start saying, "How can I do something for somebody else?" This, said Jesus, is the secret of living at peace with other people; and it works! It will stop quarreling anywhere. Try it!

Another time Jesus taught the lesson *How to Forgive*. Peter came to Him and said, "Lord, how oft shall my brother sin against me, and I forgive him? till seven times?" Matthew 18:21. It is hard to think that Peter and John ever fell out, but they must have, now and then, like most brothers. But the way to deal with it, Jesus said, was to have a forgiving spirit. "I say not unto thee, Until seven times: but, Until seventy times seven." Jesus knew that if Peter were to forgive John 490 times, and John were to forgive Peter 490 times, all ill will would disappear. So we are to keep on forgiving, over and over again, until the person who annoys us comes to love us! If your brother troubles you a great deal, try forgiving him at least a hundred times, and see what happens.

On another occasion Jesus taught His disciples *How to*

LESSONS JESUS TAUGHT

Behave at a Party. Such a simple lesson, yet how important!

"When thou art bidden of any man to a wedding," He said, "sit not down in the highest room. . . . But . . . go and sit down in the lowest room; that when he that bade thee cometh, he may say unto thee, Friend, go up higher. . . . For whosoever exalteth himself shall be abased; and he that humbleth himself shall be exalted." Luke 14:8-11. Here is a wonderful lesson indeed!

Perhaps you know some boys and girls who need this lesson. I know lots of them. They are forever pushing themselves forward. Always wanting to get attention, to "take the spotlight," as we say. But this is not the right way, said Jesus. It is not God's way. Take the lowest seat, He says, and don't worry. If you are worthy of something better, others will discover it. They will love you the more because you are humble.

Then there was the lesson He taught about *How to Give.* As He stood in the Temple one day, He watched the people bringing their gifts and putting them into the money box. Some gave a little, but "many that were rich cast in much."

Then there came along a poor widow, who put in two small coins, worth about one cent. She didn't know that Jesus was watching her, but He was. And He knew that those two coins were all she had in the world. Deeply touched by her loving sacrifice, He said to His disciples, "This poor widow hath cast more in, than all they which have cast into the treasury: for all they did cast in of their abundance; but she of her want did cast in all that she had." Mark 12:43, 44.

So it is not what we give that matters but what we have left. It is not the amount but the spirit in which we give it.

Some people may put a whole dollar into the plate in church, but if they do it carelessly, without any sacrifice, it doesn't do any good. If it means nothing to them, it means nothing to God. But when a little boy takes all his pocket money to Sabbath school and gives it to God with a smile, that is different. Jesus is pleased with that.

On another occasion Jesus taught the lesson *Always Do*

the Best You Can. This was at a home in Bethany. As Jesus sat at dinner, a woman entered the room with an expensive bottle of scent and, breaking it, poured the scent upon His head. Immediately the room was full of a beautiful fragrance, and all eyes turned toward Jesus and the woman. Some who knew what a costly scent it was were angry. "Why this waste?" they said. "That bottle was worth seventy-five dollars!"

But Jesus wouldn't let them call it waste. Nor would He let the poor woman go away disappointed, thinking she had done wrong.

"She hath done what she could," He said. And then, "Verily I say unto you, Wheresoever this gospel shall be preached throughout the whole world, this also that she hath done shall be spoken of for a memorial of her."

Nothing we do for Jesus is wasted. The smallest service we render Him will be like that little bottle of scent, its fragrance spreading and spreading till all the world is blessed

This beautiful reproduction of the Lord's Prayer is one of 28 hand-illuminated pages in Gothic lettering done in rich colors and gold in a book entitled *Sermon on the Mount*, size 22 x 30 inches, 1861 in England by W. and G. Audstey, architects.

by it. So, though we may not be able to do any great thing for Jesus, we are to do the best we can.

Perhaps the most important lesson Jesus taught was *How to Pray*. The disciples had often watched Him pray, and they had seen how it had helped Him and had given Him strength to bear His burdens. So one day they came to Him and said, "Lord, teach us to pray." Luke 11:1.

That was when He taught them the Lord's Prayer, which we all know so well. Remember?

"Our Father which art in heaven, Hallowed be Thy name. Thy kingdom come. Thy will be done in earth, as it is in heaven. Give us this day our daily bread. And forgive us our debts, as we forgive our debtors. And lead us not into temptation, but deliver us from evil: For Thine is the kingdom, and the power, and the glory, for ever. Amen."

You have prayed this prayer many times, haven't you? But have you ever stopped to think of each line? You should. This prayer begins and ends with God. It leads us to think of Him as a kind and loving Father, but also as the all-powerful, all-glorious King of heaven. That is why we are to hallow, or reverence, His name, and to pray that the day will soon come when He will reign on earth as He reigns in heaven.

In this prayer we ask but three things for ourselves— for daily bread, for forgiveness of sin, and for help against temptation—and when you come to think of it, these are what we need most.

Such a simple prayer it is, but so very beautiful. And because it is so simple and beautiful, it has lasted down the ages. Millions pray it today all over the world. In every country and in hundreds of languages, millions of fathers and mothers, boys and girls, say, "Our Father which art in heaven."

What a wonderful picture that is!

The Lord's Prayer is the greatest prayer of the Christian church. It is the one prayer nobody gets tired of saying and God never gets tired of hearing. I hope you say it every day.

STORY 53

Promises Jesus Made

~~~~~~

I SUPPOSE you have often had promises made to you. Perhaps Mother has said, "If you are at the head of your class,
I'll give you a special treat." Or Father has said, "If you
are good and behave yourself for a whole week, I'll take you
on a trip somewhere."

Most promises, as you have noticed, have a condition tied
to them. *If* you head your class, you will get the special treat.
If you don't, you won't. *If* you are a good boy, or a good girl,
for a whole week, Father will take you on a trip. If not, the
trip is off.

So it was with most of the promises Jesus made. There
was an *if* about them somewhere.

"Seek ye first the kingdom of God, and His righteousness," He said; "and all these things shall be added unto
you." Matthew 6:33. "All these things"—things to eat, things
to drink, things to wear—will be ours *if* we will seek first the
kingdom of God. If we put His kingdom last—that is, if we

397

The pure, trusting innocence of children found
kinship with the gentleness and tenderness of
Jesus. Putting His hands upon them in blessing
He said, "Of such is the kingdom of heaven."

seldom think about Him, and do not even try to do what He wants us to do—then the promise won't apply to us. We must seek *first* the kingdom of God and then Jesus will look after all the "things." We won't have to worry about them.

Another promise like this is found in John 14:14: "If ye shall ask any thing in My name, I will do it."

Does this mean that if you were to ask God for an elephant He would give it to you? Well, it *could* mean that, if

you actually needed an elephant to do something for God. But not if you merely wanted one to play with.

The condition which goes with this promise is that we ask *in His name*. This means not merely saying at the end of a prayer, "For Jesus' sake," but asking for things such as God would like to give to Jesus; things for which Jesus Himself would ask. And for what would He ask? Only things that would bring glory to God. If we ask for things like that, we will always get them. Like George Müller, of Bristol, who cared for hundreds of poor orphans, we will be surprised what God will do for us. Müller had no money to feed the children, but he prayed, in Jesus' name, that money would come. And it came—heaps of it, millions of dollars. You see, he wanted to do something that God wanted done.

The next promise fits right in with this one. "Give, and it shall be given unto you; good measure, pressed down, and shaken together, and running over." Luke 6:38. Notice the condition again. If you want people to give things to you, you

must first be generous yourself. If you want great blessings from God, you must first give yourself to Him.

Too many boys and girls are selfish, thinking of themselves all the time. When other children leave them alone and forget to give them presents they feel hurt and slighted. They say the other children are mean and unkind. But it is *they* who are at fault. Let them begin *giving* and see what happens. If you show a generous spirit to others and to God, you will be amazed how much will come back to you—"pressed down, . . . and running over."

Another lovely promise is found in Matthew 11:28, where we read that Jesus said to the people, "Come unto Me, all ye that labour and are heavy laden, and I will give you rest." This promise is for all who feel tired and sad and worried. There were many like that in the crowd around Him, and there are many like that in the world today.

Even boys and girls, though they rarely get tired, of course, sometimes get discouraged; and Jesus knows what to do about that. If we will heed His call and go to Him, He will give us rest. How? By leading us to think about something different. If things have gone wrong, He will lead us to think of His power to put them right. If we feel blue because of a tale somebody has told about us, He will help us to think of all *He* had to put up with from *His* enemies, and then our troubles will seem very small indeed.

He also made this marvelous promise: "If a man love Me, he will keep My words: and My Father will love him, and We will come unto him, and make Our abode with him."

400

John 14:23. This is almost too wonderful to understand. If we love Jesus, then He and His Father will come and make Their "abode" with us. That is, They will come and live in our hearts. This is like that other promise in the book of Revelation: "Behold, I stand at the door, and knock: if any man hear My voice, and open the door, I will come in to him, and will sup with him, and he with Me." Revelation 3:20.

There is no sweeter picture in all the Bible than this. Jesus standing at a door, knocking, knocking, waiting to come in. "If a man love Me" and "open the door," He says, "I will come in." If a boy loves Me, or a girl, and opens the door, "I will come in." Think of that!

Such are some of the precious promises of Jesus. But the greatest promise He ever made was this: "I go to prepare a place for you. And if I go and prepare a place for you, I will come again, and receive you unto Myself; that where I am, there ye may be also." John 14:1-3.

To His disciples, who had been getting very worried of late about Jesus, this meant a great deal. So much had gone wrong. When the people had tried to make Him a king, He had just walked away! This had upset many, and they "walked no more with Him." Then He had gone into the Temple and, finding a lot of people buying and selling there, He had driven them out, saying, "Is it not written, My house shall be called of all nations the house of prayer? but ye have made it a den of thieves." That had made the traders very angry with Him. The priests also had become jealous of Him because of the way the people followed Him, and they had

26

tried every way they could to hinder His work. When He raised Lazarus from the dead, right outside the gates of Jerusalem, and the whole nation buzzed with the news, these religious leaders became alarmed and determined to kill Him.

Knowing all this, the disciples were getting very depressed. That is why Jesus said to them, "Let not your heart be troubled: ye believe in God, believe also in Me." "I go away" but "I will come again."

But when would He come again? Very soon? In a year's time? In ten? Would He come while they were yet alive?

One day the disciples came to Jesus and asked Him about it. "Tell us," they said, "when shall these things be? and what shall be the sign of Thy coming, and of the end of the world?" Matthew 24:3.

Then Jesus told them. It would be a very long time. Many, many things would happen before He would come back. There would be wars and famines and pestilences and earthquakes. Jerusalem would be destroyed. There would be great trouble for all who love God. Wicked people would hurt them and put them in prison and kill them. But no matter what happened, He would never forget His promise to return for His faithful, watching people.

Then, far off down the years, when the time for Him to come back should draw near, He would cause certain things to happen so that His people would know that His coming was near. Signs would appear in the sun, the moon, and the stars. There would also be great trouble among the nations, with much suffering and fear. At last, when things had be-

403

One of the most often-repeated promises of the Bible is the wonderful assurance by Jesus Himself that He is coming back to earth again to take all His faithful people home to heaven.

come about as bad as they could be, the Son of man would be seen "coming in a cloud with power and great glory."

"When these things begin to come to pass," said Jesus, "then look up, and lift up your heads; for your redemption draweth nigh."

When a few weeks later Jesus left His disciples and went away to heaven, they remembered this promise and began to look for Him to return. Day after day, month after month, they hoped for His coming. Indeed, all their lives they talked about it and said, "He will surely come back someday. He will keep His promise." Then when they had all died, others remembered the promise, and they looked for Him too. The apostle Paul called this promise "the blessed hope," and so it has been ever since. All down the years people have looked and longed for the return of Jesus.

Today there are thousands of people all over the world with the same hope in their hearts. And it burns more brightly now than ever, because all the promised signs have appeared. In sun and moon and stars they have been seen. And all about us now are the troubles and the fears which Jesus said would be in the world just before His return. So today we can say with new meaning, "Jesus is coming again." And not only coming, but coming soon. When we see all these things, we are to KNOW that "the kingdom of God is nigh at hand." Perhaps you will live to see Him "coming in a cloud with power and great glory." Wouldn't that be wonderful!

"Watch ye therefore: . . . lest coming suddenly He find you sleeping." Mark 13:35-37.

STORY 54

Falling Shadows

~~~~~~

LITTLE more than three years had passed since Jesus had begun His ministry. Three short years. And yet already the shadows were gathering about Him. The dear old days with Mary at Nazareth seemed far, far away. So, too, the happy, peaceful hours with His disciples by the Sea of Galilee. Enemies were at work. People were criticizing His teachings, finding fault with the way He lived, ridiculing His humble birth, scoffing at His miracles.

The trouble was, of course, that Jesus had tried to change the lives of people who didn't want to be changed. He had sought to show them a better way of life, but they preferred their old ways. He had brought them light, but they chose darkness, because their deeds were evil.

Truly "the common people heard Him gladly." They loved Him for His beautiful teachings, and because He healed them of their diseases. But there were many others, like the priests and the Pharisees, whose lives were so different from

405

the pure, humble, gentle life of Jesus that they hated Him. They hated Him because He was good. They hated Him because He was loved. They hated Him because He had a power they could not understand.

So they plotted to take His life. "Then assembled together the chief priests, and the scribes, and the elders of the people, unto the palace of the high priest, who was called Caiaphas, and consulted that they might take Jesus by subtilty, and kill Him." Matthew 26:3, 4.

It is terrible to think of all those religious leaders gathered together trying to think of some way to catch Jesus secretly and murder Him. But that is what they did.

Jesus knew about it, but He did not run away. It would have been easy for Him to have done so. He knew the lonely places on the mountains better than anyone else. And there was many a humble home where He could have hidden if He had wanted to.

But He did not hide. He had come for a great purpose, and He was willing to pay the price.

He knew from the book of Daniel that Messiah would have to die. Did not the prophecy say, "After threescore and two weeks shall Messiah be cut off, but not for Himself"? And what was it Isaiah had said? "Surely He hath borne our griefs, and carried our sorrows. . . .

406

FALLING SHADOWS

He was wounded for our transgressions, He was bruised for our iniquities. . . . He is brought as a lamb to the slaughter."

Jesus remembered also the words which John the Baptist had said to Him at His baptism: "Behold the Lamb of God, which taketh away the sin of the world." John 1:29.

Every day lambs were slain by the priests in the Temple as a sacrifice for sin. All pointed to Him and the work that He must do.

So Jesus said to His disciples, "After two days is the feast of the passover, and the Son of man is betrayed to be crucified."

"To be crucified!" Surely Jesus could not mean that! What had He done to deserve so terrible a punishment? They could not believe it. They felt sure He would never let anything like that happen to Him. Why, it was only a couple of days ago that He had ridden into Jerusalem on a donkey with

all the children crying out, "Hosanna to the Son of David!" Surely He would not let Himself be put to death so soon after that. His work was only beginning!

But the shadows continued to fall. Thursday evening came—Passover night. Jesus and His disciples gathered round a table to celebrate it. Everybody was gloomy. Then when Jesus said that one of them should betray Him, "they were exceeding sorrowful, and began every one of them to say unto Him, Lord, is it I?"

He answered: "The Son of man goeth as it is written of Him: but woe unto that man by whom the Son of man is betrayed!" Soon after this Judas left. "And it was night." Night outside and night in all their hearts.

After they had eaten the Passover, they sang a hymn and walked out along the dark streets, through one of the city gates, to the Mount of Olives. But Jesus did not want to talk now; He wanted to pray. Coming to the Garden of Gethsemane, He told most of those who were with Him to rest while He went on with Peter, James, and John.

But they, too, were tired, and soon fell asleep, leaving Jesus alone. Then it was that He prayed that sad, sad prayer, "O My Father, if it be possible, let this cup pass from Me: nevertheless not as I will, but as Thou wilt." Three times He prayed, using the same words. He did not want to die.

FALLING SHADOWS

He did not want to suffer all the shame and pain of crucifixion. He shrank from the cruel torture of it. Yet He was
willing to bear it all if it was God's will.

By and by "there appeared an angel unto Him from
heaven, strengthening Him." Luke 22:43. So the angels were
watching still! Just as at Bethlehem, so now in Gethsemane.
But how different was the scene! Then all was happiness and
light; now, only darkness and sorrow.

At last Jesus heard distant shouting, and saw the light
of many torches moving in the darkness as an angry mob
surged up the hill to take Him. The end was near.

"Rise," He called to His sleeping disciples, "let us be
going: behold, he is at hand that doth betray Me."

A moment more and they were surrounded. Then Judas
came forward and kissed Jesus—the sign he had agreed upon
with the priests. Jesus said to him, with great gentleness,
"Friend, wherefore art *thou* come?"

Peter, seeing armed men about to seize Jesus, drew his

sword and struck off the ear of one of them. It was a brave deed, but useless. "Put up again thy sword into his place," Jesus said to him: "for all they that take the sword shall perish with the sword." Then He touched the bleeding ear and restored it as it was before.

"Thinkest thou that I cannot now pray to My Father," He said to Peter, "and He shall presently give Me more than twelve legions of angels? But how then shall the scriptures be fulfilled, that thus it must be?" Of course He could have called the angels to help Him! And how glad they would have been to come to His rescue and scatter that howling mob! But it could not be. The Scriptures had to be fulfilled.

"And they led Jesus away to the high priest." Down the Mount of Olives, up the slope to Jerusalem, in through the gate, and over to the palace. His hands bound, His disciples gone, Jesus walked on bravely but sadly to the fate that awaited Him in the city He had come to save.

How Jesus Died

IT WAS very late by now, but the high priest was waiting for Jesus. So were "all the chief priests and the elders and the scribes." There they sat with dark, angry looks on their faces. They had made up their minds He should not escape this time. But they had to charge Him with some crime before they could condemn Him to death. And they couldn't find any. He had not done anything wrong.

True, "witnesses" came forward to accuse Jesus, but as they did not tell the truth they kept contradicting one another. As they did so, the high priest became more and more angry. Presently, seeing that his whole plan to kill Jesus might fail if things went on like this, he turned on Jesus Himself and cried, "Answerest Thou nothing?"

Jesus kept silent. There was no need for Him to reply to false charges.

Then the high priest, white with anger, blurted out, "Art Thou the Christ, the Son of the Blessed?"

411

"I am," Jesus answered: "and ye shall see the Son of man sitting on the right hand of power, and coming in the clouds of heaven." Mark 14:61, 62.

This was too much for the high priest. Tearing his robe in fury, he cried to the whole assembly, "What need we any further witnesses? Ye have heard the blasphemy: what think ye?"

"Death!" they cried angrily. "Put Him to death!"

But they could not kill Him themselves. Only the Roman governor could do that. So they had to wait till daylight. Then, "very early" Friday morning, they hurried Jesus over to Pilate's judgment hall. Everybody went—"the whole multitude," all shouting their hatred of Jesus.

How tired the Saviour must have been! Up all night with that angry, jeering throng. Slapped, beaten, spat upon, He was now dragged and shoved toward the judgment hall.

Because it was Passover time the Jews would not go into the hall themselves, so Jesus found Himself alone with Pilate. He was glad for that. He always liked to be alone with people so that He could speak to their hearts. He had been alone with Nicodemus, with the poor woman at the well, and now, in His last moments, with the Roman governor himself.

"Art thou the King of the Jews?" asked Pilate.

"Thou sayest," said Jesus. But lest the governor should misunderstand and think He was just a common rebel against the power of Rome, He added, "My kingdom is not of this

412

world: if My kingdom were of this world, then would My servants fight, that I should not be delivered to the Jews: but now is My kingdom not from hence."

This was hard for a man like Pilate to understand. All the kings he had ever heard of fought for their kingdoms.

"Art Thou a king then?" he asked, puzzled.

"Yes," said Jesus. "To this end was I born, and for this cause came I into the world, that I should bear witness unto the truth."

"What is truth?" asked Pilate.

This was the governor's great chance to accept Jesus. But he did not take it. He was afraid. Hearing the shouting outside, he went out to the yelling mob.

"I find in Him no fault at all," he said.

At this the shouting grew louder. Pilate saw that these people were in a frenzy of rage and hatred.

Seeking a way out, he sent Jesus to Herod, ruler of Galilee, who happened to be in the city for the Passover. But Herod, after making fun of Jesus and putting a royal robe on Him, sent Him back to Pilate.

Again Pilate tried to save

Jesus. "I will . . . chastise Him, and release Him," he said.

"No!" shouted the mob. "Away with this Man, and release unto us Barabbas."

So they chose Barabbas—a murderer—rather than the Son of God.

"What then shall I do with Jesus?" Pilate asked.

"Crucify Him!" they yelled.

"Why, what evil hath He done?" said Pilate.

For answer they cried yet louder, "Crucify Him!"

At last Pilate gave way. First, he took water and washed his hands before the crowd, saying, "I am innocent of the blood of this just person: see ye to it." But no water could ever wash away his guilt. He could have saved Jesus, but he didn't.

Then the order was given that Jesus should be crucified, and the soldiers led Him away. In their common hall they treated Him so cruelly that when the time came for Him to be taken to the place of crucifixion He was half dead already. Having been scourged with a whip, and having had a crown of sharp thorns pressed down upon His head, He was so faint that He could scarcely stand.

Too weak to carry the great wooden cross that was laid on His shoulder, Jesus fell beneath it, and the soldiers looked for someone else to bear it for Him. Catching sight of a man called Simon who had come to Jerusalem from Cyrene in North Africa, they compelled him to carry the cross.

This man Simon, the Bible says, was "the father of Alexander and Rufus," and I have often wondered why those two boys are mentioned. Could it be because they were so proud that

414

their dad carried the cross for Jesus? Surely they must have talked about it the rest of their days. It was something to be proud of too.

Slowly the sad procession wended its way to Calvary. "And there followed Him a great company of people, and of women, which also bewailed and lamented Him." Luke 23:27. Many who had heard Jesus preach were there, and many whom He had healed. There were children, too, some of the very ones who had cried "Hosanna to the Son of David!" only a few days before. They looked on with sad, frightened eyes.

At last the procession stopped at the place of execution. And there they crucified Him.

Laying Jesus on the cross, the soldiers drove nails through His hands and feet. The pain of it must have been dreadful. But all Jesus said was, "Father, forgive them; for they know not what they do." The original words suggest that He kept on saying it. Over and over again, instead of cursing and swearing like the two thieves who were crucified with Him, He repeated the beautiful words, "Father, forgive them." Only the Son of God could ever have done that.

Then the cross was lifted and thrown into a hole in the ground. Again the pain must have been terrible, but Jesus whispered, "Father, forgive them." No anger, only forgiveness.

So there at last He hung, between heaven and earth, with arms outstretched in suffering love for all the world to see. It was as though, in His last dying moments, He was saying, "Look unto Me, and be ye saved, all the ends of the earth." Isaiah 45:22.

Over His head was a sign saying, "This is Jesus the King of the Jews." Though put there in jest, how true it was—their King and our King, the Great Teacher of Nazareth, the Great Healer of Galilee, the Great Friend of little children—so kind, so wise, so gentle, so undeserving of all this cruelty!

Now, in the lovely words of Stainer's *Crucifixion:*

> "Jesus is dying, in agony sore,
> Jesus is suffering more and more,
> Jesus is bowed with the weight of His woe,
> Jesus is faint with each bitter throe,
> Jesus is bearing it all in my stead,
> Pity Incarnate for me has bled;
> Wonder of wonders it ever must be,
> Jesus, the Crucified, pleads for me."

By this time a great crowd had gathered round the cross.

PAINTING BY HARRY ANDERSON
© BY REVIEW AND HERALD

HOW JESUS DIED

"And sitting down they watched Him there" (Matthew 27: 36), even as the world has been watching Him ever since.

The soldiers watched as they gambled for His garments.

The priests watched, gloating over the victory they thought they had won, and shouting, "If Thou be the Son of God, come down from the cross."

The women who had followed Him watched, weeping.

People whom He had helped and healed watched, with bowed heads and sorrowful hearts.

There must have been children there too. Perhaps a little boy and girl holding hands, looking up at the cross with big, sad eyes, and tears rolling down their cheeks, as they whispered to each other, "Poor Jesus! He was so kind to us. He told us such lovely stories. Why did He have to die—like this?"

Why? Why? How often have we all asked why? The answer is given in the words of the lovely old hymn:

> "There is a green hill far away,
>   Without a city wall,
> Where the dear Lord was crucified,
>   Who died to save us all.
>
> "We may not know, we cannot tell,
>   What pains He had to bear,
> But we believe it was for us
>   He hung and suffered there.
>
> "He died that we might be forgiven,
>   He died to make us good,
> That we might go at last to heaven,
>   Saved by His precious blood.

27

"There was no other good enough
To pay the price of sin;
He only could unlock the gate
Of heaven, and let us in.

"O dearly, dearly has He loved!
And we must love Him too,
And trust in His redeeming blood,
And try His works to do."
—C. F. ALEXANDER

STORY 56

The Boy Without a Name

CAN you imagine a baby coming to somebody's house and nobody having a name for it? I can't. Usually, just as soon as people know there's a baby coming, they begin choosing a name right away—one for a boy, and another in case it's a girl. To have no name ready at all would be very strange indeed. But it really happened once in the long ago.

When this particular baby boy turned up, his mother didn't know what to call him. Why, I don't know. Perhaps she just couldn't make up her mind whether he should be called John or Peter or Stephen or David. Maybe she read her list of names over and over again until she got into such a muddle she gave up in despair. Anyway, she gave up. And what do you suppose she did then? Well, believe it or not, she decided she would just call him Son of Papa.

What a funny name! It was. Yet, as you will see later, it was a name big with meaning, though the mother didn't know it then.

419

Hearing of the cruel death of Jesus, the children who loved Him must have been broken-hearted to find only an empty cross, the crown of thorns, and a few nails to tell the story.

Living in Bible times, this mother did not, of course, use our English words "son of papa," but the word *Bar,* meaning "son," and *Abba,* meaning "papa," or "father." So the little boy was called Barabbas.

Sad to say, he was not a good boy. He was always getting into trouble. I wouldn't be surprised if he was the ringleader of all the naughty boys in the district where he lived.

Whether Barabbas in his boyhood and early youth ever met John the Baptist or Jesus of Nazareth no one knows, though he lived at the same time and may have been among the crowds who went down to the Jordan to hear them preach. It is possible that he heard John say, "Bring forth therefore fruits worthy of repentance!" or Jesus plead with the people in His tender, gentle voice, "Come unto Me, all ye that labour and are heavy laden, and I will give you rest."

But if Barabbas ever heard these words, he did not heed them. He turned away from religion. His heart became hard and cruel. With a group of worldly young men like himself he started a riot and committed murder. For this he was arrested by the Roman soldiers and thrown into prison.

How grieved his mother must have been when she learned what had happened to the boy she had once called Son of Papa! And how worried Barabbas must have been, lying there in the dungeon, waiting in terror for his punishment!

Days passed—long, long days, and longer nights. Chained in his cell, Barabbas could hear carpenters at work in the courtyard, shaping his cross, and he knew the dreaded moment was close at hand.

THE BOY WITHOUT A NAME

Then one morning—very early—he was roused by the sound of a great commotion outside the prison. Through the window of his cell came loud, angry voices.

Louder and louder they became. It seemed as though thousands of people were shouting for vengeance on somebody. Who could it be? Who could have stirred up the whole city like this, and at such an hour of the morning?

And now, what was that?

"Barabbas! We want Barabbas!"

His name! They were shouting his name. He must die!

Suddenly he heard a rattling of keys. The guard! Perhaps they had come to hand him over to the angry crowd.

The cell door creaked open. Soldiers ordered him to rise and go with them. Tremblingly he obeyed.

Up the dark stairway, along stone corridors, marched the guard and their prisoner. Where could they be taking him? thought Barabbas. Presently, entering the governor's palace, he found himself face to face with none other than Pontius Pilate himself! And there, beyond him, was the crowd, that angry, seething crowd, still shouting, "Barabbas! Release to us Barabbas!"

Then his eyes rested upon Someone else—a sad and lonely figure standing near Pilate.

Surely I have seen that man before! he thought. Why, that is Jesus of Nazareth! That is the famous Teacher whom all the people love. What is He doing here? Surely He has committed no crime.

Then Pilate spoke to the crowd. "Whom will ye that I

release unto you? Barabbas, or Jesus which is called Christ?"

"Barabbas!" shrieked the crowd, "Barabbas!"

Pilate turned to the soldiers. "Let him go," he said. "Then released he Barabbas unto them."

Bounding down the steps, out into the crowd, Barabbas could hardly contain himself for joy. This was too wonderful for words. Instead of being crucified, as he had fully expected to be, he was free! Free! Pilate himself had released him!

By and by Barabbas noticed the crowd beginning to move away from the governor's palace. The people seemed to be moving toward the city gate, beyond which lay Golgotha, the place of execution. Rumor spread that three prisoners were to die there this day, all by crucifixion, that awful death which Barabbas had himself expected. He decided to follow the crowd.

Soon he came upon the sad procession of the condemned. Over the heads of the people in front of him he could see the crosses carried on the backs of the weary prisoners.

Who was the one in front, staggering under the weight of his cross? Why, surely, it was the same man whom he had seen that very morning in the presence of Pilate! It was the Preacher from Galilee—the kind, gentle Jesus—on His way to

422

be crucified! Yes, and carrying the very cross that might have been his!

What happened to Barabbas after that we do not know. So far as the Bible story goes, he was lost in the crowd on that dreadful day. Perhaps his wicked heart may have been touched as he realized that Jesus had taken his place and was bearing that cross for him!

Did you ever stop to think how wonderful it is that it was a man called Bar-abbas whose cross Jesus carried? Being only "Son of Papa," he stands for every boy and every girl who ever lived, no matter how bad and naughty. If his name had been John or Peter or Stephen or David, some might have thought that Jesus bore the cross just for one person in particular. Then there would have been a chance that some poor, sinful soul might have felt left out. So in the providence of God the one whose place Jesus took, whose cross He bore to Calvary, was just Bar-abbas, "Son of Papa," the boy without a name.

From that moment on, everyone could feel sure that he was included in the glorious salvation which Jesus provided. Today, two thousand years later, every son and daughter of Adam, every boy and girl in every nation under heaven, may say with confidence, "He died for me."

STORY 57

A Thief Enters Heaven

CRUCIFIED with Jesus that day were two thieves. Sometimes people think of them as old men, but most likely
they were no older than Jesus, and He was only thirty-
three. It is possible that they were much younger.

I like to think of them as just boys who had gone wrong
—boys whose mothers loved them and expected much of them
and were heartbroken when they began to lie and steal.

There was a moment in the lives of both those boys when
they left the path of goodness and started on the road that led
to horrible death by crucifixion. It may have been when they
were talking with bad companions or when they were tempted
to steal something in the house or in a neighbor's garden; but
whenever it was, that word, that deed, that evil thought, was
the beginning of a life which could have but one end, a criminal's death. How we need to watch ourselves each passing
moment that all we say and do may be pleasing to our heavenly
Father!

A THIEF ENTERS HEAVEN

Step by step those two lads plunged deeper and deeper into wrongdoing. Though brought up to believe in the Ten Commandments, they forgot all about them. Though they knew perfectly well that God had said, "Thou shalt not steal," they stole, right and left. It may even be that they lived by stealing. Then came arrest and the dread sentence of death—death on a cross, the most awful form of punishment practiced by the Romans.

Finally the dreaded moment came. Carrying their crosses, the prisoners were led to the place of execution. No doubt they were surprised to see another cross raised between theirs. Certainly they were amazed when they saw who was crucified there. They knew Jesus well. They had heard much about Him. In their hearts they believed He was a good man, though they had not, until now, thought much about His claim to be the Son of God, the Messiah of Israel. Now in their awful agony they looked at Him, wondering.

Naked, His hands and feet nailed to the wooden beams, His face drawn and haggard with His dreadful suffering, blood

running down His forehead from the crown of thorns, Jesus did not look like one who could help them. Yet there was a majesty in His bearing even on the cross as He murmured, "Father, forgive them; for they know not what they do."

Then "one of the malefactors which were hanged railed on Him, saying, If Thou be Christ, save Thyself and us."

This was no plea for help. It was a taunt, and most unkind at such a moment. This thief had no faith that the Man on the middle cross was the Son of God. He was merely mocking Him, repeating the words of the sneering priests below.

Then something beautiful happened—the one gracious deed that lighted the awful darkness and misery of that crucifixion scene. Turning on the first thief, the second thief rebuked him, saying: "Dost not thou fear God, seeing thou art in the same condemnation? And we indeed justly; for we receive the due reward of our deeds: but this man hath done nothing amiss." Luke 23:40, 41.

How the heart of Jesus must have thrilled as He heard these words and knew that He had one champion left! Most of His disciples had forsaken Him and fled. Despite all He had done for the multitudes, healing the sick and raising the dead, it seemed just then as though He hadn't a friend left. Day after day, night after night, He had poured out His love for the needy and the sorrowing, but now all His labor seemed to have been in vain. Nobody loved Him—nobody except, oh, wonder of wonders, this dying thief! Though racked with pain, this poor sinner would not let an unkind, unjust word be spoken about Him! He was more than willing to admit his own sins, but

426

would not let anyone accuse the innocent Teacher of Galilee.

Then it was that the repentant thief said, "Lord, remember me when Thou comest into Thy kingdom."

Again the heart of Jesus was deeply touched. Why, this poor thief not only believed that He was innocent; he believed that He was a king, and that beyond this dreadful death on the cross He would have a kingdom and life everlasting. In his simple way this thief had more true faith in Jesus and His mission than all His disciples put together!

If ever there was a man truly sorry for his sins, and sincerely longing to be a child of God, it was this poor, dying thief. Surely no one ever was more deserving of a place in His kingdom. No wonder Jesus said to him: "Verily I say unto thee this day: with Me shalt thou be in Paradise." Luke 23:43, Rotherham.

This promise to the repentant thief is one of the most precious in all the Bible. "Today," said Jesus, in other words, "Today, this darkest of days, when My cause seems lost, when most of My friends have left Me, and My enemies have crucified Me—today I tell you, victory is Mine, and you shall have part in it. The future is Mine, and you shall share it with Me."

427

Jesus did not, as some think, tell the poor thief that he would be in Paradise *that very day*. He could not have meant that, for He did not go to Paradise Himself that day. Three days later, after His resurrection, He said to Mary, "I am not yet ascended to My Father." John 20:17. No. When Jesus spoke that precious promise to the dying thief, He was looking into the future, to the day of His final triumph, when all who love Him and are faithful to Him will be gathered into His wonderful kingdom.

"Lord, remember me," said the dying thief.

Will Jesus remember him? Yes, He will indeed. Even if a thousand million years were to pass, Jesus would not, could not, forget this man who stood by Him in that dark and bitter day. If there is one person who is absolutely sure of a place in Paradise, it is the converted thief who in his dying moments turned to Jesus with all his heart, reached out by faith from cross to cross, and in reaching won heaven for himself.

STORY 58

Please Remember Mother

~~~~~~

IN THE dark, at the foot of the cross, stood Mary, the
mother of Jesus. How like a mother to come close to her
boy when He was suffering so much! She came as close
as she could; yet how little she could do for Him—nothing but
pray and weep!

All that had happened the past few hours had come hard-
est upon her. Nobody else could care so much as she!

Mary had expected so much of Him—right from that moment when the angel had appeared to her and said, "Behold,
thou shalt . . . bring forth a son, and shalt call His name JESUS.
He shall be great, and shall be called the Son of the Highest:
and the Lord God shall give unto Him the throne of His father
David." Luke 1:31, 32. How high her hopes had risen at the
words! And now this! Was this cross His promised throne?

She remembered Bethlehem, and the wonderful story the
shepherds had told her of the angels who had appeared to them
in a blaze of light, singing, "Glory to God in the highest," and

of the one who had said to them: "Unto you is born this day in the city of David a Saviour, which is Christ the Lord." What a thrill of happiness the words had brought to her as she lay with her Babe in the stable! But now, could this be the fulfillment of that promise? How could He be a Saviour, hanging on a cross, dying a criminal's death?

She remembered what old Simeon had said to her in the Temple as he took Jesus in his arms: "Behold, this child is set for the fall and rising again of many in Israel; . . . yea, a sword shall pierce through thy own soul also." Could this cross be the sword?

Then as she bowed her head in her misery she thought of those lovely, carefree days in dear old Nazareth. What a dear, sweet Boy He had been! What a help about the house! How kind His nature; how gentle and loving His every thought and deed! Surely He did not deserve this! Not to die like this!

She thought of His years of ministry, how He had tried to do so much for the poor, the sick, the needy. Never had He taken any time for Himself. Always He had given up everything for others. Day and night He had worn Himself out for them. Now they had done this to Him. It wasn't fair! It wasn't right!

Poor Jesus! How He must be suffering up there! Oh, if only she could do something, one little thing, to help Him, just to relieve His dreadful pain for one brief moment! But there was nothing, nothing she could do!

Now and then she peered up into His poor, scarred face. Once it seemed as though He smiled at her. Yes! He was trying to speak to her. Eagerly she caught the whispered words.

431

As the beloved disciple John looked up into the face of Jesus who was dying on the cross, he heard the gentle voice of his Master crying out of grief for Mary, "Behold thy mother!"

"Woman," He said, "behold thy son."

Then His eyes turned to John, dear, faithful John, who was standing beside her. "John," He said, "behold thy mother."

Did ever more beautiful words come from dying lips? Oh, wonderful, wonderful Jesus! In His last agonies He thinks about His mother!

Too weary, too racked with pain to say more than these few words, He said enough for both to understand. It was as though He said, "Dear John, please remember mother. Look after her—for Me—when I am gone."

"And from that hour that disciple took her unto his own home" (John 19:27)—a kindness that Jesus will surely repay ten thousandfold in that "sweet by and by" when He shall reward His own.

Do you love your mother as much as this? If you were in great trouble, would your last thought be for her and her welfare? I hope so.

You may never have to go through anything so terrible as Jesus did, and have to leave your mother for somebody else to love and care for; but day by day you may think of her with similar love and devotion. You can remember to be kind to her, and thoughtful, and affectionate, helping her in every way you can.

If she should be away from home for a little while, you can remember her with a tender, loving letter.

If she should have a headache sometime, you can remember her by being quiet as a mouse around the house.

If she should be very tired some morning, you can re-

432

PLEASE REMEMBER MOTHER

member her by taking a nice breakfast up to her in bed.

If she should be sick for a day or two, you can remember her by taking her some flowers or maybe something special that she likes to eat.

To every boy and girl in all the world comes the loving message from Jesus: "Please remember mother."

When History Broke in Two

THAT day when Jesus died upon the cross was the most important in the history of this world. It was, in fact, the day when history broke in two.

Jesus had come from heaven to reveal the love of God to the world, to men and women, boys and girls, everywhere. He had come to tell them that "God so loved the world, that He gave His only begotten Son, that whosoever believeth in Him should not perish, but have everlasting life." John 3:16.

He had revealed this love by a thousand kindly deeds, and many a gracious word of sympathy, hope, and courage. He had fed the hungry, healed the sick, opened the eyes of the blind, made the lame to walk, even raised the dead to life. There was nothing else He could have done to let the people know that the God of heaven is a God of love, and that He cares for His earthly children night and day, in sunshine and in darkness, all the days of their lives, "even unto the end of the world."

434

WHEN HISTORY BROKE IN TWO

Jesus had tried to tell everybody, too, that the love of God is so great that He is willing to forgive every sin, no matter how great, and to take into His kingdom all who truly repent of the wrong they have done. All He asks, said Jesus, is that one shall say in his heart, like the prodigal son, "I will arise and go to my father, and will say unto him, Father, I have sinned." Let any boy or girl say this, and mean it, and God will receive him gladly.

If anyone happened to say, "How can a perfectly just God overlook the breaking of His law?" Jesus replied, in effect, Don't worry; I am caring for that. Then He pointed to that beautiful passage of scripture in Isaiah 53, and applied it to Himself: "Surely He hath borne our griefs, and carried our sorrows. . . . He was wounded for our transgressions, He was bruised for our iniquities: the chastisement of our peace was upon Him; and with His stripes we are healed. All we like sheep have gone astray; we have turned every one to his own way; and the Lord hath laid on Him the iniquity of us all." Verses 4-6.

Now, to keep His promise, and to fulfill these words, He is dying on Calvary's cross. The Son of God, the Creator of the heavens and the earth, is giving His life for His one lost world. He who sat upon the throne of glory "from the years of eternity" is now hanging upon a cross. He whom angels once worshiped and adored is dying a criminal's death between two thieves!

No wonder there is "darkness over all the earth." For three awful hours, from noon till three o'clock, there has been no light from sun or moon or stars. In heaven angels veil their faces rather than look upon the dreadful scene.

Suddenly through the darkness comes a cry from the center cross, a cry as from one in great anguish. "My God, My God, why hast Thou forsaken Me?" Matthew 27:46. This is the moment of Jesus' greatest suffering. Not only is the torturing pain of crucifixion at its worst, but the whole awful weight of the sins of all mankind is pressing down upon His soul. He feels cut off from His Father's presence and companionship.

Now it is that

> "All the sins of man
> Since the world began
> Are laid, dear Lord, on Thee."

The words of that lovely hymn in Stainer's *Crucifixion* tell us:

> "Here the King of all the ages,
> Throned in light ere worlds
> could be,
> Robed in mortal flesh is dying,
> Crucified by sin for me.
>
> "This—all human thought
> surpassing—
> This is earth's most awful hour,
> God has taken mortal weakness!
> God has laid aside His power!"

436

WHEN HISTORY BROKE IN TWO

And now another cry, a "loud voice," is heard from that center cross. "It is finished!" cries Jesus. "Father, into Thy hands I commend My spirit."

The struggle is over; the victory is won. Truly Jesus is dead, but in dying He has paid the price of man's redemption. He has opened the way into the kingdom of God for all who believe in Him. He has kept the promise He made to Adam and Eve in the Garden. He has made certain that the serpent's head shall be crushed, and that Eden, glorious Eden, shall be restored as the eternal home of His children.

So, though seemingly defeated by cruel enemies, Jesus has cleared the way for a complete and glorious triumph over all evil.

Suddenly, as Jesus becomes limp and lifeless on the cross, all nature is convulsed. The earth heaves to and fro in a

mighty quake. Great rocks split open. Lightning flashes and thunder roars. The very elements seem to be shouting their fury at the wicked deed that has been done. The crowd of sneering, jeering people about the foot of the cross melts away. Priests and rulers alike flee for their lives. Only the soldiers remain, with the centurion who says, "Truly this was the Son of God." Matthew 27:54.

In the midst of all these terrible happenings the veil of the Temple is suddenly "rent in twain from the top to the bottom."

This veil separated the holy place from the Holy of Holies—the two main apartments of the Temple in Jerusalem. And when that veil—no doubt by an eager angel's hand—was ripped from top to bottom, it told the Jewish people that their services and sacrifices were no longer needed. From this moment on they would be meaningless, for the one supreme sacrifice, toward which all others had pointed, had now been made.

Even as that Temple veil was torn in two that solemn Friday afternoon in the long ago, so the whole course of history was divided by what happened then. The crucifixion of Jesus was the Great Divide in the history of the world and of the universe. From then on everything was different, not only for the Jews, but for all mankind. Till then men had been looking forward to the coming of the Messiah to bear their griefs and carry their sorrows. Now they would forever look back to a Saviour who gave His life for the world.

By dying on Calvary, Jesus gave new meaning to His birth in Bethlehem, so that His whole life began to stand out as of supreme importance in the affairs of men and nations. People began to speak of B.C.—before Christ and A.D.—after Christ (meaning *Anno Domini,* the year of our Lord). And now everybody in all the world, Christians and non-Christians alike, uses these terms. Every history book is based on them.

Today we still look back to that turning point of time. And there we see a cross, with arms outstretched in loving invitation—one toward the past, the other toward the future —taking in everyone, every father and mother, every boy and girl, from Eden lost to Eden restored. And it stands on old Golgotha, where history broke in two.

> "When I survey the wondrous cross
>   On which the Prince of glory died,
> My richest gain I count but loss,
>   And pour contempt on all my pride.
>
> "Were the whole realm of nature mine,
>   That were a tribute far too small;
> Love so amazing, so divine,
>   Demands my life, my soul, my all."

The Saddest Sabbath

ANY tears were shed when Jesus died on Calvary's cross. Not all who watched His crucifixion had jeered and mocked at Him. Among the crowd there was more than one disciple heartbroken at the turn of events. "All His acquaintance, and the women that followed Him from Galilee, stood afar off, beholding these things." Luke 23:49.

Among those who cared most were "Mary Magdalene, and Mary the mother of James and Joses, and the mother of Zebedee's children." They had been very close to Jesus in all His work the past three years, and you can imagine how they must have felt when they saw Him crucified. They hoped against hope that even at the last minute Jesus would reveal His power and surprise everybody by coming down from the cross.

Sick with fear and disappointment, they waited help-lessly, weeping their hearts out in sorrow. They saw noon be-

come dark as midnight, and for three hours they peered through the gloom at the three crosses on Golgotha's hill. They heard that last loud cry of their beloved Master; they felt the earth quake; they shuddered at the brilliant lightning and the rolling peals of thunder. Even now, they thought, amid these dreadful convulsions of nature, something might happen to raise their hopes anew. But no; it was all over. Jesus was dead. There was no hope now. There was nothing to do but go back to Jerusalem and weep.

And what would happen to His body? It would have to be taken from the cross before Sabbath; they knew that; but what would the Romans do with it? Oh, dreadful thought; would they cast it into a criminal's grave or leave it lying on the hillside for the crows and rats to devour? And what could a few poor women do about it?

Then word spread that a rich man who had been a secret disciple of Jesus had asked permission to take His body from the cross and bury it. It was Joseph of Arimathaea, "an honourable counsellor, which also waited for the kingdom of God." He had gone "boldly unto Pilate, and craved the body of Jesus," and Pilate had granted his request.

It was the first good news the disciples had heard that day and I can almost hear those weeping women murmur, "God bless him! Brave man! Thank God for Joseph of Arimathaea!"

By and by Mary Magdalene and Mary the mother of Jesus, who had lingered by the cross after the others had left, saw Joseph and his friend Nicodemus — the one who came to Jesus by night—take the body from the cross, and carry it gently to "a sepulchre that was hewn in stone, wherein never man before was laid."

It was Joseph's own sepulcher, made for himself and his family. I have been in it, or one just like it. It is close by Golgotha. Inside you can still see how it was hewn out of the rock, and how it was left unfinished, brand new, when Jesus had need of it.

There was no burial service for Jesus, such as is held for the dead today. There was too little time between His death at three o'clock and the arrival of the Sabbath at sunset. Certainly there was no time to embalm His body. So Joseph and Nicodemus did the best they could, laying Him gently inside the tomb and rolling a stone across the door.

As for the two Marys, they "beheld the sepulchre, and how His body was laid. And they returned, and prepared spices and ointments; and rested the sabbath day according to the commandment." Luke 23:55, 56.

Why did they not go right on and embalm the body of Jesus then and there? Surely nothing could have been more important than that! Had not Jesus Himself said, "The sabbath was made for man, and not man for the sabbath"? Mark 2:27. Had He not also said, "It is lawful to do well on the sabbath days"? Matthew 12:12. Had He not healed the sick on the Sabbath, and done many other good deeds on that day? True, He had. But He had never told His disciples to break the Sabbath by doing unnecessary work during its sacred hours.

443

They were cruel hands of hate that nailed Jesus to the cross of Calvary, but the hands that took His body down and prepared it for burial were hands of tender love and sympathy.

After walking with Jesus for three and a half years, the disciples knew just how He felt about the fourth commandment and Sabbathkeeping. They had no question in their minds as to which day they should keep, or how they should keep it. So, because the embalming of the body of Jesus was not absolutely necessary just then, they left the task undone, returned to Jerusalem, and waited for the holy hours of the Sabbath to pass.

And what a sad, sad Sabbath that was! Surely it was the saddest Sabbath in all history. The disciples were in despair. Some had already started back to Galilee. The rest were hiding in and around Jerusalem, afraid that now Jesus was dead the priests and rulers would try to kill them also.

It was hard to believe that only a few days ago Jesus had ridden into Jerusalem at the head of a great procession of happy people, with some spreading palm branches before Him and children crying out, "Hosanna to the Son of David: Blessed is He that cometh in the name of the Lord." Matthew

21:9. But it was so, and everyone had thought that that was the moment when He would take over the government of Israel from the Romans and let Himself be crowned king. Eagerly, hopefully, they had waited for Him to reveal His power in some wonderful way, so that everyone would welcome Him as the long-hoped-for Messiah.

Now *this* had happened! In less than a week Jesus had been arrested, tried, condemned, crucified! So suddenly had it all taken place that some thought it must be just a bad, ugly dream. It was as though a great hole had opened in the earth and swallowed all their hopes. With Jesus gone, there was nothing left to hope for, nothing left to live for. What *would* they do without Him? What could they do?

They talked together of the beautiful life Jesus had lived among them, of the wise things He had said, of the kind deeds He had done, how gracious and gentlemanly He had been to everybody, even to His enemies. They wept anew at the very mention of His name.

On Sabbath morning word spread that the priests had learned where Jesus had been buried and had gone to Pilate urging that a guard of Roman soldiers be placed around the sepulcher.

The rumor was true. A delegation of priests and Pharisees had indeed gone to Pilate, saying, "Sir, we remember that that deceiver said, while He was yet alive, After three days I will rise again. Command therefore that the sepulchre

be made sure until the third day, lest His disciples come by night, and steal Him away, and say unto the people, He is risen from the dead: so the last error shall be worse than the first." Matthew 27:63, 64.

Pilate had granted their request, saying, "Ye have a watch: go your way, make it as sure as you can. So they went, and made the sepulchre sure, sealing the stone, and setting a watch."

As the news of this reached the disciples they plunged into deeper sorrow. Now what should they do? They had planned to go to the tomb after Sabbath to embalm the body of their Lord. Now even this might be denied them. Would the soldiers let them by?

Slowly the hours of that saddest Sabbath passed by. When at last sunset came again, it found them all still mourning for their Master. They could think of nothing else but that their beloved Jesus was dead and buried, and, worst of all, a hundred Roman soldiers were guarding His body and a Roman seal was upon His sepulcher.

Twin Sunrise

~~~~~~

I DON'T suppose the disciples slept very much that Saturday night. They were too worried, too sorrowful, too afraid. Many of them no doubt spent the night getting ready to leave the city before the persecution they feared should break out. Others just went on talking of the terrible things that had happened that weekend, and of what they would have to do now Jesus had been taken from them.

But whether they slept, or lay awake, all were aroused and startled by another mighty earthquake in the early hours of the morning. Once more the earth trembled violently and all the houses shook.

What a day, what a night! they must have said.

Among those who slept little, if at all, were some of the women from Galilee, including those who had watched His burial Friday afternoon. They had one purpose in mind—to return to the sepulcher and embalm the body of the Lord. Just how early they started out on their journey nobody knows.

447

→

The Roman guards watching Joseph's tomb were startled by a mighty earthquake that put them in great fear as an angel rolled away the stone and bade Jesus come forth.

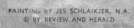

However, Luke tells us that it was "very early" (Luke 24:1); John says that they got there "when it was yet dark" (John 20:1); and Matthew says that it was "as it began to dawn toward the first day of the week" (Matthew 28:1). Evidently it was just before sunrise.

In their trembling hands the women carried the spices which they had begun to prepare before the Sabbath. They hoped that they might be able to persuade the guard to let them go into the tomb and embalm the body. Yet now, as they walked along the dark highway, a new worry troubled them. They remembered the stone which Joseph and Nicodemus had rolled in front of the sepulcher, a "very great" stone, much too heavy for women to move. "And they said among themselves, Who shall roll us away the stone from the door of the sepulchre?" Mark 16:3.

Now they are picking their way over the rough land near the place of burial. Suddenly they stop. There is the tomb, just ahead of them. But where is the stone? It is on one side; it has been rolled away!

450

TWIN SUNRISE

They can hardly believe their eyes. What can this mean? Has someone been here already and robbed the tomb of its precious body? And what of the guard? What of the Roman seal on the tomb?

They can see no soldiers. As for the seal, it is broken. Who has dared to break this seal without permission from Pilate?

Suddenly they see an angel in human form sitting on that very stone, as though daring all Rome to do its worst. His face shines "like lightning," and his raiment is "white as snow."

Terrified, the women turn to flee from the scene, but they are halted by the angel's lovely voice. "Fear not ye," he says: "for I know that ye seek Jesus, which was crucified. He is not here: for He is risen, as He said. Come, see the place where the Lord lay." Matthew 28:5, 6.

At this they enter the sepulcher and find it empty, save for another beautiful angel sitting there. The body of Jesus is nowhere to be seen. As they look around, searching for it, the angel says, "Why seek ye the living among the dead? He is not here, but is risen: remember how He spake unto you when He was yet in Galilee, saying, The Son of man must be delivered into the hands of sinful men, and be crucified, and the third day rise again." Luke 24:5-7.

"Go your way," the angel continues, "tell His disciples and Peter that He goeth before you into Galilee: there shall ye see Him, as He said unto you." Mark 16:7.

At this the women—all but one—hurry from the sepul-

cher and head back toward Jerusalem "with fear and great joy."

Can you see them running down that hillside? How they run! What a story they have to tell!

Presently, panting and untidy, they reach the place where the leading disciples have been sitting out the night.

"We have just come from the tomb!" they cry. "It is empty! His body is not there! And we saw angels who said that He is alive!" Luke 24:23.

At first the disciples will not believe them. They think that these poor women are overtired and upset by all that has happened, and their words seem to them "as idle tales." Verse 11.

"But it's true, it's true!" they cry. "We saw the angels ourselves! We heard them speak to us! One of them told us specially to tell Peter."

Peter is moved at this. So is John. Hurriedly they leave the room, determined to go and see for themselves. Full of curiosity and excitement, they run together to the tomb, with John, the younger man, gradually pulling ahead.

At last they reach the sepulcher, and John, stooping down, looks in. To his amazement he sees nothing but the linen cloth which had been wrapped around Jesus, and the napkin which had covered His head. Nothing more. When Peter comes puffing up they both go into the tomb together and find it empty.

They are puzzled. So far they have found the women's story correct. The stone is rolled away; the body of Jesus is no longer there. But what has happened to it? Has it been stolen? Yet that is impossible, for an armed guard has been outside all night. Can it be that Jesus has risen from the dead? Can it be that He is indeed alive?

They hurry back to the city to tell the others what they have found. Only Mary Magdalene lingers by the empty tomb. Alone, she stoops down and looks into the sepulcher. There she sees "two angels in white sitting, the one at the head, and the other at the feet, where the body of Jesus had lain."

They say to her, "Woman, why weepest thou?"

She says, "Because they have taken away my Lord, and I know not where they have laid Him."

Just then Mary looks around and sees someone standing near her. Supposing him to be the gardener, she says, "Sir, if thou have borne Him hence, tell me where thou hast laid Him, and I will take Him away."

Then the gardener speaks—God's Gardener. He says but one word: "Mary." But it is enough. She recognizes Him immediately.

"Master!" she says, running toward Him.

"Touch Me not," He says; "for I am not yet ascended to My Father: but go to My brethren, and say unto them, I ascend unto My Father, and your Father; and to My God, and your God." John 20:17.

Then He is gone. But Mary knows now that the story of the angels is true. She has seen Him herself! She has heard His voice! He is alive! He is risen from the dead!

Though full of weariness from the long night vigil, with wildly beating heart she rushes headlong to the city to tell the others the wonderful news. The sun is rising over the Jordan Valley, bathing all the mountains round about Jerusalem with the light of a new day.

Another sun is shining too, for Jesus is risen, the Sun of Righteousness, whose golden rays shall shine on all the earth through all the years to come. The darkness of the tomb has yielded to the morning light of eternal redemption.

Twin sunrise! Glorious dawn of a great new day for the children of men!

Knights of the Burning Heart

~~~~~~~~~~~~~~~~~~~~~~~~~~~~~~~~~~~~~~

THE disciples listened to Mary Magdalene's story, but they did not believe it. Knowing how deeply devoted she was to the Master, they supposed she had just imagined that she had seen Him outside the tomb.

Yet they were troubled. That the sepulcher was empty, there was no doubt. Peter and John had told them that. The body of Jesus was no longer there. Where was it? Who had taken it, and why?

They talked about it all day. There was nothing else to do. Most of them did not dare to go outdoors for fear they would be arrested. However, Cleopas and a friend decided to risk it and go home. They lived at Emmaus, a village about seven miles from Jerusalem.

Passing through the city streets without trouble, they started on their long, dusty walk. On the way they talked of nothing else but the events of the past weekend, how all their hopes had faded, and everything had gone dead wrong.

455

Mary turned from weeping at Joseph's tomb to see someone standing there she supposed was the gardener. She said, "Sir, tell me where thou hast laid Him, and I will take Him away."

As they journeyed another traveler joined them, and they walked along together. Noticing how sad Cleopas and his friend were, the Stranger asked them what was making them so miserable. This surprised Cleopas, for he could not understand how anyone living near Jerusalem could have failed to hear the sad news about what had happened to Jesus of Nazareth. Turning upon the Stranger, he said, "Are you the only visitor to Jerusalem who does not know the things that have happened there in these days?" Luke 24:18, R.S.V.

"What things?" asked the Stranger innocently.

"Concerning Jesus of Nazareth," said Cleopas. Then he went on to explain how Jesus "was a prophet mighty in deed and word before God and all the people," and how the chief priests and rulers had "delivered Him up to be condemned to death, and crucified Him. But," Cleopas added ruefully, "we had hoped that He was the One to redeem Israel. Yes, and besides all this, it is now the third day since this happened. Moreover, some women of our company amazed us. They were at the tomb early in the morning and did not find His body; and they came back saying that they had even seen a vision of angels, who said that He was alive. Some of those who were with us went to the tomb, and found it just as the women had said; but Him they did not see." Verses 19-24, R.S.V.

So they rambled on, telling the whole story of what had taken place over the weekend. Quietly the Stranger listened till they were through. Then, gently but firmly, He began to speak to them.

"O foolish men," He said, "and slow of heart to believe all

that the prophets have spoken! Was it not necessary that the Christ should suffer these things and enter into His glory?" Verses 25, 26, R.S.V.

Then, though He had no Bible with Him, and quoting all the texts from memory, "beginning with Moses and all the prophets, He interpreted to them in all the scriptures the things concerning Himself." Verse 27, R.S.V.

What a wonderful Bible study that must have been! Seven whole miles of it, with the two disciples marveling at the amazing knowledge of their new-found Friend.

As they drew near to Emmaus the Stranger "made as though He would have gone further," but the others, who had enjoyed His company so much, would have none of it. "Stay with us," they urged Him, "for it is toward evening and the day is now far spent."

So the Stranger stayed for supper, and Cleopas asked Him to say grace, which He gladly did. Then it was, as "He took the bread and blessed, and broke it, and gave it to them," that they recognized Him.

"Jesus! Master!" they cried. But He was gone. He had "vanished out of their sight."

So Mary Magdalene had been right! She had seen the Lord after all! He was indeed alive! Oh, wonderful news! They must tell the others right away!

Forgetting their hunger and weariness, they dashed from the table out of the house, back onto the dusty trail leading to Jerusalem.

Normally they would never have started on such a trip as late as this, with the shades of evening already falling. It was too dangerous. But what did they care, with such a story to tell the world!

No leisurely walking now. They ran; they stumbled over rocks; they fell; they picked themselves up and hurried on. On, on to Jerusalem! At all costs they must get there soon.

As they ran there was little time, or breath, for talking. But they did scold themselves for not recognizing Jesus

earlier. "Did not our heart burn within us," they said, "while He talked with us by the way, and while He opened to us the Scriptures?" Verse 32, A.V.

How different are these men from the two who set out for Emmaus only a few hours before! From being poor, sad, hopeless creatures, dragging their feet on a long and lonely journey, they are now men of faith, courage, and hope, their hearts aflame with a glorious message. Instead of fleeing in despair from their enemies, they are rushing back into the fray, Knights of the Burning Heart, to do and dare for their Master.

Puffing and panting through the city gate, they hurry to the house where they left the disciples earlier that day. Thumping on the door, they demand admittance. Gingerly someone opens it, peering anxiously into the night to make sure no enemy is there.

Through that open door Cleopas and his friend see a group of tense, excited people, one of whom, recognizing them, cries out, "The Lord is risen indeed, and hath appeared to Simon!"

But *they* have great news too, and they set out to tell it: how they met Jesus on the road to Emmaus, how He walked with them for two hours or more, and how they recognized Him as He broke the bread at supper.

Everyone is thrilled at this new evidence that Jesus is alive. Surely, they say, it *must* be true that He is risen from the dead.

Suddenly, as all are talking excitedly over this latest piece of news, someone cries out, "Look! There He is!"

All eyes turn toward the strange Person who has suddenly appeared in their midst. They hear Him say, "Peace be unto

459

you." But there is no peace in their hearts. They are filled with fear, thinking this must be a ghost. But it is no ghost, or spirit; it is Jesus Himself.

"Why are ye troubled?" He says to them. "Behold My hands and My feet, that it is I Myself: handle Me, and see; for a spirit hath not flesh and bones, as ye see Me have."

He shows them His hands and His feet, still bearing the marks of the nails that held Him to the cross.

Overcome with joy, they hardly know what to say or do. Their sadness vanishes. New hope comes into their hearts. Jesus is alive! He has come back from the grave! He has kept His promise!

Suddenly their hearts begin to burn and blaze with a great new vision and a great new purpose. From a group of discouraged, defeated disciples they become like Cleopas and his friend, Knights of the Burning Heart, ready to ride forth fearlessly for their risen Lord to the ends of the earth.

460

STORY 63

Doubting Thomas

NOT all the disciples were present when Jesus appeared among them that Sunday evening. One at least was missing. For some reason or other Thomas wasn't there. It is possible that he was among those who were busy getting ready to return to Galilee. Anyhow, he wasn't there; and so he missed being among the first to see Jesus after His resurrection.

Of course, it wasn't long before he heard about what happened that evening. Next time he met the other disciples they were full of the exciting story, and eager to tell about it.

"Jesus appeared to us!" they said eagerly. "His very self! We saw Him and talked with Him. Now we know for sure He is risen from the dead."

But Thomas refused to believe their story. Perhaps it was because he felt a little bit left out. He had heard that Jesus had appeared to Mary Magdalene, then to Peter, then to Cleopas, and finally to all the disciples in the upper room. Why, he ques-

461

tioned, if Jesus were indeed risen from the dead, had He appeared to all the others and not to him? A little bit of jealousy may well have added to his doubts.

In any case he decided he would not believe unless he actually saw Jesus Himself. "Except I shall see in His hands the print of the nails, and put my finger into the print of the nails, and thrust my hand into His side," he said, "I will not believe."

All week long he held doggedly to this idea. Nobody could move him from it.

Some have thought that it was very wicked of Thomas to doubt so long, but they forget that *all* the disciples doubted at first. When they heard the stories that the women brought from the open tomb, they called them "idle tales"! Thomas, after all, only doubted a few days longer than the rest.

And Thomas had many good points. He was a very brave man, and most devoted to Jesus during His ministry.

Now, not having seen Jesus since His crucifixion, he was in doubt. Out of loyalty to his beloved Master he did not want to make a mistake. Could the stories of His resurrection be true? He did not feel sure. "I'll believe when I see Him," he told himself, "but not before."

All that week he worried about it. As the days went by, his doubts increased. If Jesus were alive, as the others said, why did He not appear again?

Another Sabbath came, one week after that saddest Sabbath of history. There was no sadness now, but a new joy and a great new hope. In their worship that morning the disciples

462

DOUBTING THOMAS

who had actually seen Jesus no doubt told of their wonderful experience, while everybody present in the meeting hoped that He would appear again soon. Only Thomas was miserable. He was still full of doubts. "I can't believe it," he told himself; "I won't believe it; not unless I see the print of the nails in His hands."

Sabbath passed, and Sunday, with the disciples wondering what would happen next, and whether Jesus would ever come to see them again. It was now ten days since the crucifixion.

Then once more, as the disciples were all together in that upper room, "came Jesus, the doors being shut, and stood in the midst, and said, Peace be unto you."

This time Thomas was there with the rest, and what a

© BY RG

look of blank surprise came over his face! He may well have felt ashamed, too, after all his doubting. For surely this was Jesus. There could be no question now. The others had been right all the time. The Lord was indeed risen from the dead.

Then Thomas saw Jesus looking straight at him, right through him! And he heard that dear, familiar voice calling him by name.

"Thomas," said Jesus, "reach hither thy finger, and behold My hands; and reach hither thy hand, and thrust it into My side: and be not faithless, but believing."

So Jesus had read his thoughts! Jesus had known all about his doubts! Jesus had heard every word he had said about touching the wounds in His hands and feet and side!

He had no desire to touch them now. There was no need. Beyond all question this was the dear Master Himself. Kneeling humbly at His feet, he cried, "My Lord and my God."

Then Jesus said to him, so kindly, so gently, "Because thou hast seen Me, thou hast believed: blessed are they that have not seen, and yet have believed." John 20:29.

At that moment Jesus was thinking not only of Thomas but of all the people who should live from that day to this. He was thinking of all the boys and girls who would hear of Him through all the years to come, and must needs believe in Him without seeing Him. Blessed, He said, will they be.

This blessing is for you and for me, for nobody alive today has ever seen Jesus. Nobody can see Him—now. Yet we can believe in Him, you and I. The Bible tells all about Him, all we need to know. Patriarchs, prophets, and apostles have pic-

464

DOUBTING THOMAS

tured Him so clearly that there can be no mistake. They have made Him so real that we can feel Him close by us, "closer than breathing; nearer than hands and feet."

But best of all we have the word of Thomas, the man who doubted so much and then believed with all his heart. His story is recorded that you and I, not seeing, but believing, might fall on our knees before our beloved Jesus, saying, "My Lord and my God."

Breakfast on the Beach

WHAT to do now? This was the big question that faced the disciples. The Passover, which had brought them to Jerusalem, was ended. Some had their homes to think about. Most important of all, their money was almost gone. They must get back to work at once.

Then, too, had not the angels told the women at the tomb that Jesus would go before them into Galilee? Back to Galilee, then, they would go, and see what would happen there.

Seven of them walked the whole way together—Peter, Thomas, James, John, Nathanael, and two others. What a lot of things they had to talk about on that long, weary journey! How lonesome they must have felt without Jesus! The last time they had gone over this road He had been with them, their Leader, their Teacher, their Friend. Now they were on their own. True, they believed He had risen from the dead; they were sure that He was the Son of the living God; but all the same, they missed Him very much.

BREAKFAST ON THE BEACH

As they walked they passed many a place with sweet memories of their life with Him. Every now and then one would say, "This is where He gave a blind man sight," or, "This is the place where He healed a leper," or, "It was here that He said that He came not to destroy men's lives but to save them." Everywhere they looked they saw something that reminded them of the three beautiful years they had spent with Him.

As they drew near to Galilee their minds turned again to the question of what they would do next. Peter answered it for all of them by saying, "I go a fishing."

"We also go with thee," they said.

So they went down to the little wharf at Tiberias, or maybe Capernaum. There were the boats, the dear old boats, just as they had left them. Some of their old friends were there, too, glad to see them back. How wonderful to be home once more!

And there was old Galilee itself, so calm, so peaceful, so very beautiful, and quite unchanged by all that had happened.

I have been on a boat on Galilee. I have seen the sun rising behind the eastern hills, driving back the shadows and filling all the tiny wavelets with sparkling jewels. I have seen the fishermen hauling in their nets loaded with fish, big fish, and I know how Peter and the rest of the disciples felt that evening they arrived.

Those boats were so tempting, the disciples could hardly wait to get into one of them again. The Bible says, "They went forth, and entered into a ship immediately." I am sure they did. They couldn't help it.

But a disappointment awaited them. They couldn't catch

any fish. Time after time they threw out their nets and hauled them in only to find them empty. It was very discouraging, especially as they so badly needed the money a good haul would bring them. Probably they said to one another, "We've forgotten how to do it. We've lost our skill all these months we've been away."

The stars came out, and still there were no fish. Midnight passed, and their nets were yet empty. Dawn began to break, and there was nothing to show for the whole night's toil.

As the morning light grew brighter they noticed a man standing on the shore.

"Who can that be standing there at this time of the morning?" one asked.

"Can't tell," said the others. "Seems to be a stranger in these parts."

Then to their surprise the Stranger spoke to them, His voice carrying across the water separating them.

© BY RGH

BREAKFAST ON THE BEACH

"Children, have you any fish?" He called.

"No," they said sadly.

Then to their amazement the Stranger said, "Cast the net on the right side of the boat, and you will find some."

Should they, or shouldn't they? How could this Stranger know where the fish were to be found? And so near shore, too. Had they not toiled all night and caught nothing? Oh, well, they might as well try. So they cast the net overboard once more, "and now they were not able to haul it in, for the quantity of fish."

"It is the Lord!" John whispered to Peter.

Peter took one look and saw it was indeed Jesus.

Throwing his coat about him, Peter leaped into the water and waded ashore, the rest following in the boat.

How glad they were to see Him again! And how kind of Him to give them all these fish when they needed them so much!

Then they noticed something else. There beside Him was "a charcoal fire . . . , with fish lying on it." Oh, wonder of wonders! The Lord Jesus, though risen from the dead in power and glory, was still so much their friend that He even had their breakfast ready for them!

"Bring some of the fish you have just caught," Jesus said in that gentle, kindly voice they knew so well.

So Peter got back into the boat and hauled in the netful of fish, which had been completely forgotten in the excitement of seeing Jesus again. It was full of large fish, "a hundred and fifty-three of them."

Then Jesus said to them, "Come and have breakfast." (R.S.V.) And He came "and took the bread and gave it to them, and so with the fish."

What a lovely, unforgettable scene! Jesus, Lord of glory, waiting on His poor, tired disciples, who had been up all night fishing!

And is there any more beautiful invitation in all the Bible than this, "Come and have breakfast"?

Truly there is the important invitation to Noah: "Come thou and all thy house into the ark."

There is the loving invitation to sinners: "Come now, and let us reason together, saith the Lord."

There is the tender invitation to the toilworn and weary: "Come unto me, all ye that labour and are heavy laden, and I will give you rest."

There is the urgent invitation to supper: "Come; for all things are now ready."

470

BREAKFAST ON THE BEACH

But surely one of the best of all is this sweet, simple invitation to breakfast—an invitation that every boy and girl can understand. For we all love breakfast, don't we? Whatever would we do without it? And it is the first meal of the day. In its strength we go forth to do our work and fulfill our duties, at home or at school.

And so it was then. That breakfast was the beginning of a great new experience for all those disciples.

Their fishing days on Galilee were over forever. From now on they were to start on the great work for which Jesus had been preparing them so long.

That call to breakfast was the call to a new work and a new life for every one of them. From this day forth they were to "catch men" for the kingdom of God.

And so may it be with us. When we are tired and worried, wondering what to do next, let us heed that kindly call of the Master—"Come and have breakfast." There, in His presence, feeding on His Word, we shall find strength for the next task He wants us to do for Him.

The Last Good-by

~~~~~~~~~~~~~~~~~~~~~~~

FOR forty days after His death on Calvary, Jesus met with
His disciples. Precious days!

True, He was not with them all the time, but they
felt He was very near to them, likely to appear among them
any minute; and it was always so good to see Him when He
came.

After He had met with the seven fishermen by the lakeside, and invited them to breakfast, news of it spread all over
Galilee. Hundreds of people who knew Jesus wanted to see Him
again.

Many of them had not been able to go to Jerusalem for
the Passover, and they were eager to know what had happened
there. Rumors had reached them that Jesus had been arrested
and crucified, and then had risen from the dead. Could it all
be true?

From far and near they began to move toward one cen-
tral meeting place—"a mountain," the Bible says—perhaps

where Jesus had met with them so many times before. Soon there were more than five hundred present, all talking eagerly about the great events of the past few weeks, and all wondering whether Jesus would appear to them now.

Some thought that, seeing He was risen from the dead, He might reveal His power in a very wonderful way and set up the kingdom of Israel again, with Himself as King. They were sure He would appear among them in a blaze of light and glory. Then suddenly someone caught sight of a familiar figure walking there on the mountainside, just as Jesus had come among them so many times in the dear old days they remembered so well.

At once the cry went up, "It is the Lord; it is the Lord!" All five hundred saw Him at once, so that there could never be any question about His having risen from the dead.

Now it is that He says to them, "All power is given unto Me in heaven and in earth. Go ye therefore, and teach all nations, baptizing them in the name of the Father, and of the Son, and of the Holy Ghost: teaching them to observe all things whatsoever I have commanded you: and, lo, I am with you alway, even unto the end of the world."

This, then, is what He wants them to do. Not to stay around Galilee, working at their old jobs, but to go everywhere

telling others of the beautiful things He has taught them. How good it is to know that, though He has "all power . . . in heaven and in earth," He will never forget them! Never! He will be one with them in all their joys and sorrows "even unto the end of the world." They are never to feel alone. Always He will be thinking of them in love.

Something Jesus says at this time leads the eleven apostles to return to Jerusalem. At any rate, that is where we find them next in the Bible story, and here Jesus meets with them once more, "Eating together with them." Acts 1:4, margin. Now it is that He promises to give them power to preach and teach His message, saying, "And ye shall be witnesses unto Me both in Jerusalem, and in all Judaea, and in Samaria, and unto the uttermost part of the earth."

This is a new idea. Fancy a group of poor, humble fisher-folk like them witnessing in Jerusalem, of all places, where the priests and Pharisees live! And how can they, with no money and no possessions, ever go to the uttermost part of the earth?

THE LAST GOOD-BY

Still wondering what Jesus can mean, they walk with Him to Bethany, a little way out of Jerusalem. This is where Mary and Martha live, and where Lazarus was raised from the dead only a few weeks before.

Now Jesus is looking at His disciples with a special tenderness. The hour of parting is at hand. He knows that He must soon leave them and return to heaven.

There is sadness in His heart. He loves these dear men, every one of them. He has lived with them for more than three years. He knows all about them; how much they have given up for Him, and how much they soon must suffer for His sake.

Dear Peter! Dear James! Dear, dear John! And Thomas, too, bless him, despite his doubts. And Matthew, Philip, and all the rest. Such good men and true, with all their faults!

"Bless you, bless you, every one!" He says, and there are tears in His voice, I think.

Suddenly they notice that He is rising into the air. He is going away! Yes! Up, up, up He goes, farther and farther, until at last a cloud receives Him out of their sight.

He has gone, but still they look, their eyes peering into the depths of space, hoping against hope that they may catch one more glimpse of Him. But He is gone, gone! And the dreadful feeling comes over them that He is gone for good. For a moment a desperate sadness fills their hearts.

Then all of a sudden they notice two strangers standing near them, both dressed in white. Who can they be?

"Ye men of Galilee," say the strangers, "why stand ye gazing up into heaven? this same Jesus, which is taken up from

475

you into heaven, shall so come in like manner as ye have seen Him go into heaven."

Now they know! Surely these two men are really angels, sent by their beloved Master to comfort their hearts with the promise that someday He will come back again.

How kind, how thoughtful of Him! On His way to the glory land, with all the shining host of heaven around Him, He has remembered His friends left behind on earth!

And they "returned to Jerusalem with great joy."

All sadness gone, they are "continually in the temple, praising and blessing God." Had not the angels said He would return? And that it would be "this same Jesus" who would come back, not another?

Beautiful, blessed hope! "This same Jesus" is to come again. The very same Jesus who healed the sick, raised the dead, loved the children, and told such beautiful stories—He is coming again. The same dear Jesus of Nazareth, Capernaum, and Cana, who did so many kind deeds for the poor and needy, who was always so gentle and gracious and good—He is coming again.

It will not be another Jesus, a different Jesus, but "this same Jesus." Time will not age or alter Him, for He is "the same yesterday, and to day, and for ever." When He comes back down that shining pathway through the skies, it will be the same Jesus who went away, unchanged by the changing years. We shall know Him by the smile on His face, by the sweet melody of His voice, and by the marks of the nails in His hands.

477

← PAINTING BY HARRY ANDERSON   © BY REVIEW AND HERALD

As the disciples were earnestly asking Jesus about the future He was suddenly taken up from them into heaven and two angels appeared telling them that He would come again.

House Afire!

CROWDED into the little upper room in Jerusalem are a hundred and twenty disciples. All are talking excitedly about the ascension of Jesus. Those who saw Him go up into heaven are eager to tell the wonderful story to the others, while they, full of questions, are just as eager to hear it.

"Did you really see Him go up into the sky?" asks one. "How far up did He go before you couldn't see Him any more?" "And the cloud that received Him—was it a cloud of angels?" asks another. "And what about those two young men in white—are you sure Jesus sent them? Did they really say that He would come back?"

For hours and days they talk about this latest miracle, and all the other wonderful things that have taken place since Jesus rose from the dead after His crucifixion.

Then they remember how Jesus told them to wait in Jerusalem until they should receive "power from on high." More

478

questions come to their minds. What can this mean? What power? What for? How will it happen? And when? And what will it do to them?

Nobody can answer these questions. They will have to wait and see. But they all feel that if Jesus is going to send them power from heaven, they must get ready to receive it. So they begin to pray and continue in prayer.

They have some wonderful prayer meetings. I can almost hear them all thanking God for sending Jesus from heaven to earth to live among them and die for them. I believe I can hear them too, thanking Him for the friendship of Jesus and all the lovely times they had together with Him.

And I think I can hear them telling God how much they need courage and strength to be witnesses for Jesus, as He told them to be, and how they want to be brave and good and true.

As they get closer to God, so they get closer to one another. Some begin to ask forgiveness for hasty words they have said, or unkind deeds they may have done. There are tears in many eyes as some clasp hands, saying, "Of course, I forgive you; please forgive me!" And so they all begin to know something of the joy that comes from keeping that beautiful commandment of Jesus: "That ye love one another, as I have loved you." John 15:12.

© BY RGH

Day after day they tarry in that upper room, waiting for Jesus to keep His promise to send power from heaven. Then, just seven weeks after the crucifixion, when the day of Pentecost has fully come, a strange thing happens.

Suddenly there is a sound of a rushing mighty wind, rattling the windows, slamming the doors, shaking the house. The room where they are sitting is filled with this gale from God, as all wait tensely for what may happen next.

Then upon every one of them there appears a tongue of fire. Those at the back of the room see it flaming upon Peter, James, John, and the rest of the apostles, while they in turn see it flashing from the humblest disciple present.

For a moment it seems as though the whole house is on fire. And so it is! On fire for God.

Until this moment the room has been hushed and quiet. Only the voices of people praying have been heard. Now, with this rushing, mighty wind and these tongues of flame, all is changed. In one swift moment everybody is filled with zeal and activity. All begin talking at once about the wonderful love of Jesus.

They feel they have prayed enough; now they must go out and tell the world about their risen Lord.

Opening the door, they pour out into the streets of Jerusalem, a light on their faces and a purpose in their hearts they have never known before. To their surprise they find they can make themselves understood by people from other countries. Wonderful!

PAINTING BY HERBERT RUDEEN
© BY R&H

The people who hear them think it is wonderful too. Indeed, they are all amazed, "saying one to another, Behold, are not all these which speak Galilaeans? And how hear we every man in our own tongue, wherein we were born?"

Some, of course, just laugh. There are always people like that. These disciples of Jesus are drunk, they say.

But they are not drunk, as Peter soon tells them. Standing bravely before the growing crowd, he preaches his first sermon. With great power he tells about Jesus and His love.

Fearing nobody, neither priest, nor scribe, nor Pharisee, he boldly cries, "Therefore let all the house of Israel know assuredly, that God hath made that same Jesus, whom ye have crucified, both Lord and Christ."

The crowd listens enthralled. The people can hardly believe their ears. Nor can the disciples. Can this be Peter, the fisherman, whom they have all known so well? How can he preach like this? Why, here he is holding thousands of people spellbound! What can have happened to him?

Something has happened! The power of God has come upon him. His heart has been set on fire by the Holy Spirit. Peter the coward, who denied his Lord, has become Peter the fearless, a mighty witness for Jesus.

When Peter asks how many will give their hearts to Jesus and accept Him as their Saviour, three thousand people respond. The Christian church is born!

This day, from that fire-filled upper room, ten dozen men and women go forth, aflame for God, eager to carry the light of His love to the uttermost parts of the earth.

STORY 67

Exciting Days

~~~~~~~~~~~~~~~~~~~~~~~~~~

EXCITING days followed. With the coming of the fire of God into the hearts of the disciples they discovered that they could not only preach but heal! Besides being able to talk in several languages, they could make people better from all sorts of diseases. They had become both preachers and doctors at once.

Now, instead of one person performing miracles, there were a hundred. The work that Jesus did alone was now done by His many followers whom He had filled with His Spirit. No wonder the whole city of Jerusalem was stirred.

As for the disciples themselves, they were amazed at the power that flowed through them to bless the people. They were thrilled to think they were now able to do things as wonderful as Jesus did while He was with them.

Going up to the Temple one day, Peter and John saw a lame man being carried by his friends to the gate, where he used to sit all day asking passers-by for money.

They had seen him there many times before, and had felt sorry for him. Now they could really help him.

"Look at us," said Peter, to call the lame man's attention.

The lame man looked, expecting a gift, but the apostles had something far better for him than money.

"Silver and gold have I none," said Peter; "but such as I have give I thee: In the name of Jesus Christ of Nazareth rise up and walk."

Taking the lame man by the hand, Peter lifted him up. Immediately his feet and anklebones received strength. "And he leaping up stood, and walked, and entered with them into the temple, walking, and leaping, and praising God."

You can imagine what happened next. As the healed man clung to Peter and John in joy and gratitude, "all the people ran together unto them . . . , greatly wondering." Pushing and shoving, the crowd pressed forward to see the beggar and the man who had healed him.

Everybody knew this poor man. They had seen him begging at the Temple gate for years—since he was a boy. For forty years he had been lame. Yet here he was walking and leaping about in the most amazing way. What a miracle!

As the people crowded around, Peter saw another opportunity to tell them about Jesus. "Ye men of Israel," he cried in a voice that could be heard above the hubbub, "why marvel ye at this? or why look ye so earnestly on us, as though by our own power or holiness we had made this man to walk?"

Then he went on to tell them that it was really Jesus who had done it. "His name through faith in His name hath

485

Outside the Gate Beautiful of the Temple a poor beggar who had been lame all his life was healed by Peter, who said, "In the name of Jesus Christ of Nazareth rise up and walk."

made this man strong" and "given him this perfect soundness in the presence of you all."

Then he pleaded with the people to repent of their sins and give their hearts to Jesus.

As he spoke, more and more people joined the crowd, until almost everybody in the Temple was there. Many of the priests came to listen too, and they were anything but pleased—especially when they heard Peter say, "Ye denied the Holy One and the Just, and desired a murderer to be granted unto you; and killed the Prince of life, whom God hath raised from the dead; whereof we are witnesses."

Here was the very thing of which they had been so much afraid. The disciples of Jesus were claiming that He had been raised from the dead! This must be stopped at once.

So while Peter was speaking, the captain of the Temple, with a group of priests, forced his way through the crowd and arrested both him and John, and led them away.

With the two apostles gone the crowd melted away, but as the people went to their homes many of them made up their minds that these men were right, and that Jesus was indeed the Christ, the Saviour of the world. Many decided that they would join the disciples and help to tell the good news to others.

Next morning there was a big meeting of the Temple leaders. Annas the high priest was there, also Caiaphas—the very ones who had presided at the trial of Jesus. Presently Peter and John were called before them.

"By what power, or by what name, have ye done this?" asked the high priest.

Without a trace of fear Peter replied, "By the name of Jesus Christ of Nazareth, whom ye crucified, whom God raised from the dead, even by Him doth this man stand here before you whole."

Then Peter told his story once more, speaking so freely and boldly that the priests and rulers were astonished. They couldn't understand how a poor, uneducated fisherman could talk like this. As for the miracle that had been wrought, they couldn't say a thing. Not only was the man who had been healed known to every one of them, but here he was in their midst, ready to speak any minute.

"What shall we do to these men?" the priests asked of one another when the council room had been cleared. "For that indeed a notable miracle hath been done by them is manifest to all them that dwell in Jerusalem; and we cannot deny it."

Finally they decided that they would tell the apostles that they must not preach about Jesus any more, then let them go. But they did not realize the kind of men these fishermen had become.

Called back into court, and hearing the decision of the priests and rulers, "Peter and John answered and said unto them, Whether it be right in the sight of God to hearken unto you more than unto God, judge ye. For we cannot but speak the things which we have seen and heard."

"You had better not," said the high priest. But the apostles went away with no thought of stopping their work. Later, in their upper room, they had a wonderful time together, thanking God for the way He had helped them in their first trouble with the authorities, and praying for strength to witness yet more boldly in the future.

"Now, Lord," prayed one of them, "behold their threatenings: and grant unto Thy servants, that with all boldness they may speak Thy word, by stretching forth Thine hand to heal; and that signs and wonders may be done by the name of Thy holy child Jesus." Acts 4:29, 30.

The prayer was answered. More power came from heaven. More people were healed. More great sermons were preached. "With great power gave the apostles witness of the resurrection of the Lord Jesus: and great grace was upon them all." Verse 33.

"By the hands of the apostles were many signs and wonders wrought among the people. . . . Insomuch that they brought forth the sick into the streets, and laid them on beds and couches, that at the least the shadow of Peter passing by might overshadow some of them." Acts 5:12-15.

It was just like the days when Jesus had been there! People began flocking into Jerusalem from nearby villages "bringing sick folks, and them which were vexed with unclean spirits: and they were healed every one."

This was too much for the priests and rulers. They became very angry. They could not bear to see these followers of Jesus so much more popular than themselves. So once more they had them arrested and put in the common prison. But these men couldn't be imprisoned. They wouldn't stay put. No sooner were they in than they were out again.

"The angel of the Lord by night opened the prison doors, and brought them forth, and said, Go, stand and speak in the temple to the people all the words of this life."

So Peter and John went straight from the prison to the pulpit, as it were. And there in the Temple they went on witnessing for Jesus just as though nothing had happened.

The best of it was that the priests knew nothing about the apostles' escape. They made ready for their trial and "sent to the prison to have them brought." But there were no prisoners there. In a great fluster the officers returned, saying, "The prison truly found we shut with all safety, and the keepers standing without before the doors: but when we had opened, we found no man within." Verse 23.

You can imagine the feelings of everyone in that council

489

room. What! The prisoners gone? Where could they be? And how did they escape through locked doors?

Suddenly a messenger comes panting with the astounding news that the escaped prisoners are actually "standing in the temple, and teaching the people."

"Fetch them in!" cries the chief priest, and the guard goes in search of them.

They are soon back, this time with Peter and several other apostles.

"Did not we straitly command you that ye should not teach in this name?" asks the high priest hotly. "And, behold, ye have filled Jerusalem with your doctrine."

"We ought to obey God rather than men," says Peter, which makes the priests and rulers more angry still; so much so that they begin to talk of killing them. On second thought, however, after listening to the wise counsel of Gamaliel, they decide to let them off with a beating.

It isn't a nice thing to think about, but one by one all those good men were given a lashing. It was the first time they had ever been in trouble like this. How those lashes must have hurt! But the Bible says that "they departed from the presence of the council, rejoicing that they were counted worthy to suffer shame for His name. And daily in the temple, and in every house, they ceased not to teach and preach Jesus Christ."

Scattered Seeds

~~~~~~

THAT cruel beating, far from being the last of their troubles, was only the beginning of worse things to come. As some of the apostles went daily to the Temple to preach about Jesus—right under the noses of the priests—and others went from house to house telling the story of His love, they soon began to find that all was not well. Opposition was growing.

The wonderful success they had had right after Pentecost had been too good to last. Shadows were beginning to fall. The chief priests and rulers, fearful that the new movement would become too powerful, had made up their minds to stamp it out if they could.

The first to suffer was Stephen, a fine young man, one of the first deacons of the church. For a time he was almost as strong a preacher as Peter himself. The Bible says that "full of faith and power," he did "great wonders and miracles among the people." Once, getting into a debate with some learned

491

rabbis, he so completely defeated them that "they were not able to resist the wisdom and the spirit by which he spake." Acts 6:10.

Alas, this was his undoing. In order to get even with him, those rabbis accused him of blasphemy. He was brought before the council, just as Jesus and the apostles had been.

All sorts of false charges were made against Stephen, but he listened to them calmly, trying to show the spirit of Jesus in all his conduct. "And all that sat in the council, looking sted-fastly on him, saw his face as it had been the face of an angel." Verse 15.

Told that he could defend himself, Stephen spoke with great power. With his wonderful knowledge of the Scriptures he told of the way God had led His people from the days of Abraham to that moment. The priests and rulers listened pa-tiently until he began to speak of Jesus, then they refused to hear more. Shouting and shrieking, they rushed upon him, while he, looking up, called out, "I see the heavens opened, and the Son of man standing on the right hand of God."

This maddened them still more and "they cried out with a loud voice, and stopped their ears, and ran upon him with one accord, and cast him out of the city, and stoned him."

© BY RGH

SCATTERED SEEDS

As the rain of stones began to fall, Stephen knelt down saying, "Lord Jesus, receive my spirit. . . . Lord, lay not this sin to their charge." Then "he fell asleep."

Stephen was the first martyr of the Christian church, but not the last. Thousands upon thousands of men and women, boys and girls, have given their lives for Jesus' sake. They have loved Him unto death.

The killing of Stephen made the rest of the disciples very sad. They never thought that the priests and rulers would go this far in trying to stop their work. But they made up their minds that whatever might happen they would not cease telling the wonderful story of Jesus and His love.

Soon the dreadful news spread that all followers of Jesus were to be arrested and imprisoned. The Bible says that "at that time there was a great persecution against the church which was at Jerusalem; and they were all scattered abroad throughout the regions of Judaea and Samaria, except the apostles." Acts 8:1.

Hundreds of people must have left Jerusalem at that time, trying to get away before they should be jailed. Some went north toward Syria, others south toward Egypt. Some perhaps took ship from Caesarea or Tyre and sailed for Italy, Spain, or even England.

As the priests and rulers saw them go, no doubt they rubbed their hands in glee. "This is the last we shall hear of that Jesus doctrine," they may well have said. "Now we shall be rid of that Man at last." But they were mistaken, for "they that were scattered abroad went every where preaching the

493

word." Instead of persecution stamping out the church, it gave it new life. Like seeds blown about by the wind, the Christians fleeing from Jerusalem began to take root in a thousand towns and villages throughout the Roman Empire.

Months earlier the priests and rulers had thought to finish with Jesus by nailing Him to a cross, only to learn that He had risen from the dead and ascended to heaven, alive forevermore. Now as they tried to crush the work He had left behind they saw it growing up everywhere, bigger and stronger than ever. By trying to kill it they made sure that it would never die.

Roadside Conversion

O NE of the worst enemies of the early Christians was a man called Saul. He was a Pharisee, and he hated the followers of Jesus. He "made havock of the church, entering into every house, and haling men and women committed them to prison." Acts 8:3.

Having done his worst in Jerusalem, he thought he would follow those who had left the city and were preaching about Jesus in other parts of the country.

"And Saul, yet breathing out threatenings . . . against the disciples of the Lord, went unto the high priest, and desired of him letters to Damascus to the synagogues, that if he found any of this way, whether they were men or women, he might bring them bound unto Jerusalem." Acts 9:1, 2.

With his mind full of plans for wiping out the Christians in short order, he starts on his journey, leading a company of men who are to help him in his wicked work. For several days they travel northward over the dry, dusty roads.

They are almost at Damascus, within sight of the city, when a wonderful thing happens. It is midday and the sun is beating down fiercely upon them all. Everybody is hot and tired and thirsty. Suddenly a light "above the brightness of the sun" shines about them. Everyone is struck to the ground and the caravan comes to a dead stop.

Blinded by the dazzling light and unable to rise, Saul hears a voice calling to him, "Saul, Saul, why persecutest thou Me?"

"Who art Thou, Lord?" he asks.

"I am Jesus whom thou persecutest."

Saul is astounded. How can Jesus be here on the Damascus road? Can this be the very Person whom the Christians declare has risen from the dead? If so, then what a dreadful mistake he has made in persecuting His followers!

A few moments before, Saul was a proud, self-important man; now he is humble; he sees how foolish he has been.

"What shall I do, Lord?" he asks.

"Arise, and go into Damascus," says Jesus, "and there it shall be told thee of all things which are appointed for thee to do."

At this Saul staggers to his feet, while his friends, still trembling with fright, crowd around, offering their help. But there is nothing they can do save lead him by the hand. He is blind.

And so Saul arrives in Damascus. Not as he had planned, striding proudly at the head of this group of men sworn to stamp out the Christian faith, but stumbling forward, humble and penitent, to learn the will of Jesus and serve Him faithfully forever.

In the city at last, Saul goes to stay with a man called Judas and there, for three days and nights, he neither eats nor drinks. Shocked by what happened to him on the Damascus road, sorry for all his mistakes and foolishness, he wants only to pray. And

there on his knees he asks Jesus to forgive him and show him what to do next.

About this time Jesus appears to one of His disciples in Damascus, and says, "Arise, and go into the street which is called Straight, and enquire in the house of Judas for one called Saul, of Tarsus: for, behold, he prayeth."

Ananias is alarmed. The last person he wants to meet is Saul of Tarsus. He knows him well, and all his cruel deeds. "I have heard by many of this man," he says, "how much evil he hath done to Thy saints at Jerusalem."

But Jesus replies, "Go thy way: for he is a chosen vessel unto Me, to bear My name before the Gentiles, and kings, and the children of Israel." Acts 9:15.

Ananias obeys. He finds Saul in the home of Judas, praying, as Jesus said. There, putting his hands on him, he says, "Brother Saul, the Lord, even Jesus, that appeared unto thee in the way as thou camest, hath sent me, that thou mightest receive thy sight, and be filled with the Holy Ghost."

At once Saul's eyes are opened. He can see again. And the first person he looks upon is a disciple of Jesus, who baptizes him into the church.

498

That was a very lovely thing that Ananias said, "Brother Saul." It is hard to call someone brother who has been unkind to you. To Saul's ears it must have sounded very beautiful indeed. It may have helped more than we know in leading him to make his decision for Christ.

His sight restored, and a baptized member of the church, Saul begins to witness for his Lord. "Straightway," he preaches Christ in the synagogues, "that He is the Son of God."

Some of the disciples refuse to have anything to do with him, remembering how he persecuted the Christians in Jerusalem. But he insists that he now loves Jesus as much as they do.

As for the Jews who had expected him to stamp out the Christian faith in Damascus, they are at first amazed, then angry. They plan to take Saul's life, but news of the plot is brought to Saul, and while the Jews watch the city gates night and day to kill him, some of the disciples put him in a basket and in the dead of night let him down over the city wall.

Thus Saul of Tarsus escapes from Damascus to become Paul the apostle to the Gentiles, one of the greatest champions Jesus ever had.

Escape From Prison

〰〰〰〰〰〰〰〰〰〰〰〰〰〰〰〰〰〰〰〰〰〰

A FTER the conversion of Saul the disciples of Jesus enjoy a little time of peace. "Walking in the fear of the Lord, and in the comfort of the Holy Ghost," they grow and multiply. Already the little company of fire-filled men who hurried from the upper room on the day of Pentecost has become a host of believers. Groups of Christians have sprung up all over Palestine. The more daring ones are pressing on with the gospel to the limits of the Roman Empire and beyond, eager to tell the wonderful story of a crucified and risen Saviour.

But the good times do not last long. Persecution comes again, this time from King Herod. To please the Jewish leaders, he arrests James the brother of John and has him killed with a sword—the first of the apostles to die a violent death. Then he arrests Peter and puts him in prison, intending to kill him after the Passover.

Having heard how Peter got out of prison once before, Herod gives orders that four squads of soldiers shall guard him

500

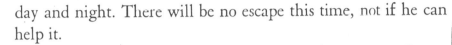

day and night. There will be no escape this time, not if he can help it.

Meanwhile the disciples in Jerusalem, having seen James executed, are doubly worried about their beloved Peter. Will he suffer the same dreadful fate? They decide to have special prayer for him. From early morning till late at night, yes, and all through the night, they cry to heaven on his behalf. I can almost hear them praying, "O Jesus, please save Peter. Don't let them kill our beloved Peter!"

Day after day, night after night, Peter remains in the prison, while the church prays without ceasing for his release. The last night comes, the night before he is to die. Unless something happens soon, the morning will see him executed.

Chained in his cell, Peter thinks back over his past life, how he first met Jesus in Galilee, how he followed Him for more than three years and then, in the last crisis, denied Him. He sorrowfully remembers how he had said in angry tones, "I know not the man!" and then how the cock crowed. Has Jesus

501

forgiven him for that? Will He come and save him now?

It seems impossible. What can anyone do now? Look at these chains on his hands and feet; the two soldiers in his cell, the locked door, the soldiers outside, the mighty iron gate at the entrance to the prison. What hope of escape is there? Who could possibly rescue him from such a place?

Peter is dozing, half asleep, when suddenly he feels a thud upon his side. He starts up, wondering who struck him.

Hark! What is that? Someone is whispering in his ear.

"Get up quickly!"

Peter staggers to his feet and sees a stranger in his cell. Mysteriously his chains drop with a clank on the floor.

"Dress yourself and put on your sandals," says the stranger.

Wondering what it all means, Peter obeys, dressing as quickly as he can. Scarcely has he put on his clothes when the stranger speaks again.

"Wrap your mantle around you and follow me," he says, as he leads the way.

ESCAPE FROM PRISON

Silently the stranger opens the cell door and passes through it, Peter following, wondering if it is all real.

Past the first guard they go, past the second, then into the courtyard. All is still, save for the dull snoring of the soldiers who seem to be dead asleep.

Ahead looms the great iron gate, beyond which is the city, and freedom. Can they get through that? Does this stranger have the key?

As they approach the gate, to Peter's amazement it opens as it were of its own accord.

Through the gate they go, down to the end of the street. Peter turns to thank the stranger who has rescued him, but there is no one there. "Now I am sure," he says to himself, "that the Lord has sent His angel and rescued me from the hand of Herod and from all that the Jewish people were expecting." Acts 12:11, R.S.V.

Left to himself, Peter, thankful for his cloak so that he can hide his face from any chance passer-by, hurries through the darkened city to the house of Mary, the mother of John Mark, where many disciples are gathered in prayer for him.

He knocks on the door, and, to make sure that the people inside will not be afraid to open to him, he calls out his name.

A girl named Rhoda comes to open the door and recognizes Peter's voice. However—just like a girl!—she is so happy to think that Peter is there that she forgets to let him in, and runs back into the room where the prayer meeting is going on.

"Peter's here—outside the door!" she cries. "I heard his voice."

"You're mad!" they say to her.

"But I heard him!" she says. "I know it is Peter."

Still they refuse to believe her. Meanwhile Peter is getting impatient, afraid that he may be discovered out there on the street. He goes on knocking.

At last they all go to the door and open it. And there he stands. They can hardly believe their eyes. Then they give him such a welcome that he has to beg them to be quiet, lest the soldiers come and find him there. Then he tells them the wonderful story of how an angel rescued him from the prison.

In the morning all Jerusalem is agog with excitement. At the prison there is "no small stir" over what has become of Peter. But search as they will, neither priests nor soldiers can find him anywhere. He has vanished. No one, not even Herod, can explain it.

But Peter understands. He knows how it all happened. Once more he has seen the tender love of Jesus for him. And now, saved from death by a miracle, he goes forth again to do an even greater work for God.

STORY 71

Endless Adventure

≈≈≈≈≈≈≈≈≈≈≈≈≈≈≈≈≈≈≈≈

FARTHER and farther spreads the wonderful story of Jesus and His love. Peter went one way with it; Paul, another; Thomas, another. And so with all the disciples. They went everywhere preaching the Word. And everywhere they went they found people glad to listen to their message.

In many parts of Europe, Asia, and Africa people began to believe in Jesus. Not only big, important people, but little people too. Hundreds and thousands of boys and girls came to think of Him as their Saviour and Friend.

Guided by their parents, these children learned how Jesus had come in fulfillment of the prophecies in the ancient Scriptures; how He was the one to whom Adam and Eve had looked forward from the gates of Eden; the one of whom Enoch, Noah, Abraham, Moses, Isaiah, and all the prophets had written. They learned, too, of the beautiful life that Jesus had lived, of the perfect example He had set from His boyhood onward, then of His sad, terrible death on the cross "that whosoever

505

Rhoda answered the knock and heard Peter calling. Forgetting to let him in, she ran back to the disciples with the happy announcement, "Peter is at the door; I recognized his voice."

believeth in Him should not perish, but have everlasting life."

They learned, also, about His rising from the dead, that He was not lying buried in a tomb, but alive, sitting at the right hand of God, waiting in heaven till it should be time to return to gather His people home.

As this lovely story was told and retold around the world, new hope came into people's hearts. They could see that God, far from forgetting them, had given them His best and greatest gift, and was planning more marvelous things for them in the days to come.

As years passed by, this blessed hope burned brighter and brighter. Many people began to pray that Jesus would return soon. They longed to see Him, as the first disciples had seen Him in Galilee of old. They yearned for the day when He would keep His promise to take them to the many mansions He once said He would prepare for His loved ones.

Sometimes they wondered what this heavenly home would be like. That it would be very beautiful, they had no doubt; Jesus, having all power in heaven and earth, would see to that. Nothing would be too good for Him to give to those who loved Him. But what sort of home would it be?

True, they had read what God had said through Isaiah: "Behold, I create new heavens and a new earth: and the former shall not be remembered, nor come into mind"; and they were happy to think that they would "build houses, and inhabit them. . . . Mine elect shall long enjoy the work of their hands." But was this all they could know about the coming kingdom?

Knowing the longings of His people, Jesus one day drew

507

Jesus said, "And I, if I be lifted up from the earth, will draw all men unto me," and countless millions from every walk of life have yielded to the appeal of His outstretched hands.

back the curtain and let them see what is in store for them. And because John was the beloved disciple, the vision was given to him. He saw it just as you and I might see it on a television set.

Describing the beautiful homeland of the children of God, he said: "I John saw the holy city, new Jerusalem, coming down from God out of heaven, prepared as a bride adorned for her

husband." "Having the glory of God: and her light was like unto a stone most precious, even like a jasper stone, clear as crystal."

This city, as he saw it, had twelve gates, all of pearl. As for its streets, they were of pure gold. And the foundations were "garnished with all manner of precious stones," gleaming and sparkling in the light from the throne of God. For "the city had no need of the sun, neither of the moon, to shine in it: for the glory of God did lighten it, and the Lamb is the light thereof."

As the picture shimmered there before his eyes, John noticed that there was a "pure river of water of life, clear as crystal, proceeding out of the throne of God and of the Lamb," while on either side of the river was, wonder of wonders, the tree of life, "which bare twelve manner of fruits, and yielded her fruit every month."

This must be Eden, he thought, dear old Eden, the lovely home that Adam lost in the beginning. More glorious than ever, it was awaiting the redeemed, to be their home forever.

As John, enthralled, watched this dazzling scene, he heard "a great voice out of heaven saying, Behold, the tabernacle of God is with men, and He will dwell with them, and they shall be His people, and God Himself shall be with them, and be their God. And God shall wipe away all tears from their eyes; and there shall be no more death, neither sorrow, nor crying, neither shall there be any more pain: for the former things are passed away."

Wonderful home! Not only because of its golden streets and pearly gates, but because of its everlasting peace and hap-

509

In exile on Patmos, the beloved John was given a vision of the triumphs of the gospel message to that time when the New Jerusalem would come down from God out of heaven.

piness. Within its borders there will be no worry or sadness, and no one will ever cry again.

Best of all, Jesus will be there. "And they shall see His face." His kind and tender face, so noble and serene, so full of majesty and gentleness, the face of a King and of a Friend. How good it will be to look upon the face of Jesus and see Him smiling back in recognition, as He greets each one of us by name, saying, "Tom [or Mary], I am so glad you are here!"

And Jesus will not only smile at us and greet us with gladness. He will lead us "unto living fountains of waters." Revelation 7:17. Where that will be, I do not know; but I think I can see Him leading His children on all sorts of wonderful expeditions. Who knows—when we have been "caught up . . . to meet the Lord in the air"—He may take us on many a thrilling trip to the planets, or even the most distant stars, all over His great creation. Sometimes, perhaps, He will take the boys and girls by themselves. How perfectly thrilling! Can't you picture them, hundreds of thousands of them, all beaming with joy, overflowing with health and happiness, streaming through the gates of the Holy City with Jesus at their head?

Then, after a thousand years in heaven, when the New Jerusalem rests at last upon the earth made new, there will be still more adventures with Jesus. Endless adventures. With Him as our Teacher and Guide we shall explore the universe, delving into all the secrets of nature, forever learning more and more of the greatness of His power, the marvel of His wisdom, the wonder of His love. This is the glorious future He is planning for all who love Him.

511

In that promised land of fadeless day about which we so often sing, our Saviour who sacrificed His life that we might have right to the tree of life will be our constant joy.

Such was the picture that John saw in the long ago—a picture that brought new courage to the disciples in those far-off days, and made them long for the day when He should return and make this dream come true. And such is the picture before our eyes today. Only now it is not far away. Now there is not long to wait. Soon the hope of all the ages will be realized. Soon Jesus, "this same Jesus," dear, wonderful Jesus, will come back in power and glory for His own.

Today to every boy and girl in every nation under heaven He sends the message: "Be ye also ready: for in such an hour as ye think not the Son of man cometh." Matthew 24:44. He wants to find us ready when He comes, to go home with Him to the place He has prepared for us.

Are you ready? Have you given your heart to Him? Have you made up your mind, with His help, to be good and kind and true, the sort of boy and girl Jesus wants in His kingdom, the kind that He can trust with the treasures of the New Jerusalem, who will be happy forever and ever in His homeland of tomorrow?

Shall we not pray that Jesus will make us ready, and keep us ready, for the great day of His appearing?

© BY RGH